Hewlett-Packard
Official Recordable CD
Handbook

Hewlett-Packard® Official Recordable CD Handbook

Mark L. Chambers

IDG Books Worldwide, Inc.
An International Data Group Company

Foster City, CA ■ Chicago, IL ■ Indianapolis, IN ■ New York, NY

Hewlett-Packard® Official Recordable CD Handbook

Published by
IDG Books Worldwide, Inc.
An International Data Group Company
919 E. Hillsdale Blvd., Suite 400
Foster City, CA 94404
www.idgbooks.com (IDG Books Worldwide Web site)

ISBN: 0-7645-3474-2

Printed in the United States of America

10 9 8 7 6 5 4 3 2

1B/QV/QW/QQ/FC

Distributed in the United States by IDG Books Worldwide, Inc.

Distributed by CDG Books Canada Inc. for Canada; by Transworld Publishers Limited in the United Kingdom; by IDG Norge Books for Norway; by IDG Sweden Books for Sweden; by IDG Books Australia Publishing Corporation Pty. Ltd. for Australia and New Zealand; by TransQuest Publishers Pte Ltd. for Singapore, Malaysia, Thailand, Indonesia, and Hong Kong; by Gotop Information Inc. for Taiwan; by ICG Muse, Inc. for Japan; by Intersoft for South Africa; by Eyrolles for France; by International Thomson Publishing for Germany, Austria, and Switzerland; by Distribuidora Cuspide for Argentina; by LR International for Brazil; by Galileo Libros for Chile; by Ediciones ZETA S.C.R. Ltda. for Peru; by WS Computer Publishing Corporation, Inc., for the Philippines; by Contemporanea de Ediciones for Venezuela; by Express Computer Distributors for the Caribbean and West Indies; by Micronesia Media Distributor, Inc. for Micronesia; by Chips Computadoras S.A. de C.V. for Mexico; by Editorial Norma de Panama S.A. for Panama; by American Bookshops for Finland.

For general information on IDG Books Worldwide's books in the U.S., please call our Consumer Customer Service department at 800-762-2974. For reseller information, including discounts and premium sales, please call our Reseller Customer Service department at 800-434-3422.

For information on where to purchase IDG Books Worldwide's books outside the U.S., please contact our International Sales department at 317-596-5530 or fax 317-572-4002.

For consumer information on foreign language translations, please contact our Customer Service department at 800-434-3422, fax 317-572-4002, or e-mail rights@idgbooks.com.

For information on licensing foreign or domestic rights, please phone +1-650-653-7098.

For sales inquiries and special prices for bulk quantities, please contact our Order Services department at 800-434-3422 or write to the address above.

For information on using IDG Books Worldwide's books in the classroom or for ordering examination copies, please contact our Educational Sales department at 800-434-2086 or fax 317-572-4005.

For press review copies, author interviews, or other publicity information, please contact our Public Relations department at 650-653-7000 or fax 650-653-7500.

For authorization to photocopy items for corporate, personal, or educational use, please contact Copyright Clearance Center, 222 Rosewood Drive, Danvers, MA 01923, or fax 978-750-4470.

Library of Congress Cataloging-in-Publication Data

Chambers, Mark.
    Hewlett-Packard official recordable CD handbook / Mark L. Chambers.
        p.   cm.
    ISBN 0-7645-3474-2 (alk. paper)
    1. CD-ROMs. 2. Compact discs. 3. Laser recording.
    4. Sound--Recording and reproducing--Digital techniques. I. Title: Official recordable CD handbook.
II. Title.
TK7895.C39 C47   2000
621.389'3--dc21   00-024337

ABOUT IDG BOOKS WORLDWIDE

Welcome to the world of IDG Books Worldwide.

IDG Books Worldwide, Inc., is a subsidiary of International Data Group, the world's largest publisher of computer-related information and the leading global provider of information services on information technology. IDG was founded more than 30 years ago by Patrick J. McGovern and now employs more than 9,000 people worldwide. IDG publishes more than 290 computer publications in over 75 countries. More than 90 million people read one or more IDG publications each month.

Launched in 1990, IDG Books Worldwide is today the #1 publisher of best-selling computer books in the United States. We are proud to have received eight awards from the Computer Press Association in recognition of editorial excellence and three from Computer Currents' First Annual Readers' Choice Awards. Our best-selling *...For Dummies®* series has more than 50 million copies in print with translations in 31 languages. IDG Books Worldwide, through a joint venture with IDG's Hi-Tech Beijing, became the first U.S. publisher to publish a computer book in the People's Republic of China. In record time, IDG Books Worldwide has become the first choice for millions of readers around the world who want to learn how to better manage their businesses.

Our mission is simple: Every one of our books is designed to bring extra value and skill-building instructions to the reader. Our books are written by experts who understand and care about our readers. The knowledge base of our editorial staff comes from years of experience in publishing, education, and journalism — experience we use to produce books to carry us into the new millennium. In short, we care about books, so we attract the best people. We devote special attention to details such as audience, interior design, use of icons, and illustrations. And because we use an efficient process of authoring, editing, and desktop publishing our books electronically, we can spend more time ensuring superior content and less time on the technicalities of making books.

You can count on our commitment to deliver high-quality books at competitive prices on topics you want to read about. At IDG Books Worldwide, we continue in the IDG tradition of delivering quality for more than 30 years. You'll find no better book on a subject than one from IDG Books Worldwide.

John Kilcullen
Chairman and CEO
IDG Books Worldwide, Inc.

WINNER

Eighth Annual Computer Press Awards ≥1992

WINNER

Ninth Annual Computer Press Awards ≥1993

WINNER

Tenth Annual Computer Press Awards ≥1994

WINNER

Eleventh Annual Computer Press Awards ≥1995

IDG is the world's leading IT media, research and exposition company. Founded in 1964, IDG had 1997 revenues of $2.05 billion and has more than 9,000 employees worldwide. IDG offers the widest range of media options that reach IT buyers in 75 countries representing 95% of worldwide IT spending. IDG's diverse product and services portfolio spans six key areas including print publishing, online publishing, expositions and conferences, market research, education and training, and global marketing services. More than 90 million people read one or more of IDG's 290 magazines and newspapers, including IDG's leading global brands — Computerworld, PC World, Network World, Macworld and the Channel World family of publications. IDG Books Worldwide is one of the fastest-growing computer book publishers in the world, with more than 700 titles in 36 languages. The "...For Dummies®" series alone has more than 50 million copies in print. IDG offers online users the largest network of technology-specific Web sites around the world through IDG.net (http://www.idg.net), which comprises more than 225 targeted Web sites in 55 countries worldwide. International Data Corporation (IDC) is the world's largest provider of information technology data, analysis and consulting, with research centers in over 41 countries and more than 400 research analysts worldwide. IDG World Expo is a leading producer of more than 168 globally branded conferences and expositions in 35 countries including E3 (Electronic Entertainment Expo), Macworld Expo, ComNet, Windows World Expo, ICE (Internet Commerce Expo), Agenda, DEMO, and Spotlight. IDG's training subsidiary, ExecuTrain, is the world's largest computer training company, with more than 230 locations worldwide and 785 training courses. IDG Marketing Services helps industry-leading IT companies build international brand recognition by developing global integrated marketing programs via IDG's print, online and exposition products worldwide. Further information about the company can be found at www.idg.com. 1/26/00

Credits

Acquisitions Editor
Kathy G. Yankton

Project Editor
Christopher C. Johnson

Technical Editors
Peter Tengerdy
Mary Hart

Copy Editors
Robert Campbell
Marti Paul

Project Coordinators
Linda Marousek
Danette Nurse
Joe Shines

Graphics and Production Specialists
Robert Bihlmayer
Jude Levinson
Michael Lewis
Dina F Quan
Ramses Ramirez
Victor Pérez-Varela

Book Designer
Kurt Krames

Design Specialist
Kippy Thomsen

Illustrators
Mary Jo Richards
Gabriele McCann
Karl Brandt

Proofreading and Indexing
York Production Services

Cover Designer
Deborah Reinerio

Floral Photography
Sandy Rodrigues

About the Author

Mark L. Chambers has been a computer consultant, technical writer, and hardware technician for more than fifteen years. His first book, *Running a Perfect BBS*, was published in 1994. He's now a full-time author, writing several books a year ✳ and spending entirely too much time on the Internet. His other books include *Computer Gamer's Bible*, *Teach Yourself the iMac Visually*, *The Hewlett-Packard Official Printer Handbook*, *Building a PC for Dummies*, *Recordable CD Bible*, *Official Netscape Guide to Web Animation,* and *Windows 98 Troubleshooting and Optimizing Little Black Book*. You can reach him at http://www.geocities.com/SiliconValley/Bay/4373/.

✳ they must be crap if he's writing ≥3 a year!

This book is dedicated to the one-and-only "Funny Aunt Joan," my wonderful sister-in-law, Joan Judycki.

Foreword

Less than five years ago, the idea of recording Compact Discs (CDs) was only a reality for businesses that could afford to spend $5,000 or more on the technology. Today, thanks to the innovation of Hewlett-Packard Company, recording CDs is becoming almost as commonplace in the home or office as PCs are.

In 1996, HP introduced the first affordable CD-Recorder, making it possible for a much broader audience to store data, audio, and video files with reliable and durable media. Since then HP has continued to lead the personal desktop storage market and has more than 6 million CD-Recorder/CD-Rewritable (CD-R/CD-RW) drives installed worldwide.

HP continues to improve the performance of CD-RW drives and technology through faster read/write speeds and through easier-to-use and more innovative features at affordable prices. HP has made the possibility of creating custom CDs a reality for novice and expert PC users the world over. Through HP's investment and leadership, the CD-Writer market is continuing to balloon, and more people than ever before are seeing both the practical storage applications and the unique entertainment options of custom CD creation.

We're very pleased that author Mark Chambers uses this book to make the once complex idea of creating CDs easy enough for the novice to follow, while providing useful information to the expert. Whether you are using your CD-Writer for home or office, for MP3 files or check registers, for school or work presentations — or anything else you can think of — this book is sure to help you simply get more out of your CD-Writer.

Enjoy!

£19 and no CD—what a rip-off!

John Spofford
General Manager
Hewlett-Packard Company
Colorado Personal Storage Solutions

Preface

When I wrote *Recordable CD Bible* for IDG Books Worldwide in 1997, CD recording was still relatively unknown for most first-time computer owners. CD recording technology was much more expensive than today, and the idea of selling a retail computer with a CD recordable drive (CD-R) — let alone a CD rewritable drive (CD-RW) — as standard equipment would not have been viewed as economically feasible. Rewritable drives were on the horizon, but still not generally available. You wrote data once at 2x or 4x *and* you kept your fingers crossed until the entire process had completed successfully!

Today, CD-R and CD-RW drives are the norm, and they're often found on retail computers, such as the Hewlett-Packard Pavilion line of personal computers. Hardware and software have advanced tremendously. The combination of today's faster processors, larger hard drives, and sophisticated software, like Adaptec's Easy CD Creator, Toast, and DirectCD, have helped make recording a CD as automatic and trouble-free as possible. And the explosive popularity of MP3 digital audio, MPEG video, and digital cameras has created a demand for recordable CDs that dwarfs anything I would have imagined in 1997. After all, those audio, video, and image collections need to be stored somewhere . . . and a CD-RW disc is the most cost-effective solution when it comes to removable media!

Whether you're a first-time computer owner or an experienced computer user introducing yourself to CD recording, you're probably asking yourself a host of questions regarding recordable CD technology. What kind of features do I need? How do I know I'm getting the best equipment for my money? How do I install a recordable CD drive? Compared to familiar computer hardware like your hard drive, a CD recorder is still a relatively new animal, accompanied by a host of new terms, formats, standards, and features. If your computer didn't come with a CD recorder, you'll need to install that new hardware. Troubleshooting a problem with CD recording hardware can cost you money — blank discs are inexpensive, but they're certainly not free — and many computer owners want to understand what's going on inside their computer and their CD recorder to help determine where problems can arise. You need to make choices when recording — for example, you need to know how to select the right data and audio format, how to create discs for other computers, and how to format, erase, and reuse your rewritable discs. Finally, what types of projects are available for today's CD recorders — what's involved in recording a Video CD, and how can you permanently transfer those digital images that you took with your camera to a CD-ROM?

You're in luck! You're holding the book that provides all that information, answers those questions, and guides you through those projects, step-by-step! In this comprehensive guide to CD recording, I show you how to select and buy the right drive, how to set it up and maintain it, and how to create a wide variety of audio and data discs.

Who Should Read this Book?

I'm the owner of a Hewlett-Packard CD recorder, but I certainly don't assume that *you* are! Although Hewlett-Packard drives are used as examples for step-by-step projects and product features, the *Recordable CD Handbook* is *not* specifically geared towards owners of Hewlett-Packard CD-RW drives. No matter what brand or model of CD recorder you own or how old it is, I'm confident that you'll benefit from the information you find here.

The *Recordable CD Handbook* was designed for any owner of a PC or Macintosh who's interested in recording different types of CDs, but I've written it with the following readers in mind:

- First-time computer owners and those who have just purchased a CD recorder. No prior experience with any program or operating system is required.

- Computer owners who are interested in the technical details of CD recording.

- Computer owners who are experiencing problems with installing, configuring, or using a CD recorder.

- Those who are shopping for a recorder.

How This Book is Organized

I've divided this book into four parts, which are composed of 14 chapters. Each of the first twelve chapters deals with a specific topic, while the last two chapters provide you with a series of step-by-step projects that lead you through the creation of discs using basic and advanced recording formats.

The chapters are organized like this:

- **Part I, "CD Recording 101,"** starts you off quickly, showing you how to record an audio CD using Adaptec's Easy CD Creator. You also learn how your CD-RW drive can record data, the mystery of the X factor, and how to store, handle, and clean your discs. In Part I you also discover some of the many advantages to CD recording, find out how to shop for the right CD recorder, and learn how to install it once you've bought it.

- **Part II, "Recording a CD-ROM,"** helps you prepare for CD recording. You learn how to select the type of disc and the format that's correct for your material and to optimize your hardware and operating system. You also use the popular Windows recording programs Easy CD Creator and DirectCD to record data and audio CDs, create bootable CDs, and copy an existing disc using CD Copier. If you are a Macintosh user, don't worry. In Chapter 10, I show you how to use Adaptec's Toast recording program. You see how to record data CDs and audio CDs, how to configure your preferences, and how to create a temporary hard drive partition for volume recording.

- **Part III, "Advanced Recording Topics,"** focuses on the process of adding an HTML menu system to your recorded CDs, including details on HTML editing applications, menu design, common HTML commands, and the conversion of word processing files to HTML code. You also learn how to create both types of multisession data CD-ROMs and how you can use Session Selector to access the different volumes on a multivolume multisession disc.

- **Part IV, "Recording Projects,"** gives you the opportunity to apply what you have learned step-by-step. You create a new employee orientation disc, archive your old vinyl album collection to an audio CD, and record your family's genealogy. In addition, you learn how to record a Video CD, a photo album slideshow disc, a Mixed-Mode CD (with both computer data and digital audio) and a CD Extra disc. I also demonstrate how to create and print a custom disc label and jewel case insert for an audio disc, and how to create a basic HTML menu for a data CD.

The back of the book includes a troubleshooting guide covering problems you may encounter recording and reading CDs, as well as a glossary of terms found throughout the book.

Helpful Icons

This book uses four types of icons as visual cues to annotate the contents of the text:

Cross-Reference

Most people won't read this book from cover to cover, but instead will zero in on the chapter or section that they need. The Cross-Reference icon tells you where information relevant to the topic you're reading about is located in the book.

Note

The Note icon offers an aside or extra information about the topic.

Tip

The Tip icon is perhaps the most important icon. It signals the kind of information that saves you time, money, and aggravation.

Warning

The warning icon cautions you to watch out or to take particular care when performing a procedure.

Where to Go From Here

Will you miss out on important material if you skip the first chapters of the book? On the other hand, why read introductory material if you're already experienced with CD recording? Because this book is designed for both novice and intermediate computer owners, I can suggest four starting points:

- *If you're itchin' to record your first CD,* start right at Chapter 1 and record a custom audio disc using MP3 files downloaded from the Internet.

- *If you're new to the world of CD recording and you're interested in how the technology works,* begin with Chapter 2.

- *If you've already purchased a CD recorder and you're ready to install it,* jump to Chapter 5 — then once you've installed your new drive, take your time and read the rest of the book.

- *If you're experienced with CD recording and you'd like to try the projects I've included,* jump to Chapters 13 and 14 — then return to the other chapters whenever you're ready.

Acknowledgments

This book is the second that I've written in the Hewlett-Packard Press series, and I find myself indebted to many of the same knowledgeable folks who helped me write the Hewlett-Packard Official Printer Handbook! Now that the work is done, it's a good time to step back and offer my heartfelt thanks to everyone who pitched in to assist me on this project. (Forgive me if this seems somewhat like an Academy Awards acceptance speech, but every person I'm about to name deserves recognition!)

First, I'd like to express my deep appreciation to all at Hewlett-Packard who supported my writing with specifications, driver software, test units, and troubleshooting suggestions. I can honestly say that this company is proof positive that great people produce great products.

Next, it's time to thank the hard-working people at IDG Books and Hewlett-Packard who helped me polish the rough edges of the manuscript, including Peter Tengerdy and Mary Hart for their technical edit of the manuscript; Bob Campbell and Marti Paul, who copy edited the book; all the hard working folks in the production department responsible for design, layout, and coordination; and Viviane Abudayeh at Castlewood Systems for providing some last-minute artwork. A special note of thanks is reserved for my good friend Pat Pekary, who has supported all of my work as a Hewlett-Packard Press author. The success of this series is a credit to her vision and her organization.

And as always, I end this roll call by acknowledging the two people at IDG Books Worldwide who were most responsible for delivering this book into your hands: Kathy Yankton, my Acquisitions Editor, and Chris Johnson, my Project Editor. I won't forget their tireless efforts to make this book the best it could be, and I sincerely hope that I'll be able to work with them again in the future — that is, once they've recovered from this project!

Mark L. Chambers

Contents at a Glance

Contents

Chapter 9: Introducing Adaptec's DirectCD Step-by-Step 153

Chapter 10: Introducing Adaptec's Toast Step-by-Step 169

Part III: Advanced Recording Topics   179

Chapter 11: Adding HTML Step-by-Step 181

PART

I

CD Recording 101

CHAPTER
1

Quick Start: Record Your MP3 Files!

IN THIS CHAPTER

- Recording your first audio CD
- Using Adaptec's Easy CD Creator for the first time

Have you already installed your CD recorder, or did your computer arrive with one already installed? Have you already installed the popular recording program Easy CD Creator? If so, try your hand at creating a custom audio disc from those MP3 files that you've downloaded from the Internet!

You'll be able to play your new disc in any standard audio CD player as well as on your computer, and you'll be able to delete those MP3 files and save the space they're using on your hard drive . . . and later in the book, you'll learn how to create a custom jewel box design for the disc you record now.

You'll need the following:

- **A blank CD-R disc.** Note that you should *not* use a CD-RW (rewritable) disc — the CD player in your stereo system won't be able to read it. Because standard CD-R blank discs are cheaper than CD-RW blanks, you save money as you expand your audio collection.

- **Version 4.0 of Easy CD Creator.** If you have an older version of this program, you can still record MP3 files — however, you have to convert them to Microsoft WAV format first using an audio editing program.

Cross-Reference

If you have yet to install you new CD recorder, and you want to first learn about how CDs and CD recorders work, start by reading Chapter 2, "How Does a CD-ROM Work?"

Recording MP3 Files on a CD

Without further ado, let's have some fun! To record MP3 files on a CD using Easy CD Creator:

1. From the Start menu, open the Programs menu, select Easy CD Creator, and then click Create CD.

2. When the Welcome dialog appears, as shown in Figure 1.1, click Audio and then select Audio CD.

3. Easy CD Creator displays the Audio Layout screen, which is shown in Figure 1.2. I cover this screen in detail later in the book, including all the buttons and controls you see. For now, just remember that this is the main window where all of the action takes place when you're recording audio CDs. At the top of the screen, you can see a smaller version of the familiar Windows Explorer display; click the drive that contains your MP3 files.

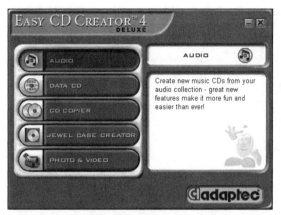

Figure 1.1 The starting point for many custom-recorded audio CDs

Figure 1.2 The Easy CD Creator Audio Layout screen

4. To display directories on the selected drive, click the plus sign to expand the directory tree. Locate the directory with your MP3 files and click it, and you'll see the files appear in the list at the top right section of the screen, as shown in Figure 1.3.

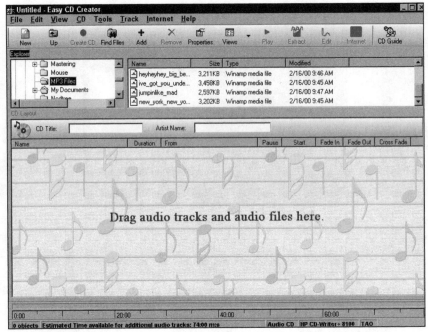

Figure 1.3 My collection of MP3 files displayed in the Explorer window

5. Now click the MP3 files that you want to add to your new audio CD. To select multiple files, hold down the Ctrl key while you click.

6. Once you've selected five or six MP3 files, click the selected filenames and drag them within the CD Layout window while holding down the left mouse button. Release the mouse button to "drop" the files.

7. Notice that Easy CD Creator now lists the files as tracks in the CD Layout window—this is the play list for your new audio CD, as shown in Figure 1.4. Also, be aware of the Estimated Time bar at the bottom of the screen: this bar increases as you add files to indicate how much time remains to be filled on your audio CD. A standard CD-R disc can hold a maximum of 74 minutes of music.

8. Continue to add MP3 files until you've reached the maximum this disc can hold.

9. Now it's time to reorder the songs the way you want them. To move a song to a new position in the track list, simply click and drag the song title entry to the new location and release the mouse button.

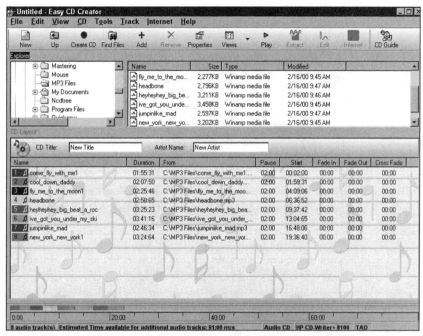

Figure 1.4 The play list shows the songs you've added to your new audio CD.

10. Satisfied with the track list? Good: Now click in the CD Title field and type the name of your new audio CD. You can also click in the Artist Name field and enter the artist's or band's name. (If you design a jewel case liner for this CD, these fields are automatically carried over as text fields.)

11. If you're like me and you have a large collection of MP3 music, you probably need to preview songs from time to time before you record them. To play a song, double-click the track entry; Easy CD Creator displays the control panel shown in Figure 1.5, which operates just like an audio CD player. To change the volume level, move the slider at the bottom right. To close the control panel, click the Close Window button at the top right.

Figure 1.5 Previewing an MP3 song in my track layout

12. Once you're ready to record, click the Create CD button on the program's toolbar. Easy CD Creator displays the confirmation dialog shown in Figure 1.6.

Figure 1.6 Starting the recording process

13. Leave the settings as is on the CD Creation Setup dialog, and just click OK.

14. If you haven't loaded a blank CD-R yet, the program automatically opens your drive and prompts you, as shown in Figure 1.7. Load a blank CD-R disc, wait a second or two, and click Retry.

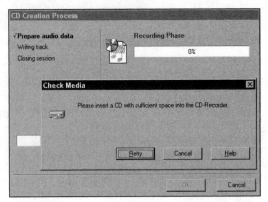

Figure 1.7 If you haven't loaded a blank disc, Easy CD Creator asks for one.

15. Once the recording process has started, sit back and relax. The program announces that recording has finished — you can eject the disc and listen to it in your audio CD player (or you can leave it in the drive and listen to it through your computer's audio system)!

That's all there is to it! Thanks to Easy CD Creator and your CD recorder, you've created a custom commercial-quality audio CD — with exactly the music you want in the order you want it — in less time than it would take most folks to drive to the mall.

Remember, I cover the audio recording process later in the book (including the details on many features that you didn't use in this Quick Start project).

How Does a CD-ROM Work?

IN THIS CHAPTER

What really goes on inside a CD-ROM drive and a CD recorder? How is laser light used to store and retrieve information? What's the difference between the commercial data CD-ROM that you buy in a store and the recorded CD-ROM that you create on your computer?

Okay, I'll be honest with you: You don't *really* need to know the answers to those questions! You can jump right in and start recording your own data and audio CDs without any background in this technology at all—there are no pre requisites for the programs and applications that I discuss and demonstrate later. With that in mind, if you feel like skipping most of this chapter, go right ahead! (You still need to read the last section, "CD-ROM Care and Feeding," however.)

Still with me? Good! That means that you're curious about how compact disc technology actually works, and you'd like to learn more. (Personally, I think laser storage is the neatest thing since sliced bread, but then again I make small talk about my cable modem at parties.) If you're interested in what's happening inside your CD-RW or DVD-RAM drive, get ready for a grand "behind the scenes" tour of CD recording!

What Is a CD-ROM?

First things first: Let me introduce you to the compact disc itself. CDs are commonplace these days, and you have to go as far back as 1980—when Sony and Philips first introduced the compact disc—to remember just how revolutionary they were. In case you've been hiding in the Amazon rainforest for the last twenty years, a standard CD is a polycarbonate plastic disc 12 centimeters in diameter, with a thickness of up to a millimeter, with an opaque top and a reflective coating.

Discs created for use on a computer are commonly called CD-ROMs (short for *compact disc–read-only memory*), but they have the same physical structure as a standard audio CD that plays in your home or car stereo. Figure 2.1 illustrates a cross-section of a standard mass-produced commercial compact disc.

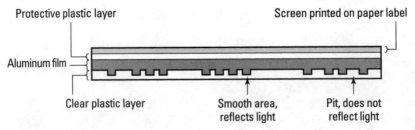

Figure 2.1 The hidden beauty of a very familiar object—a commercially made compact disc

misleading: the aluminium film is quite thin and the lower plastic layer is thick. This means it is probably more important to protect the top of the CD than the bottom, playable surface.

The Structure of a Compact Disc

Although it's not apparent to the naked eye, there are several layers to a disc. From the top layer down, they include:

■ **A screen-printed label.** CD labels are printed using a technique similar to T-shirts; it's called *screen printing,* where layers of ink are applied on top of one another through custom-made stencils to create a single multicolored image (Figure 2.2). The more colors, the more expensive the label design. Although the label isn't necessary — the CD can be read without it — it's practically a requirement for a manufactured disc.

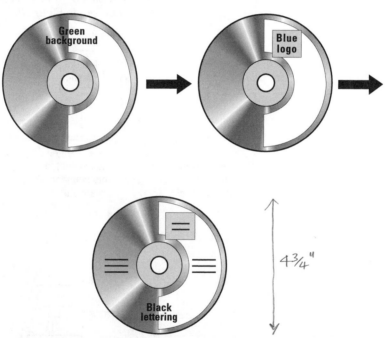

Figure 2.2 Screen printing involves applying layers of ink to create a single image.

■ **A layer of opaque protective plastic.** Because the label offers no protection to the materials below it, the next layer consists of a scratch-resistant polycarbonate plastic. The bottom of this layer is covered with microscopic indentations called *pits* that travel in a single spiral microscopic groove. This groove is so small that if you unraveled it into a straight line, it would stretch almost three miles! (I tell you more about this later in the chapter.)

- **A layer of aluminum film.** You may already know that a compact disc works by reflecting laser light, and this layer does the job nicely. Although very thin (and easily damaged if scratched), the aluminum coating is chemically very stable, so it doesn't degrade over time.

- **A layer of clear protective plastic.** Unlike the top layer of polycarbonate plastic, which is usually opaque, the bottom layer is crystal-clear to enable the laser light to pass through. It's also extremely tough and scratch-resistant to help minimize the effects of wear — refraction must be kept to a minimum to guarantee that the data can be retrieved from the disc.

What's involved in mass-producing hundreds of thousands of copies of a single disc? As you might expect, every step demands a high level of precision, but the process is not very complex at all, as you can see in Figure 2.3.

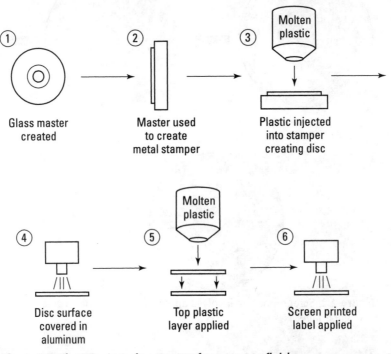

Figure 2.3 The CD mastering process from start to finish

In fact, producing compact discs is very similar in some ways to the manufacturing process for "antique" vinyl record albums:

1. First, a photoetching process creates the prototype glass "master" disc—a laser beam recorder actually burns the data into a photoresist layer on top of the glass surface. The surface of the master disc carries the specific pattern of pits that will later be translated into digital data, such as music or a software program.

2. This master disc is used to create metal molds called *stampers;* the stampers carry a reversed copy of the pattern of pits on the master disc.

3. The stampers are fitted to an injection press and molten polycarbonate plastic is introduced. As the material cools, it creates an exact plastic duplicate of the surface of the original glass master disc—the layer immediately above the aluminum film.

4. The polycarbonate disc is covered with a layer of aluminum.

5. A second layer of clear plastic is applied to the bottom of the disc.

6. Finally, a screen-printed label is applied to the top of the disc.

The Structure of CD-R and CD-RW Discs

As you can see in Figure 2.4, the cross-section of a CD-R (short for *compact disc–recordable*) disc is somewhat different from that of a commercial disc. Although the physical structure is very similar, there's now a layer of green or blue reactive dye under the reflective surface (both aluminum and gold are used in a CD-R disc). The top plastic layer of a CD-R disc has no pits, but it does have the same groove as a stamped commercial disc.

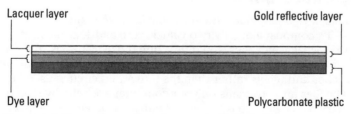

Figure 2.4 The cross-section of a standard CD-R disc

Finally, Figure 2.5 illustrates the cross-section of a CD-RW (short for *compact disc–rewritable*) disc. The dye layer in a CD-R disc is replaced by a crystalline layer with "amorphous" properties — talk about a mouthful! (Don't worry, you won't be tested on this stuff.) Normally, the layer is clear, but a beam of laser light can transform this material into an opaque material — and back to clear again.

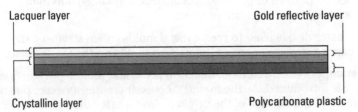

Lacquer layer   Gold reflective layer

Crystalline layer   Polycarbonate plastic

Figure 2.5 The CD-RW disc shows off its infamous crystalline layer.

So we have three similar structures for commercial CDs, CD-R discs, and CD-RW discs — what's the significance of those different layers? Well, as you're about to find out in the next section, the layer of dye or crystal determines whether the disc is recorded once or recorded many times!

Inside CD-ROM and DVD Drives

Now that you know all about the media used in CD recording, let's explore the process of reading and writing data to these different types of discs.

Reading Data from a Disc

Are you familiar with *binary* data? Binary is the language "spoken" by computers — it's composed of only two values, zero and 1, as illustrated in Figure 2.6. An electrical engineer would describe those values as "off" and "on," in that they date back to the days when computers were composed of huge banks of switches and relays rather than the integrated circuits used in today's computers.The files and programs on your computer are actually stored as long strings of binary data — and so is the digital music on an audio compact disc (which is why the word "digital" is tacked in front of practically every piece of stereo equipment these days). Computers and audio CD players can read digital information and convert it to data or audio. Thankfully, this is not a computer programming book, so that's all you need to remember about binary data.

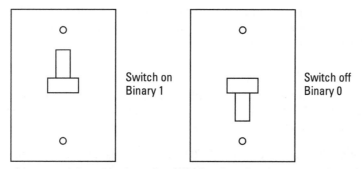

Figure 2.6 Binary data can be thought of as the two states of an electric switch.

However, compact discs don't store binary information electronically, and they don't use a magnetic field as your computer's hard drive or an audio cassette does; instead, the "on" and "off" states of our binary switch are represented by the presence of (or lack of) laser light! To illustrate, remember those microscopic pits I mentioned on the surface of the reflective layer in a commercial disc? As you can see in Figure 2.7, when laser light hits a pit, it scatters, and most of it isn't reflected back — think zero in binary data. However, when that same laser beam hits one of the flat surfaces (called a *land*), it's reflected cleanly back like your reflection in a mirror. The transition between a pit and a land represents a 1 in the stream of binary data. This is the technique used by your CD-ROM drive to read the data encoded on a disc as pits and lands.

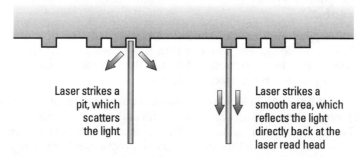

Figure 2.7 The reflective properties of pits and lands within a compact disc

Remember that three-mile-long groove I mentioned earlier in the chapter? All the pits and lands appear in that groove — just like the groove of a vinyl record album. (Most people don't know just how similar vinyl albums and audio CDs really are—a laser beam simply replaced the needle!) The groove in a disc, however, runs in the opposite direction from that of a record; it starts at the center and spirals to the outside of the disc.

What's Inside My CD-ROM Drive?

Before I continue to an in-depth description of the actual read process, you need a little background. It's time to introduce you to the various parts inside your CD-ROM drive. Every CD-ROM drive has these components:

- **A tray or disc carrier.** Every CD-ROM drive needs a method of loading and ejecting discs; most drives use a *tray* system that slides out to receive the disc. Some drives simply have a slot for loading: the disc is automatically drawn into the drive, and it reappears when you eject it. Older CD-ROM drives used separate *caddies,* which were thin plastic boxes about the size of a disc. To load a disc, you first loaded it into the caddy, and then you inserted the caddy into the drive. These days, caddy drives are considered antiques. Many CD-ROM *changers* are also available, where multiple discs are stored in a cartridge. CD-ROM changers are very convenient, because you can load any disc in the cartridge without ejecting it. Although these drives are used on computers, they're actually similar to the audio CD changers used in car stereo systems.

- **Front panel controls.** All CD-ROM drives have an eject button, a headphone jack for listening to audio CDs, and a volume control. Some drives also have audiophile controls such as pause, play, next track, and previous track. Drives with these extra controls usually cost a little more, but if you often use your computer system to play audio discs, the convenience factor is worth it.

- **A variable-speed motor.** Your drive has a high-speed electric motor connected to a spindle system, which in turn holds the disc. The speed of this motor can be precisely controlled, because the laser lens must move at ~~dif-~~ the same ~~ferent~~ speeds across the surface of the disc.

- **A laser read head.** A CD-ROM read head is a combination of the laser lens, which focuses the beam upward toward the surface of the disc, and the optical pickup and prism system, which determines whether the beam was reflected or not (more on this later). This complete assembly is mounted on a movable track so that it can cover the entire surface of the disc.

- **An emergency disc eject hole.** Last but certainly not least—especially if you've ever experienced problems with your CD-ROM drive—is the tiny hole on the front of every CD-ROM panel. If you insert a paper clip or a piece of stiff wire into this hole and push, your drive will eject the disc—even without power to the drive! This feature comes in handy if your computer is "locked up" and won't eject the disc in a normal manner.

Reading a Disc: the Detailed Description

The procedure of reading data from a CD-ROM is the same no matter what model of drive you're using. To read a CD-ROM:

1. Load a disc into your computer's CD-ROM drive — by the way, use the Eject button to close the drive tray, rather than pushing the tray with your finger (a bad habit that can eventually result in alignment problems). The spindle locks the disc in place, and the motor spins the disc to the proper speed. The actual speed varies according to the position of the drive's laser read head. Because the outside area of a spinning disc is moving faster relative to the inside area, the motor must vary the speed to ensure that the surface of the disc is always moving at the same speed underneath the laser read head, as shown in Figure 2.8.

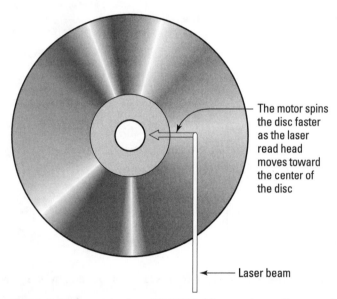

The motor spins the disc faster as the laser read head moves toward the center of the disc

Laser beam

Figure 2.8 The motor in a CD-ROM drive must vary the speed at which the disc spins.

2. The laser read head is activated, and the laser beam is focused on the reflective surface of the disc. It passes through the clear plastic layer.

3. One of three events can happen now, depending on the type of disc you're reading:

   - If you're reading a commercial disc created by a stamper, the beam will strike either a physical pit or a land in the reflective surface of the disc. As you can see in Figures 2.9 and 2.10, the beam is scattered by a pit but reflected back by a land.

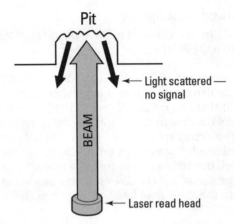

Figure 2.9 The laser beam is not reflected by a pit.

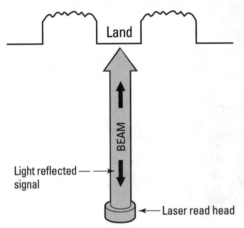

Figure 2.10 The reflected light from a land can be read by your drive.

- If you're reading a CD-R disc, the beam strikes the reactive dye. If the dye layer has not been changed, the beam is reflected by the gold layer behind the dye—just as it would be by a land. If the dye layer has been altered, the beam is scattered as it would be by a pit. (I tell you more about how these changes are made in the dye layer in the next section.) Figures 2.11 and 2.12 illustrate how pits and lands work on CD-R discs.

- If you're reading a CD-RW disc, the beam will strike the crystalline layer, and the effect will be the same as with the CD-R disc. If your CD-RW drive has turned the crystalline material opaque, the beam is scattered; if the crystalline layer is still clear, the beam is reflected by the next layer.

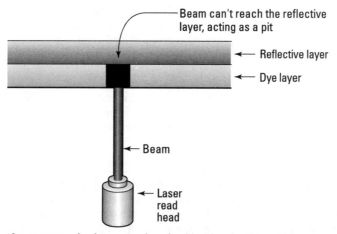

Figure 2.11 The beam is absorbed by the dye layer to create a pit.

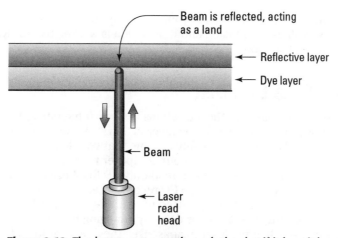

Figure 2.12 The beam can pass through the dye if it hasn't been altered.

As you can see, the end result is the same no matter how the lands and pits are created — the beam is either scattered or reflected. The transition between a pit and a land represents a 1 in the stream of binary data stored on the disc.

4. If the beam is reflected cleanly by a land, it returns to a system of prisms in the laser read head, which in turn pass it to a light sensor that can detect the presence or absence of the beam.

5. The light sensor returns a signal representing the pattern of lands and pits — now converted into a stream of binary data — to the CD-ROM drive, which in turn sends it as an electronic signal to your computer.

6. The entire process is repeated until all of the data has been read from the CD-ROM drive.

7. Finally, your computer takes the incoming data and completes the task — whether it be copying a file, loading program data, or converting the digital signal to the analog audio you hear through your computer's speakers.

Tip

It's important to remember that most older read-only CD-ROM drives made more than a couple of years ago will *not* be able to read the data on a CD-RW disc. If you need a CD-ROM drive that will read both older CD-R discs and CD-RW discs that you've recorded, look for a drive with the MultiRead symbol. If you're creating a disc for distribution to others or you're not sure whether a drive will read a CD-RW disc, use CD-R discs — they're less expensive, too.

Congratulations! You've earned your easy degree in compact disc technology. However, we still haven't talked about how data is written to a CD-R or a CD-RW, so on to the next section.

Writing Data to a Disc

By now you're familiar with the alterations that must happen to the dye layer within a CD-R (and to the crystalline layer in a CD-RW): But how do those changes happen? (I think I can safely assume that you don't have a photoetching lab and a plastic injection press in your computer room.)

Compared with the laser unit in a read-only CD-ROM drive, the laser in a CD recorder is more powerful. In fact, **a CD** recorder needs two power settings: low and high. The low power setting **is us**ed to read the disc. The high power setting is used to record the disk, which is done by changing the physical characteristics of the disc — when the laser beam strikes the dye layer in a CD-R disc at high power, it permanently changes that spot. Most discs use a dye that darkens or discolors when the beam hits it, as illustrated in Figure 2.13. But some discs use a dye that actually melts or bubbles.

On a CD-RW disc, the amorphous quality of the crystalline layer means that it can be altered back and forth between clear and opaque, over and over, so the disc can be completely rewritten. A CD-RW disc must be formatted before it can be completely rewritten. The formatting process clears the entire surface of the disc, essentially returning the disc to a "factory-fresh" state like a CD-R disc.

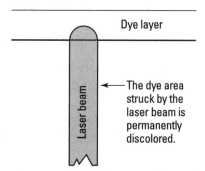

Figure 2.13 A high-powered laser beam makes a permanent change to a CD-R disc.

Because the reactivity of the crystalline layer is reduced slightly each time you use it, a CD-RW disc is no longer reliable after 1,000 to 1,500 uses or so. The number of times the disc can be rewritten varies slightly from manufacturer to manufacturer. Because most CD-RW discs aren't reformatted anywhere near that often, however, this usually isn't a problem.

What's Inside My CD-RW Drive?

Your CD-RW drive has the same components as a standard read-only CD-ROM drive, but two key additions are necessary for recording:

- **A laser write head.** Along with the standard read head that I covered earlier in the chapter, many CD-RW drives have a separate laser write head that's used only for recording. Other drives use a single laser that does double duty, both recording and reading. Whichever method your drive uses, it can toggle the recording beam between two states: high and low frequency (which we think of as the "power" of the beam).

- **The recording buffer.** Every drive has an internal memory buffer to hold data from your hard drive until it's ready to be recorded. With the speed of today's processors and hard drives, the buffer is no longer as important as it once was, but it still helps maintain an efficient flow of data to the recorder.

Writing a Disc: the Detailed Description

Here's the recording procedure in depth, step by step:

1. You load a blank disc into your computer's CD recorder. The spindle locks the disc in place, and the motor spins the disc to the proper speed.

2. The laser write head is activated, and the laser beam is focused on the underside of the disc. It passes through the clear plastic layer.

3. Your computer sends the data to be recorded to the drive, where it's stored temporarily in the recording buffer.

4. One of two actions occurs, depending on the type of disc you're recording:

   ● If you're writing a CD-R disc, the beam strikes the reactive dye. The laser write head alternates between high and low power to create the pits and lands on the dye layer, as shown in Figures 2.14 and 2.15.

   ● If you're writing a CD-RW disc, the beam will strike the crystalline layer, and the surface will turn opaque when hit by the high-powered beam.

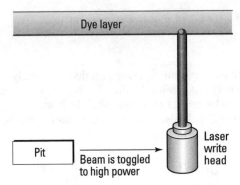

Figure 2.14 A pit is created when the laser write head is toggled to high power.

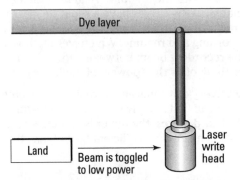

Figure 2.15 At low power, the dye layer isn't changed, and the spot becomes a land.

5. The entire process is repeated until all of the data has been read from the CD-ROM drive.

The Structure of DVD-RAM Discs

DVD-~~RAM~~ discs can store an amazing ~~2.6~~ *4.7* or ~~5.2~~ *9* gigabytes of data, but they're really only an improved version of a CD-RW disc. In fact, a DVD-RAM disc looks very similar to a CD-RW disc, except there is no "up" or "down." Because ~~most~~ *some* DVD-~~RAM~~ discs are double-sided, they don't have labels.

Other differences between DVD-~~RAM~~ and CD-RW:

■ **An increase in storage capacity.** Figure 2.16 illustrates the difference: On a DVD-~~RAM~~ disc, the pits and lands are much closer together, and the groove that holds the data is also more tightly compressed.

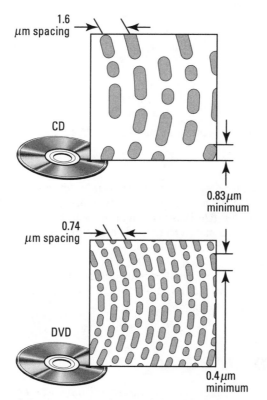

Figure 2.16 Now that's tightly packed data!

■ **Double-sided media.** Two-sided DVD-RAM discs can hold a total of ~~5.2~~ *9* gigabytes. Some drives require you to manually flip the disc over, while other drives actually have twin read/write heads so that both sides can be recorded without flipping.

■ **Multiple data layers on one disc.** As you can see in Figure 2.17, a DVD-RAM disc can have more than one reflective layer, and the laser can penetrate the first data layer to reach the second!

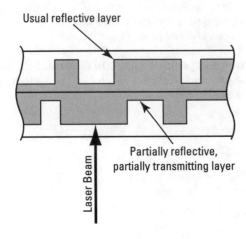

Figure 2.17 DVD-RAM discs provide multiple reflective layers for additional storage.

DVD-RAM is best suited for storing digital video and multimedia, as well as backing up the larger hard drive arrays used on a typical office network. At this time, a single 5.2 gigabyte DVD-RAM disc is still about $20, so the technology ⁵⁰ᵖ hasn't reached a price point to match the typical computer owner's budget. (Also, the typical computer owner probably doesn't need that amount of storage quite yet.)

Because the duplication of copyrighted material is still an important issue with the producers of films and videos, the future of DVD-RAM is still somewhat uncertain at the time of this writing.

The X Factor Explained

The X factor is the speed at which data is both read from and recorded to a disc. When you see a drive advertised as 8x/4x/16x, that means the drive has an 8x CD-R recording speed, a 4x CD-RW recording speed, and 16x read-only speed. As you might have guessed, the faster the X factor, the faster that data can be retrieved or recorded.

Technically, the X factor is actually a multiplier of the original transfer rate for a single-speed drive (the first drive to hit the market back in 1980), which was 150 kilobytes per second. A 2x CD-ROM drive, therefore, can transfer data to your computer at 300 kilobytes per second, and a 40x CD-ROM can transfer data at a whopping 6,000 kilobytes per second!

Should you pay more for a drive that records at 8x? That's up to you, of course. If your new recorder will be teamed with a standard read-only CD-ROM drive, you already have a fast drive for reading discs, so you don't have to spend additional cash for the third X factor. (Most multimedia games only need an 8x read speed, anyway.) A 4x CD recorder can finish a typical 600-megabyte disc in well under 20 minutes, which is quite fast as far as I'm concerned. However, I don't create more than two or three discs a week. The more discs you record, the more that extra speed will come in handy. Just remember: The faster drive is not always the best pick for your needs!

CD-ROM Care and Feeding

Attention, please, here comes a very important announcement: No matter what you've heard in the past, CD-ROM discs are *not* indestructible! Granted, they are tough—they were designed to take typical wear and tear—but it's easy to ruin a compact disc and the data it contains unless you treat it properly.

In this section, I show you the correct way to handle, clean, protect, and store your CD-ROMs.

Handling Your Discs (the Right Way)

"Is there *really* a right way to hold a compact disc?" You bet; ask anyone who's tried to install a program from a disc that's smudged by fingerprints, grease, oil, or even paint! As you just learned, the laser beam in your CD-ROM drive must be able to pass through the clear layer of plastic (not once, but twice) if the drive is to read data successfully from the disc. Your fingers can transfer all sorts of contaminants just by holding your discs incorrectly. Sure, you can take time to clean a disc, but holding it the right way is a simple step you can take to save yourself the trouble.

Figure 2.18 and Figure 2.19 show the two proper methods of holding a disc: by the outside edges, and by inserting a finger into the spindle hole.

Never touch the reflective underside of a disc, and don't lay a disc label side up on a table. If you need to set a disc aside for a few seconds, lay it label-side down (or better yet, put it back in its jewel case).

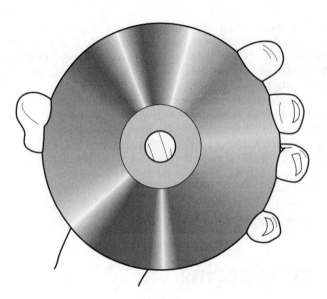

Fingers grip on outside edge

Figure 2.18 Holding a CD-ROM by the outside edges

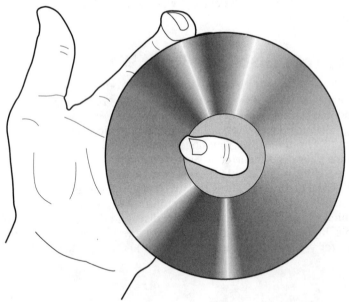

Figure 2.19 Holding a CD-ROM with a finger through the spindle hole

How Not to Care for Your Discs

Now that you're holding your discs properly, you should keep them far away from:

- **Heat.** The classic example is your hot car seat on a summer day— CD-ROMs can fall prey to high temperatures just like your cassettes or videotapes.

- **Dust.** Because the laser read head passes so close to the disc and acts on reflected light, you can understand why dirty discs tend to skip (or suddenly turn unreadable). Keep your discs in their jewel cases or store them properly to keep them dust-free, and be careful to avoid fingerprints on the surface of your discs.

- **Liquids.** Yes, even water! Even if a liquid doesn't naturally stain, keep those discs dry – a disc normally doesn't require any liquid to clean, as you'll see in a moment.

- **Sharp objects.** A surface scratch on either side of a disc can ruin the reflective coating inside a disc, usually rendering it unreadable!

Tip

Don't use a ballpoint pen to label the top of a recorded CD! That pen can easily damage the disc. Instead, use an alcohol-free felt-tip pen to label your CDs.

Some CD-ROM drives feature automatic cleaning of the laser lens. If your drive doesn't include such a feature, you can use a CD-ROM drive laser lens cleaner. Do not use one of these cleaners on a CD-RW drive, however; you could damage the drive! The complex laser and lens system inside a CD-RW drive doesn't require any cleaning.

Storing Discs

What do I use to store my discs? Unfortunately, jewel boxes can take up more room than you may think, especially if you're an audiophile or you really enjoy your computer games. For the best protection for the most discs in the least space, I recommend a disc binder like the one shown in Figure 2.20.

These binders store each disc in an individual plastic sleeve, so you can toss the jewel case. CD binders are available in sizes that range from 10 discs to more than 250 (all in the space of a typical briefcase)!

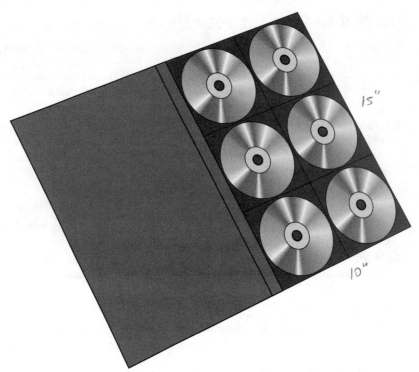

Figure 2.20 A CD storage binder can pack an amazing number of discs into a ~~very~~ small space.

Whatever storage method you choose for your discs, make sure that it meets these three criteria:

- **It must protect your discs from dust.** Avoid any storage method that leaves your discs exposed.

- **It must protect your discs from scratches.** If your discs are stored in sleeves, make sure that they don't rub against each other, and avoid sleeves that are all plastic (instead, look for lined sleeves that prevent scratches).

- **It must be expandable.** If you're leaving your jewel boxes behind, you're probably running out of room anyway—don't make the mistake of buying a storage system that can't expand in the future!

Cleaning Discs

Sure, you can spend a fortune on a compact disc cleaning machine, but I'd recommend you forget that! Compact discs were designed to be easy to clean. All that's really required to clean your discs is a lint-free *photographer's lens cloth,* which will handle your dusting chores. You may need a spray or two of disc cleaning fluid if the disc has picked up a stain from a sticky liquid — next time, leave the peanut butter sandwich on the plate.

Figure 2.21 illustrates how you should wipe the bottom surface of a CD: Always move from the center spindle hole straight toward the outside of the disc, and always apply only fingertip pressure to avoid causing scratches to the disc surface.

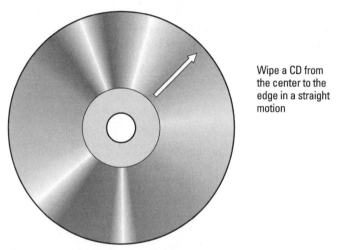

Wipe a CD from the center to the edge in a straight motion

Figure 2.21 The correct method of wiping a disc clean of fingerprints and dust

Never wipe a compact disc in a circular motion (Figure 2.22), which can scratch the surface and result in lost data!

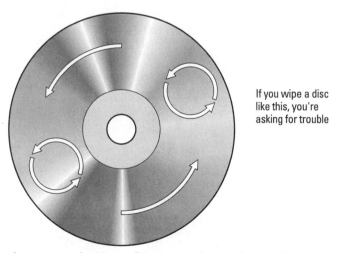

If you wipe a disc like this, you're asking for trouble

Figure 2.22 Cleaning a disc incorrectly may damage its surface.

In Review

In this chapter, you saw what's happening "behind the scenes" of your CD-ROM drive and CD recorder, learning how data is read from a disc and how a CD-RW drive stores data on a disc. You also compared the difference between a commercial disc created at a factory and the discs you record on your computer, considered DVD-RAM and how it differs from standard CD-RW technology, and studied the X factor and how the computer industry uses this measurement to rate the speed of a CD recorder. Finally, we covered how you should store, handle, and clean your discs to keep them ready for use.

Introduction to
CD-ROM

IN THIS CHAPTER

■ Comparing CD-RW to other recording media

■ Exploring the advantages of CD-RW

■ Applying CD recording technology

No more than five years ago, CD recording was an expensive proposition. When I first began using my state-of-the-art 2x2 CD recorder, the drive was as expensive as an entire modern computer system, with a price tag well over $1,000. The software I used for recording was hard to find, and it was more expensive than a typical office productivity suite. Even a single blank CD-R disc might cost $15 or more!

Today, however, the CD-RW drive is practically considered standard equipment by most computer manufacturers, and recorders are replacing the traditional CD-ROM drive in most of the retail computers on the market today. If you're shopping for a CD recorder to upgrade your system, you'll find that many recorders are cheaper than standard hard drives, and a spindle of 50 blank discs will set you back less than $40. Plus, the number of recording applications has mushroomed, with dozens of commercial and shareware offerings (including some that specialize in specific types of recording, such as creating audio CDs from MP3 files).

A major factor in this price drop has been the rapid acceptance of CD recording over the last few years. The floppy disk has all but disappeared, and recorded CDs have become the standard for carrying data. Naturally, CD-RW technology must be a clear choice to have earned this popularity . . . but why? Why are recorded CDs so superior to other storage media, and what factors have led to their appeal among computer owners?

In this chapter, I provide you with the reasons why CD-RW has taken the computer world by storm, and I compare it to other forms of removable media. I also list a number of applications for computer owners of every experience level that take special advantage of CD-RW technology.

Examining the Advantages of CD-RW

Quick—can you name a single program that you've installed in the last year from a single floppy disk? Probably not! The venerable floppy drive holds a mere 1.44 megabytes of data, and it's less than reliable; data on floppies tends to become unreadable over time, and placing a floppy disk with important files on top of a magnetic source like your monitor or a stereo speaker is a sure recipe for disaster. For these reasons, floppy disks are following punch cards and cassette tape to computer oblivion. (You read that correctly—I'm a proud member of the computer generation that remembers when Atari, Radio Shack, and Commodore computers used cassette drives to store programs and files!)

The Apple iMac shown in Figure 3.1 is an example of this phenomenon— although the iMac doesn't come with a floppy drive, it continues to be a great success. The computer comes with USB ports (short for *Universal Serial Bus*)— if an iMac owner needs removable storage, it makes more sense to add an external Iomega Zip drive (which I discuss later in this chapter), an Imation SuperDisk, or a CD recorder. Apple, always a trendsetter, has recognized that most of us rarely use a floppy drive these days, and the company has taken the bold step of removing the "appendix" from their computers. As an iMac owner myself, I can tell you that I haven't missed it yet!

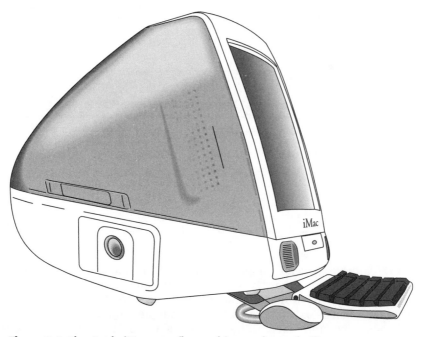

Figure 3.1 The Apple iMac—no floppy drive, and proud of it

In this section, I discuss the specific advantages that have made the CD-RW drive such a success story in recent years.

Cost-Effective

CD-RW is the computer owner's dream-come-true: a near-perfect combination of *high capacity* and *low cost*. For less than five dollars, your CD-RW drive can store up to 650 megabytes of data—the equivalent of over *450* floppy disks—and you can erase and reuse the disc hundreds of times. If you don't want to rewrite over the data you're recording, a standard CD-R disc is an even better bargain, storing that same 650 megabytes of data (or 74 minutes of audio) for an incredible 75 cents! The cost of a CD-RW drive has also dropped tremendously over the last five years, so that now you can buy a recorder for less than most other types of removable media drives.

In fact, the cost-efficiency of mass storage is so important that it's usually measured as *cost-per-megabyte* by the manufacturers of hard drives and removable drives. Cost-per-megabyte is calculated by determining the number of cents it costs to record one megabyte of data. For example, at the time of this writing a typical 10-gigabyte hard drive costs around $200, which works out to two cents per megabyte (remember, a gigabyte equals 1,000 megabytes). However, a 650-megabyte CD-RW disc costs approximately four dollars, which works out to an incredible six tenths of a cent per megabyte! Table 3.1 illustrates a number of popular removable media technologies and their approximate cost-per-megabyte figures.

Table 3.1 Storage Media: Cost-per-Megabyte			
Media Type	*Number of Megabytes*	*Typical Price*	*Cost-per-Megabyte*
DAT tape	4,000MB (4GB)	$10.00	0.25 cents
CD-RW	650MB /800MB	$4.00 50p	.61 cents .08p
ORB drive	2,200MB (2.2GB)	$40.00	1.8 cents
ZIP disk	250MB	$20.00	8 cents

CD-RW drives haven't completely replaced the hard drives in today's computers — a typical hard drive can store dozens of gigabytes of data. Yet why buy a hard drive to store data that you won't need to change in the future, or that you'll change only infrequently? For example, would you buy a hard drive to store your tax return data for the last several years? And why risk damage to a hard drive by transporting it from place to place when you could bring a virtually indestructible compact disc instead?

Archival storage and transport: Those are the two of the roles that CD-RWs play so well on today's computers.

Reliable

As you know, CD-RW discs are far more reliable than backup media such as floppy disks and tapes. They're not affected by magnetism, and the "recording medium" on a CD-ROM doesn't stretch or lose cohesiveness over time. In fact, you can safely store your compact discs for decades without losing a single byte of data. Unlike a hard drive, a CD-ROM has no moving parts to wear out over time, either.

To illustrate the advantages of CD-ROM for archival storage and retrieval, consider the local radio stations in your area, which used to rely on tape cartridges for music storage (and before that, of course, on vinyl albums). Within the last few years, most radio stations have moved to an all-CD format — discs are much cheaper than tape cartridges, they last much longer, and the quality of the sound that listeners hear is much better from a compact disc.

Companies and organizations are also turning to CD-RW as a means of safe-guarding important data; of course, a 650-megabyte disc may not hold enough, but the latest DVD-RAM drives can hold 5.2 gigabytes!

Efficient

Next, let's consider two other important advantages that CD-RW has over traditional backup media: *rapid access* and *random access*.

Today's CD-RW drives read and write data many times faster than floppy disks, Zip drives, or QIC-format tape backup drives — and that access speed translates into faster backups (and, in case you actually lose a directory of files, faster restoration of lost data). But access speed is also important for people who would like to run programs or read data directly from their archival backup; even if a program did actually fit on an old 1.44-megabyte floppy, for example, would you want to run it from that floppy? CD-RW is fast enough to enable your computer to read multimedia content directly from the disc, saving you time and trouble.

CD-RW also has the advantage over tape drives when it comes to the access method used to retrieve data. For example, the tape drive uses a sequential access method, like that illustrated in Figure 3.2. This means a tape drive must rewind or fast-forward through information that you don't need before it reaches the file and can actually read the data you need.

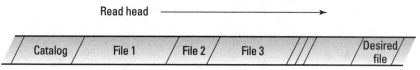

Figure 3.2 The sequential access method used by tape drives is slow and inefficient.

A CD-RW, on the other hand, uses the random access method shown in Figure 3.3. In plain English, random access means that a CD-RW drive can jump directly to a file no matter where it's recorded on the disc. As you might expect, random access is much faster and more efficient, which is why hard drives also use a similar method.

Convenient

The most revolutionary improvement in CD recording has been the arrival of *packet-writing*, which is discussed in depth later in the book. With packet-writing software like Adaptec's DirectCD, which is shown in Figure 3.4, you can drag and drop files directly to the CD-RW drive icon. In other words, your CD-RW drive becomes as easy to use as a floppy disk drive! You can even record data to a

CD-ROM in the background, while you use your word processor or read e-mail. In fact, it's no longer necessary to load recording software at all, unless you want to create an audio disc or build a special directory system. Without these convenience refinements in the CD recording process, CD-RW would never have become as popular and universal as it is today.

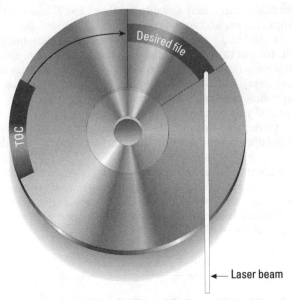

Figure 3.3 A CD-ROM uses random access for faster and more efficient data transfer.

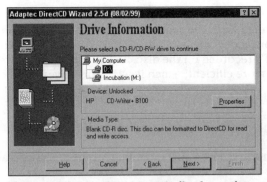

Figure 3.4 Formatting a CD-RW disc for packet-writing with Adaptec's DirectCD

Optimizing Your Computer

In the early days of CD recording — a mere six or seven years ago! — your computer had to be fine-tuned to *perfection* to ensure a successful recording. The processor and hard drive in a typical 386-based computer running Windows 3.1 weren't fast enough to guarantee that data could be sent to the CD recorder in a steady stream. If that data stream was interrupted, you were rewarded with buffer errors and a shiny coaster. When I first started recording discs, I left a sticky note attached to my monitor that read "Optimize Or Perish!" as a reminder. This optimizing procedure could easily take 30 minutes ... and then you'd have to run your recording software and build the disc image. Finally, you'd wait another 30 to 45 minutes for the recording process to finish, during which you'd be unable to use your computer!

Despite the great improvements to CD recording technology, it still important to optimize your computer, but now it's a simple process that you can take care of in five minutes every month or so. Computers are light-years ahead of that 386 system, with superfast processors and hard drives, and Windows 98 is a much more efficient operating system. With the hardware and software available today, a system with a CD-RW drive rarely encounters buffer errors (even at 8x or 10x speeds)!

Cross-Reference

To learn how to optimize your computer for fast, efficient, and effective CD recording, take a look at Chapter 7, "Preparing Your Computer."

Flexible and Compatible

Now let's consider the flexibility of CD-RW . . . no, not the disc itself! (Bending a CD-RW is hard work, and you'll ruin the disc.) By flexibility, I'm referring to the amazing variety of data a CD-ROM can hold. No other type of removable medium can store so many different types of data. For example, consider this list:

- **Computer data.** You can store files and programs on a CD-ROM, including images and video clips.

- **Digital audio.** A CD recorder can create standard audio CDs that you can play in your stereo.   CD-RoM not CD-RW

- **Digital video.** Your CD-RW can record video CDs that you can use with a video CD player.

- **Electronic pictures.** Most CD-RW drives can create picture CD-ROMs.

- Digital audio MP3. Some audio equipment can play MP3 files. You can hold over 10 hours of audio on one CD-RoM! (Approx. 1MB per minute.)

Only the CD-R and CD-RW can deliver all of those different formats and data types — unless, of course, you've figured out how to load your hard drive into your car's CD player.

CD-R and CD-RW discs are also the recognized kings of compatibility. Except for the floppy disk (which I've already committed to a museum of prehistoric computer hardware), no other form of removable medium comes anywhere near the universal acceptance of CD-R and CD-RW. Virtually every computer made in the last five years has a CD-ROM drive — and although many older drives can't read a CD-RW disc, they can read a CD-R disc. Naturally, today's MultiRead CD-ROM drives can read both types of recorded discs.

Comparing CD-RW with Other Forms of Storage

Although most computer owners consider CD-RW to be the best technology for removable storage, there *are* a number of other choices. . . . In this section, I introduce you to the best of these alternative removable storage solutions and compare them to the advantages of CD-RW that I cover earlier in this chapter.

The Zip Drive

The venerable Zip drive from Iomega shown in Figure 3.5 has been around for many years now; in fact, many computer manufacturers include both a floppy drive and a Zip drive on their PCs.

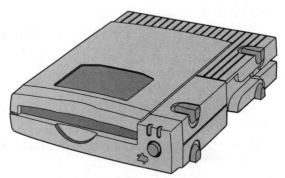

Figure 3.5 The popular Iomega Zip drive

In its original form, the Zip drive held 100 megabytes, which sounds like very little space today — but when the drive was first introduced, that same 100 megabytes could store most of the contents of a hard drive. A new version of the drive can hold 250 megabytes on one disk, and it's backward-compatible with the lower-capacity disks.

From the front, a Zip disk looks very similar to a 1.44-megabyte floppy — but it's twice as thick, much stronger, and considerably heavier. Zip drives come in many forms: external drives with connections for parallel ports, USB, and SCSI, and internal EIDE and SCSI drives. (As I explain later in more detail, these are the interfaces used to connect your CD-RW drive to your computer — SCSI and EIDE are the two most popular interfaces in the Windows world.)

Cross-Reference

To learn more about SCSI, USB, EIDE, and other connections, check out Chapter 4, "Buying a Recorder."

Because Zip disks are used just like a floppy, they're well suited for quick storage jobs. However, Zip disks fall short when compared to CD-RW:

■ **Capacity is limited.** A CD-RW holds over twice as much data as a 250-megabyte Zip disk.

■ **Storage is expensive.** For the price of a single Zip disk, you can buy two or three blank CD-R discs.

■ **Transfer rates are slow.** Only the SCSI and IDE Zip drives offer transfer rates that are somewhat comparable to a CD-RW drive.

■ **Availability is limited.** Although Zip drives are common, they're still not as well accepted as CD-ROM drives.

The Jaz Drive

The Iomega Jaz drive is a good example of a removable drive that's actually a hard drive — each Jaz cartridge, which holds two gigabytes, is simply a protective case surrounding a set of magnetic platters like those in a regular fixed hard drive. When you load a cartridge, the platters are exposed and data can be read and written to them. Figure 3.6 illustrates the Jaz drive and cartridges.

Because the Jaz drive is essentially a traditional hard drive, it's exceptionally fast at accessing and saving data. Also, it can hold over twice as much as a standard CD-RW disc. The Jaz drive is available in both internal and external versions, but only for computers with SCSI support.

Jaz drives are a good pick for those working with multimedia such as digital video or audio; for example, a single two-gigabyte cartridge can hold over three hours of CD-quality digital music, or 111 minutes of MPEG video. Compare the technology to CD-RW, though, and the Jaz drive falls short in a number of important criteria:

■ **SCSI is required.** If you don't have SCSI support already, you'll have to add a SCSI adapter to your computer.

■ **Storage is expensive.** With a street price of over $300 for the drive and $100 per two-gigabyte Jaz cartridge, a Jaz drive is much more expensive than a CD-RW drive.

■ **Availability is severely limited.** Good luck in finding a Jaz drive in a typical office, much less a typical home computer. The cost and SCSI support necessary to use a Jaz have made them a niche product.

Figure 3.6 An Iomega Jaz drive and cartridges

The Orb Drive

Castlewood Systems' Orb drives, which are shown in Figure 3.7, have only been available for a short time compared to the Iomega products, but they beat the Jaz drive in capacity, delivering 2.2 gigabytes of space. Like the Jaz drive, an Orb can deliver data at transfer rates similar to those for a fixed hard drive.

Unlike the Jaz drive, the Orb drives are available in a wide variety of interface connections, including external drives for parallel port, USB, and SCSI, and internal IDE and SCSI drives. The drive itself is much less expensive, with a street price of around $175 to $200 for the internal models. Orb disks are approximately the size of a Zip disk, and they carry a retail price of about $40.

Like the Jaz drive, Orb drives are best suited for multimedia and Web professionals who need to store and transfer large amounts of data. However, Orb drives do have a couple of disadvantages compared to CD-RW drives:

■ **Storage is still expensive.** Although far less expensive to use than a Jaz drive, the Orb still can't beat the cost of a typical CD-RW drive and blank discs.

■ **Difficult to find.** Unlike CD-RW drives and discs, which you can find at any computer store, the Orb drive and its disks are still mail-order material for most computer owners. Because the Orb hasn't been around for long compared to the Zip and Jaz drives, you'll be hard-pressed to find an Orb drive on another computer.

Figure 3.7 The Orb family of recordable drives from Castlewood Systems

Using CD Recordings

"Great, but what can *I* do with a CD recorder?" That's a good question. Naturally, a home computer owner has different applications for a CD-RW drive than the multimedia professionals who pioneered CD recording.

Because CD-RW is a true rewritable medium, it's suitable for just about any job that needs high capacity and fast access. Because of its compatibility with audio CD players and older CD-ROM drives, CD-R is the best pick for recording audio CDs and distributing data to others.

Besides the obvious (creating data CD-ROMs, recording audio CDs, and backing up your existing hard drive), here are a number of other possible applications for CD-R and CD-RW:

■ **Audio CDs.** It's easy to create your own audio CD—and yes, it will have the same great sound quality you're used to hearing from discs you buy at your record store. You can arrange the music tracks in any order you prefer, and you can even "extract" music tracks from different discs and create compilation discs!

■ **Digital "photo albums."** You can take those images from your scanner or digital camera and record them on a CD-R—complete with a shareware program to display them—and create a digital photo album for family, friends, and special events like reunions.

■ **Web-site-on-a-CD.** Are you using your Web site for a demonstration or presentation? Why worry about network connections and remote access when you can save your entire Web site to a CD-ROM? Both Internet Explorer and Netscape Navigator can display *offline* sites from disk files. Your audience will never know that you're not online.

■ **Video CDs.** Because most CD-RW drives can record video CDs, you can archive your home movies to disc (safeguarding them permanently) and reuse all of those VCR tapes.

■ **Travel.** If you're traveling with a laptop computer and you're running short on hard drive space (or you'd like to safeguard your data from damage), burn that data onto a CD-RW. Your data is both backed up and easily accessed, and you can delete that material from your laptop's drive. Also, you can easily copy the data to a customer's computer if necessary, without hassling with cables or network connections.

■ **Network storage.** The savvy network administrator does everything possible to conserve valuable disk space, and if you have a home network or a small network at your office, consider the time and trouble you'll save by archiving data on a CD-ROM for use on your file server! If a particular directory of files is always being accessed but rarely changed, save the data on a CD-RW rather than a hard drive, and you'll never have to back that data up!

Cross-Reference

You can practice some of these applications by doing the projects in Chapters 13 and 14.

In Review

This chapter familiarized you with the advantages of recording your own CD-ROMs. You learned why CD recording has become such a popular method of storing all kinds of data, and how CD-RW technology compares to other forms of mass storage. Finally, you now know the many applications for CD-ROM recording for both novice and experienced computer owners.

CHAPTER
4

Buying a Recorder

Okay, it's time to take the plunge. You know how a CD recorder operates, and you're familiar with all of the advantages of CD-RW technology; so you're ready to buy a recordable disc drive.

After an hour browsing through the CD recorders available from your favorite online computer Web site (or, if you prefer hands-on shopping, your local computer store), you'll come to one certain conclusion: The market has a huge range of CD-RW drives!

Naturally, the popularity of CD recording has resulted in a seemingly endless variety of brand names, interfaces, and features for you to choose from — and, as with any other piece of computer hardware, the specifications printed on the box may not be what you need for your system. Which drive is easiest to install? Which one is best for audio recording? Are those audio CD controls really necessary?

If you're a computer power user or you're experienced with recording, the idea of researching these questions for a potential CD-RW purchase might be exciting — and you may want to simply skim this chapter as a quick refresher. (Of course, if your computer came with a CD-RW built-in, you won't need all of the information in this chapter either.)

However, if you do need to buy a drive and you're a recording novice, or you'd like someone else to show the way, then this chapter is for you! Be sure to take notes on the specifications that meet your needs. I also explain the extra features that define the best drives, help you choose the right interface for your system, and provide tips about what to look for and what to avoid. Finally, I end the chapter with tips for buying online and buying locally.

Are you ready to buy some hardware? Then let's go!

Evaluating Recordable CD Features

If you have already done some shopping for CD recorders, you may think that no two CD drives are exactly the same. A list of specifications for a CD-RW drive is chock-full of terms you may have never heard before: For example, you'll be hit with "internal/external," "interface type," "recording speed," "data buffer," and "recording formats." What do all these tech terms mean — and more important, how do you evaluate a recorder to determine which is the right one for you?

Take my word for it, buying a drive without fully evaluating its features is asking for trouble later on. For example, when your new drive is a month old and you discover that it can't record in disc-at-once mode (more on this later), it's too late! I'm a firm believer in fully researching a purchase beforehand. In this section, I cover the features that you should look for *before* you buy.

Choosing an Internal or External Drive

Here's a fundamental decision that everyone needs to make at the planning stage: Will you be shopping for an internal or an external recorder? An internal drive fits inside your computer's case, much like your floppy drive, whereas an external drive has a separate external case and power cord.

At first glance, the internal drive might appear to be the clear choice; after all, it takes up no space on your desktop, doesn't require a separate AC power connection or external data cable, and is usually significantly less expensive than an external drive. So why would someone pay the extra cost for an external recorder? Here are a number of reasons:

- **Saves room.** If you own a laptop computer or an Apple iMac, it may be impossible to add an internal drive. (In fact, most Macintosh computers can only use an external recorder.) Or perhaps you've already used all the slots in your desktop PC and have no more room for another drive. In these cases, an external recorder is a good solution.

- **Easy to install.** If you're a computer novice — or you'd simply rather not open the case on your computer — it's a lot easier to add an external CD-RW drive to your system. It is as simple as plugging in the proper connector and loading the software.

Tip

If you'd like to install an internal recorder and you'd like help, I can heartily recommend another of my books, *Building a PC for Dummies,* 2nd Edition, from IDG Books Worldwide. You'll also learn about all of the other peripherals you can add to a computer, and how to build a PC from the ground up.

- **Easy to share.** Unlike an internal recorder, an external CD-RW drive can be shared by everyone in an office. For example, an external parallel port or USB CD-RW drive makes a great backup device for individual computers that aren't connected to your office network.

- **Stays cool.** Luckily, overheating isn't as much of a problem as it once was — older computers could overheat when they were crammed full of drives and devices. (If you're running a Pentium II or Pentium III computer with several drives and only a single standard fan, your system is probably not properly cooled, and you may be risking component failure! I recommend you install a second fan in your case as quickly as possible.) An external recorder will have its own fan if the manufacturer deems it necessary.

So which is right for you? Unless you need to transport your drive, or your case simply can't hold another drive, I usually recommend an internal recorder. You save money and space on your desktop (and in an office environment, an internal drive is far less likely to be "misplaced" than an external model).

Picking an Interface

Ready for a list of really weird acronyms? Okay, try these on for size: EIDE, SCSI, PCMCIA, USB, and parallel! (Okay, that last one's not an acronym, but it belongs in this list, as you'll see later in the chapter.) These word jumbles actually stand for the most popular *interfaces* for CD-RW and DVD-RAM drives. (If you're unfamiliar with the word *interface,* it refers to the type of connection through which data flows between your system and your recorder.) I've talked to many novice computer owners who would look nervously at that list and think, "Oh boy, it's techno-nerd time . . . how am I ever going to decide which is which? Do I really have to know this stuff just to record discs?"

Good news: Although you do need to know a little about each of these interfaces, you certainly don't have to be an electrical engineer to select the right model. Besides, you've got me to help! In this section, I discuss each interface in turn, and it should be a snap to determine which one you need for your system.

EIDE: The Popular Favorite

I start our quick connectivity tour with the interface of choice for virtually all modern CD-RW hardware: EIDE, which is short for *Enhanced Integrated Drive Electronics.* (You may want to write that down in case you ever challenge a computer hardware technician to a trivia match.)

Most computers built these days use EIDE hard drives and CD-ROM drives; a typical PC has both a primary and a secondary EIDE connector. Each connector can handle two EIDE devices for a total of four drives. Because most home computers have only a single hard drive and a single CD-ROM drive, your computer is likely to have a spare EIDE connection that you can use for your recorder.

Note

EIDE drives are exclusively internal, so if you're shopping for an external drive (or if you're using a Macintosh), you should skip to the next interface in this section.

Because I describe the complete installation procedure for an EIDE drive later in the book, I'll simply point out that an EIDE drive has only a single configuration jumper that you have to set, as shown in Figure 4.1. If you've never installed hardware, a jumper is a little plastic connector that's used to configure hardware, and the fewer jumpers you have to set, the easier it is to install your drive. Therefore, EIDE is easier to configure than SCSI (the other most popular interface, which I cover next). I generally recommend EIDE for most home computer owners.

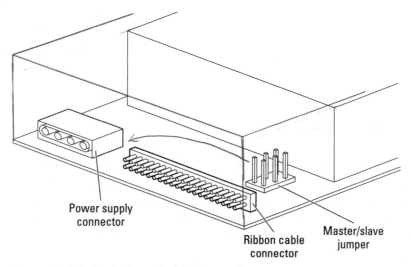

Power supply
connector

Ribbon cable
connector

Master/slave
jumper

Figure 4.1 The back of a typical EIDE recorder

SCSI: Speedy but Tricky

Our next stop is the SCSI interface, another strange acronym that stands for
Small Computer System Interface. SCSI has been around for many years now, and
it's available in several different versions. Older Macintosh computers used SCSI
hard drives, and it's been a popular interface for external peripherals for both PC
and Macintosh.

SCSI has two important advantages over the EIDE interface:

- **It's fast.** SCSI drives can transfer data significantly faster than an ordinary
  EIDE drive, so most early CD recorders used SCSI to ensure a high transfer
  rate during recording. If you use a drive that can record at 6x or even 8x,
  this speed increase makes a difference.

- **It supports more devices.** A standard SCSI adapter can control anywhere
  from 8 to 14 devices, depending on the version you're using, which means
  you can expand your system farther with a SCSI interface than with a typical EIDE interface. Unlike with an EIDE connection, data can be transferred
  between multiple SCSI devices at the same time, making it an ideal pick for
  power users who sometimes use other applications at the same time
  they're recording a disc.

Now for the bad news: Although Windows 95/98 and Windows 2000 automate
as much as possible, SCSI is still significantly harder to configure than EIDE,
because it requires the correct arrangement of terminators and a unique SCSI ID
number for each device. Also, SCSI hardware is often more expensive than similar EIDE hardware.

Again, I explain the complete installation procedure for a SCSI drive later in the book. Suffice it to say that SCSI is a more powerful interface, but it requires more work to configure and it may cost you a little more than an EIDE solution. I would recommend SCSI for experienced computer owners who are looking for the best performance and are comfortable with installing and configuring hardware.

PCMCIA: The Road Warrior's Friend

If you don't own a portable computer, stop reading right here and skip to the next interface—PCMCIA cards are used to support peripheral devices for laptop computers. PCMCIA stands for *Personal Computer Memory Card International Association,* but thankfully, PCMCIA cards are also commonly called PC cards. Generally, PCMCIA devices, like the one illustrated in Figure 4.2, include modems and hard drives that fit internally inside your laptop, but PCMCIA adapters are also available for external devices such as CD-ROM drives.

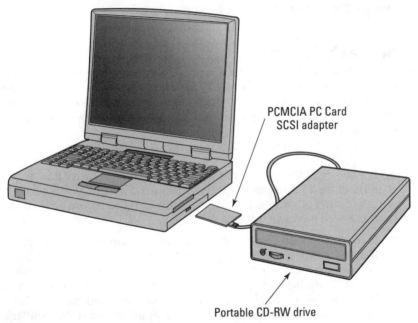

PCMCIA PC Card
SCSI adapter

Portable CD-RW drive

Figure 4.2 A PCMCIA card for a laptop

Because portable computers don't have internal drive bays, a PCMCIA CD-RW drive is about the only choice that notebook and laptop owners have when it comes to CD recording. Unfortunately, PCMCIA drives are usually somewhat slower than an EIDE or a SCSI drive, so you probably won't find a PCMCIA recorder capable of burning discs any faster than 2x or 4x. Also, PCMCIA drives are usually cost $50 to $100 more than a typical EIDE or SCSI recorder.

USB: The Easiest Option

Ladies and gentlemen, our last acronym — USB, which is short for *Universal Serial Bus* — is definitely the winning approach to installing just about anything! Figure 4.3 illustrates the Hewlett-Packard CD-Writer Plus 8210e portable CD-RW drive, which uses a USB connection. This is a great example of a plug and play drive that's perfect for use on the road. The 8210e is a 4x/4x/6x drive, meaning that it can write both CD-R and CD-RW discs at 4x and can also perform as a 6x CD-ROM drive.

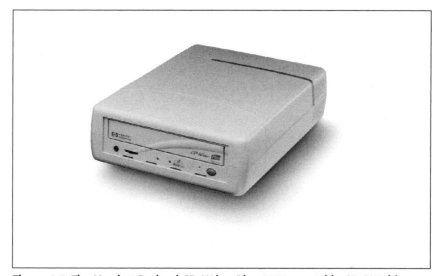

Figure 4.3 The Hewlett-Packard CD-Writer Plus 8210e portable CD-RW drive

Because the USB port shown in Figure 4.4 has become standard equipment on new PC and Macintosh computers, these peripherals have exploded onto the home computer scene. You can choose from literally hundreds of different USB hardware devices . . . and, of course, among them is our favorite peripheral, the external CD recorder. Although a USB connection is much slower than an EIDE or SCSI connection, it's still fast enough for most of the recorders currently on the market.

Here's why USB is so popular:

■ **It's plug-and-play.** Windows 95/98, Windows 2000, and Mac OS 9 all fully support USB (if your computer has them), so all you have to do is plug your new CD-RW drive into your computer's USB port and it's automatically recognized and configured by the operating system. I can actually call this process "no hassle" with a straight face. No hardware installation is required, and you won't have to open your computer's case.

■ **It doesn't require rebooting.** USB devices can be *hot swapped,* meaning that you don't even need to reboot or shut down your computer when you connect your drive. (This is also a great feature for portable computers.)

■ **It can be used by both Mac and PC folks.** Because USB is supported across different operating systems, the same drive can work on both types of computers — a real boon for offices that need to share a CD-RW drive between different platforms.

■ **It doesn't need a power supply.** If you're using a portable, many USB drives can draw their power supply through the USB connector, so they don't need an external power supply. If you're like me, one less electrical cord makes a difference on long trips.

This plug-and-play convenience typically comes with a slightly higher price tag, but most of the novice computer owners that I know are happy to pay $50 extra for a USB CD-RW drive.

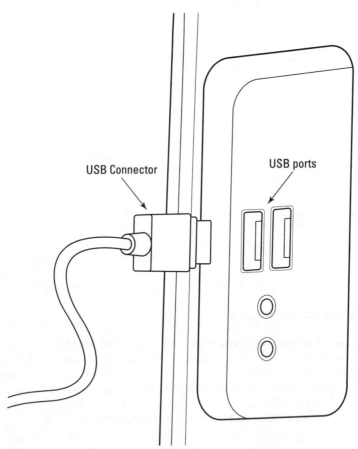

USB Connector

USB ports

Figure 4.4 The USB port and connector . . . truly plug-and-play!

Tip

Because most computers have only two USB ports, you may have to add a USB *hub* to expand your system. A hub converts one of your USB ports into four ports.

Naturally, I recommend USB for all computers, including portables with a USB port.

Parallel: When Nothing Else Works

What if your system doesn't have USB ports or a PCMCIA slot, and you'd still like to add an external drive? You have one last option: You can add a parallel port CD recorder, which connects to your computer's printer port, as shown in Figure 4.5. This only works for PC owners, because Macintosh computers don't have a 25-pin parallel printer port.

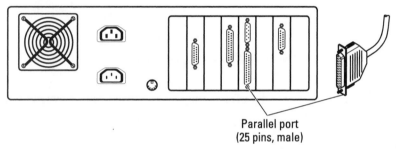

Parallel port
(25 pins, male)

Figure 4.5 The standard 25-pin parallel port can support a recorder, but it's no superstar!

I don't recommend these drives, unless you have no other choice, because:

■ **Parallel port drives are slow.** The IBM parallel printer port was originally designed for just that: to connect a printer to your computer. To enable faster transfer of data in both directions, a number of improvements have been made to the standard parallel port over the years. However, parallel port technology is still much slower than any of the other interface choices I've listed. Because the computer's data transfer rate is so important to recording, parallel port drives are inherently slower and more prone to errors than any other type of drive. They do work, but parallel port technology is nowhere near an efficient solution.

■ **No access to your printer port.** Many parallel-port devices claim that they offer *pass-through* (also called *daisy-chaining*) connections for your printer, as shown in Figure 4.6. Pass-through connections enable both your printer and your CD recorder to "share" the same port. However, this type of connection doesn't work with some printers. If you already have a parallel port scanner or Zip drive on the same port as your printer, they're not likely to work reliably with yet a third device connected to the same port! Often, PC owners that use this technology end up performing the dance that I call "the Parallel Port Twist" as they constantly unplug one parallel port device and connect another (which requires a reboot and involves moving their computer each time).

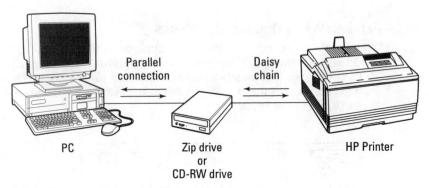

Figure 4.6 A parallel-port pass-through connection

I recommend parallel port CD-RW only for those computer owners who can't use another interface.

And the Winner Is . . .

. . . completely up to you! With the information and the recommendations that I've provided in this section, you should be able to make the right choice for your system. To recap, remember that your interface choice depends on these criteria:

■ The number and types of ports available on your computer

■ The number of free internal drive bays in your case (if any)

■ The amount you're willing to spend

■ The performance you want (as well as the top rated speed of your drive)

■ Whether your drive is an internal or external model

■ The type of computer you're using (PC or Macintosh)

Considering Speed

I've already discussed the X factor earlier in the book—but how does a person shopping for a CD-RW drive decide on the best possible recording and playback speeds? Of course, the fastest recording speeds are attractive, if your computer can handle the load, but is a 6x or 8x drive worth the extra money you'll spend?

Cross-Reference

To learn more about recording speeds, check out Chapter 2, "How Does a CD-ROM Work?"

At the time of this writing, I feel that the best bargain in recording speeds is definitely 4x. The reasons are simple:

- **For most of us, 4x is fast enough.** Although you won't break any speed records, you'll record at twice the speed of an "antique" 2x drive and burn an entire 74 minutes of digital audio in less than 20 minutes. Certainly, faster is better — but consider the amount of recording you'll do, and how fast you need to finish a disc.

- **Prices have dropped.** As you may have noticed, 2x drives are becoming harder and harder to find, and 4x recorders are now the most common variety on the market. That popularity has resulted in a lower price point for 4x drives that would have been unheard-of four or five years ago.

- **Could your computer handle 6x or 8x?** Remember, I'm not talking about just the processor speed when I bring up your computer's overall performance — you also need to consider the data transfer rate of your hard drive and controller. Your choice of interface may also limit you as well; for example, reaching 8x on a parallel port drive would be a tricky matter indeed. In fact, even an older Pentium-based PC with an original IDE drive (the ancestor of EIDE) might be hard-pressed to deliver data fast enough to record reliably with a superfast CD-RW drive — but that same computer could probably record at 4x without problems.

To sum up, I'd suggest a minimum of a 4x drive for just about every computer owner, unless recording speed is all-important to you and you can afford to spend the additional cash on a faster drive. After all, do you really need to eat out once a month?

Examining Data Buffers

Next, let's consider one of the least understood (and yet most important) features on any CD recorder: the *data buffer,* also commonly known as a *cache* or *internal RAM.* Every CD recorder made these days carries a certain amount of internal memory as a buffer; this buffer storage is designed to hold data that's already been read from your hard drive until your recorder is ready for it, as shown in Figure 4.7. Because the hard drive in your system can read data faster than the drive can record it, storing the data helps ensure a steady, efficient flow of information to the drive.

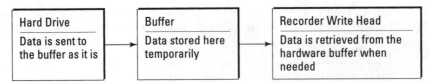

Figure 4.7 Your recorder's data buffer helps minimize recording errors.

As I said, virtually all CD-RW drives have a data buffer, but not all drives are created equal—some drives might include only 512K of buffer memory, while another drive might have 1, 2, or 4 megabytes. Here's the rule: *The larger the buffer, the better the drive and the fewer problems you're likely to encounter* (especially if you're recording at 8x or 10x, or if you'll be using a PC with an older Pentium CPU). If you're considering two drives with similar features and prices and one drive has a significantly larger data buffer, that's the model I would recommend.

Surveying Formats: the More the Merrier

Another set of specifications that are very important when shopping for a CD-RW drive are the *recording formats* it supports. Any drive you buy should be able to create a data disc with computer files or an audio disc that conforms to the Red Book standard (the international standard for the digital "structure" of audio CDs and how they're recorded). However, many other specialized alternate recording formats and methods are used to create special types of discs, and not all drives support all formats.

As a general rule, the more formats a drive can record, the better it is and the more likely you'll be able to create specialized CD-ROMs in the future. Naturally, you'll also need recording software that supports the same alternate formats. These formats include:

■ **Packet-writing.** Unlike formats that require you to burn the entire disc in one or more sessions, packet-writing enables data to be added to the disc incrementally, one or more files at a time, just as you would save data to a floppy disk. Packet-writing even enables you to erase data from a disc; the data is essentially "overwritten" so that it can't be retrieved. Windows 95/98, Windows 2000, and Mac OS support packet-writing, and packet-writing is the format used by programs like Adaptec's DirectCD. It's a good idea to limit your shopping to drives that support packet-writing.

■ **CD-ROM XA.** These discs are recorded in *multisession* mode, which means they can carry separate recording sessions on the same disc. For example, one session might be the first release of a program, and the second session would contain the second version. All of the sessions on a multisession disc can be accessed, but only one at a time. Multisession mode used to be a neat trick for updating information that had already been recorded on a disc, but CD-ROM XA is seldom used these days; packet-writing is better supported, and it's much more convenient. Also, older CD-ROM drives may not be able to read discs recorded in this format.

■ **Video CD.** If your recorder supports the VideoCD format, you can create high-quality video discs for a video CD player, complete with menu system and freeze-frame.

■ **CD Extra.** Because a CD Extra disc can contain both audio and data tracks; a single disc can contain both the music and a music video, or song lyrics, or even a multimedia interview with the artist that you can watch on your computer. As more and more computer owners now have high-quality audio, this format has really become popular in the last few years. Another neat feature: Because the audio track is recorded first on the disc, a CD Extra disc can also be played in a regular audio CD player.

■ **Photo CD Image Pac.** This format is often used to create image clip art libraries. If you have a high-resolution scanner or digital camera, you can create discs that can display photo-quality pictures on your computer.

Note

The Kodak PhotoCD format used by PhotoCD players is proprietary, so you won't be able to create them using your recorder.

Tip

"Where can I get all these specifications?" Your first stop should be the manufacturer's Web site — if you can't find a complete description of the drive there, visit www.buy.com or www.computershopper.com and check out the product information. Also, computer magazines often publish hardware comparisons online, so it's worth a foray onto the Web to read them.

Adding Audio Extras

For me, the ideal computer system has two drives: One is a CD-RW or DVD-RAM, but there's also another CD-ROM or DVD read-only drive dedicated to playing games and multimedia applications. Why the second drive? Two reasons:

■ **CD copying is easier.** If you'll spend most of your time copying existing discs, it's much easier and more convenient to copy drive-to-recorder instead of creating a disc image file, swapping the original for a blank disc, and then recording.

■ **Recorders aren't the fastest readers.** Today's 48x and 52x read-only CD-ROM drives are much faster than a typical 24x CD-RW drive, so chores like installations and multimedia games perform better.

However, let us not forget that many computer owners shopping for recorders will actually replace their existing CD-ROM drive with a CD-RW or DVD-RAM drive. If you fit into this group and you're an audiophile, I would suggest that you invest in a CD recorder with audio controls. Virtually all recorders feature a volume control and headphone jack, but some drives also offer the same drive controls that you'd find on an audio CD player or a high-end CD-ROM drive — these generally include track-forward and track-reverse, pause and play. Audiophile controls are very convenient if you like to listen to music played through your computer's audio system while you're working.

Assessing the Software

Don't forget to look at the software that is included with any drive that you are evaluating. I've noticed that many computer owners will buy a piece of hardware without considering the software they receive with the drive — it's a "surprise bonus" for these folks. Unfortunately, the value of the software packages that accompany CD-RW drives can vary tremendously, so it's very important to evaluate the software as you look at different drives! (Some people just want the basics and do not want to pay for a lot of "extra" packages; others want added flexibility.)

Determining Your Minimum Software Requirements

Besides required software drivers, any CD-R or CD-RW drive you're considering should come with *at least* two programs:

- **Basic recording software.** The drive should come with a program for recording discs in all of the formats supported by your drive; if you're buying a CD-RW drive, this software should also be able to erase and format CD-RW discs. Figure 4.8 illustrates the main window from one of the most popular recording programs around, Adaptec's Easy CD Creator, which ships with Hewlett-Packard recorders. (I use this program throughout the book.)

- **Drive diagnostic software.** You'll need some way to check the operation of your drive and make sure that it's been correctly installed and configured. Many recording programs have this function built in, so it may not appear as a separate program on the box.

That's not a long list, but in my opinion any recorder that ships without at least those two programs should be given a wide berth. (Personally, I like as many nice extras as I can get, too.)

o Nero Burning.

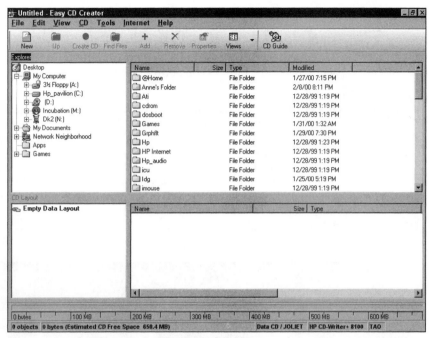

Figure 4.8 A familiar site to most recorder owners: Adaptec's Easy CD Creator

Finding Software Extras

Speaking of extras, here's a list of the programs that I've seen accompanying the better drives on the market today. Of course, not every recorder ships with all these programs, but the more the merrier (and the more favorably I would consider that drive while shopping). As I mentioned before, some of these features may be built into a comprehensive program like Easy CD Creator.

- **Label software.** If you'd like to label your discs once they've been recorded, a number of programs enable you to design and print professional-looking results. If simple text isn't enough, you can import line art or images to use as label backgrounds.

- **Packet-writing software.** Because part of the idea behind packet writing is to avoid running a recording program, packet-writing software is usually packaged separately. For example, Adaptec's DirectCD can be installed separately from the rest of Easy CD Creator. Under Windows, these programs usually run in your Taskbar, so they're always ready to initialize a disc for packet-writing.

■ **Backup software.** As I've mentioned earlier in the book, a CD-RW drive works great as a backup device. Some programs may back up the contents of your entire system, whereas others are specifically designed for disaster recovery and back up only the critical files on your computer (which, of course, is much faster). Either type of program is a welcome addition to a recorder package.

■ **Multimedia editing and retrieval software.** One of the primary uses for CD recording in the past has been multimedia file storage. For this reason, drive manufacturers often package a graphics editor or a digital video viewer with their drives. Figure 4.9 illustrates Paint Shop Pro, a very popular shareware image editor and browser that I've been using for years. Another favorite is the multimedia retrieval program. To help you find just the file you need for your presentation or document, these programs can organize and display (or play) an entire collection of digital photos, sound files, and digital video clips.

Figure 4.9 Browsing my image collection with Paint Shop Pro

■ **Jewel box insert software.** If you're recording discs for distribution or you want to add a finishing touch to your recording projects, you'll want to print an attractive cover for the front of the *jewel box,* the plastic case in which the CD is stored. Some programs can also create a custom-printed insert for the back of a jewel box containing audio track descriptions for your audio discs or file descriptions for data discs. Figure 4.10 illustrates the jewel box insert feature in Easy CD Creator.

■ **Audio CD/MP3/WAV player.** An all-in-one audio player is a good find when you're buying a recorder. In fact, you should have one even if you're not buying a drive! The best audio players handle anything that today's music industry and the Internet can throw at them, including the extremely popular MP3 format for CD-quality digital music, audio CDs, Windows WAV files, and Macintosh AIF files. Figure 4.11 illustrates my favorite player, the jack-of-all-trades program WinAmp from Nullsoft, Inc.

Figure 4.10 Creating a jewel box insert using Easy CD Creator

Figure 4.11 Listening to my favorite MP3 files with WinAmp

Locating Recording Shareware

Before I leave the topic of software, I should also mention that the popularity of CD recording has resulted in a wide range of excellent *shareware* programs. The idea behind shareware is practically as old as the personal computer itself: You can download and try a shareware program free of charge for a specified time, and if you like the software and want to continue using it, you simply register it by paying the program's author directly. The author also provides technical support and product upgrades for those who have registered the software.

Some shareware recording programs are specifically designed for certain applications. For example, a number of programs record an audio CD directly from MP3 files—whereas others are as fully featured as a commercial recording program. These programs have no set look and feel, so some are harder to use than others.

Tip

If you're looking for a specific type of shareware recording application and you have an Internet connection, try entering that application as a keyword on a major search site such as Yahoo! or Infoseek. For example, you could enter "MP3 CD recording" as your search phrase.

Buying Hardware: The No-Frills Guide

If you're asking which is better—buying locally from a store or buying your recorder over the Web—you're not alone; it's one of the questions that I receive most often from readers. I cannot give you one "correct" answer: The right decision depends more on your experience level and the money you can afford to spend. In this section, I provide you with a quick guide to the advantages of both local and online purchasing.

Oh, by the way, if you've never bought anything online, there are basic precautions that you can take to help ensure that your credit card number is safeguarded; I discuss them as well.

Buying Online

First, let's do the "e-" thing—after all, more consumers are buying merchandise online than ever before, and you can't pick up a newspaper or watch television news without tripping over "e-commerce" and "e-marketing!" Computer-savvy shoppers now surf the Web first, and many of my friends don't even consider entering a store unless they need a particular program or hardware component immediately.

The advantages of buying online include:

■ **A broader selection.** Even the largest local store can't boast the selection you'll find on the Web. By searching a site like www.pricewatch.com, you can even compare prices asked by competing online stores for the same drive! Naturally, you'll also find more bargains than you would shopping locally, because many more online stores offer clearance merchandise.

■ **Lower cost.** If you want to buy that CD-RW drive as cheaply as possible, you're certain to find a better price online than you would by shopping in a physical store. After all, the local store has overhead costs and has to pay salespeople. Online Web stores are mostly automated and don't require a traditional storefront — they do not have to incur the same overhead costs traditional stores do. Although you'll have to pay shipping, it still generally works out to less than you'd pay locally.

■ **Convenience.** If you're like me, the idea of bypassing the crowd at the mall — especially during the holiday season — is a big point in favor of online shopping! (It's not that I don't like people, it's just that I don't have to leave my computer when I'm shopping on the Web.)

■ **You *may* not need to pay sales tax.** Once upon a time — four or five years ago — no one charged sales tax on the Web. Now, however, many states have caught on and are starting to tax online purchases.

■ **Fun!** At least it is for many computer owners. As I said before, researching the right purchase online is easy, and the actual purchase is a breeze.

Taken singly, each of these perks might not sound so revolutionary, but taken as a whole, you can see why online shopping has become such a compelling alternative to traditional shopping in a store.

Buying Locally

E-commerce hasn't quite replaced the corner store or the gargantuan shopping mall, however, and I don't think anyone honestly thinks it ever will. Of course, you may rather shop at your local store, and there are a number of reasons to do so. The advantages of shopping in a local store include:

■ **Immediate gratification.** Now this is an important point! You can install a drive that you've bought locally the same evening and be recording that night. No matter how much money and driving time you save by purchasing a recorder online, you're not going to get it immediately.

■ **Hands-on shopping.** If a local store carries exactly the model of recorder that you've selected, you can see the drive in action (or at least get a good look at the box) before you buy.

■ **Personal service.** Depending on the training and experience of the salespeople, you may be able to ask questions and elicit opinions about the hardware you're buying — in fact, it never hurts to ask whether or not the drive has proved reliable, and whether other customers were satisfied with it.

■ **Returns easier.** Woe unto the poor customer who buys a defective recorder over the Web. It doesn't happen often, but returning an item to an online store can be a hassle! At most sites, you'll have to call the company's customer support number for RMA approval, repack the drive, and ship it back at your expense; eventually (read that as a week or two) you'll receive a replacement. On the other hand, returning an item to a local store is a breeze by comparison, as is any warranty work necessary later.

Tip

If you have a friend who's a computer expert (or someone who has extensive experience in CD recording), ask him or her to accompany you on your shopping trip. It never hurts to have an educated opinion along for the ride!

Still unsure about which method is really right for you? Not everyone is a perfect fit into either category, so here's my personal recommendations on who should buy locally and online.

I recommend online shopping if you are an experienced computer user who has bought hardware before, doesn't need any personal assistance, and wants to save money. If you want that recorder immediately, prefer assistance from a salesperson, or would like to return the drive locally if it turns out to be defective, I recommend going to a local store.

Buying Tips to Remember

If you've never bought computer hardware before, you need to consider a number of possible pitfalls. Some of these hazards apply to one type of shopping experience, and others apply no matter whether you're buying online or locally—for example, I always recommend that you avoid buying a "no-name" brand from a manufacturer you've never heard of before, no matter whether you shop locally or online.

■ **Don't buy online without a secure connection.** Both Internet Explorer and Netscape Navigator tell you if a site has an encrypted (or secure) connection. When information is encrypted, it's much harder for a hacker to intercept your data as it's being transmitted to the Web site. If the Web site asks for personal information, such as your credit card, as you are buying your drive, check to see that your browser is displaying a closed padlock icon on the status bar at the bottom of the screen; if it isn't, I recommend finding another site!

■ **Beware of refurbished merchandise.** Many computer owners don't mind buying refurbished (or used) hardware, especially if the price is right and it's being offered for sale by the original manufacturer. If you decide to buy a refurbished drive, consider what warranty coverage you receive with it. If the price on a "new" drive seems too good to be true, make sure you read the entire description, including any fine print—you may be looking at a refurbished item. If you're buying locally, make sure the drive works before you leave the store. Ask the salesperson to hook up the drive and test it for you.

- **Use common sense at auctions.** If you're considering a recorder from an online auction, check the feedback rating for the seller. I recommend buying only from individuals who have accumulated positive feedback from other transactions. Also, look out for ridiculously high shipping charges (which are generally paid by the purchaser), and get a full description of the item before you bid on it.

- **Don't pay more for shipping than necessary.** Unfortunately, I've visited a few online stores that offer next-day or overnight shipping as the default. If you can wait a few more days for your hardware, why spend $30 or more extra simply to have it the very next day? I usually pick the least expensive shipping method (typically UPS Ground), wait a day or two more, and keep my hard-earned cash in my wallet!

- **Attack of the Creeping Restocking Fee.** Most online and local computer stores now charge a restocking fee if you return an item. I've seen everything from 5 percent to a whopping 20 percent of the amount you spent charged for restocking! Make sure that the company will accept the return of a defective item without charging any fee. Also, it pays to shop around for a store that charges a minimum for restocking (or make very certain that you've made the right choice before you buy).

Above all, remind yourself: *Take your time shopping and don't be shy about asking questions!* You're not running a race. If you're buying your recorder from a local store, no one should pressure you. If you're not sure about how something works or why you should pay extra for a specific feature, you deserve an answer. After all, that's why the salesperson is there, and that's one of the advantages of buying locally.

Looking for Warranty and Support

As with any other piece of computer hardware, it's important to compare the lengths of the manufacturers' warranties while shopping for your drive. Most companies offer a one-year warranty, but I have seen drives with as much as three years of warranty coverage. Check these points while comparing warranties:

- Will the manufacturer pay for returning the drive?
- Is the entire drive covered, or just certain parts and subsystems?
- Is an extended warranty offered? (Don't forget to compare both price and length of an extended warranty.)

Even more important, however, is the help you may need after you've bought your drive. Most manufacturers have both voice technical support and a Web site. Is voice support free, or will the company charge you? Is an 800 number available? Is support offered 24 hours/7 days a week, or only during certain times? Most of the answers should be available through the company's Web site (as well as the contact e-mail address for the Sales department, if you have specific questions that you'd like to ask). As always, reputation is important — if you've heard that a company has a good track record for support, you may feel that paying for help is worth it if the problem is resolved quickly and reliably.

Speaking of the Web site, it's an often-overlooked litmus test for many manufacturers. For example, it's a good idea to check the download section on the Web site: How often are software drivers and firmware updates posted? I'd consider it a bad sign if the latest driver update file you can find is dated 1997! Does the Web site feature valuable content such as a FAQ (short for *Frequently Asked Questions*) file, or a searchable knowledge base of tech support solutions?

I know that not every computer owner devotes time to researching the manufacturer's warranty and technical support. You'll find, however, that reading the side of the box is not always the best indicator of what you can expect. Because the Web makes it easy and yes, even a little fun, take a few minutes to check out these details — you may save yourself considerable trouble later on!

In Review

In this chapter, you learned how to find the right CD recorder for your system; determine which features it should include; and make sure the best software is bundled with your drive. If you have never shopped for computer hardware, you now know the plusses and minuses of shopping online or at your local computer store. In addition, you now know the hazards of hardware shopping and how you can avoid them.

CHAPTER

5

Installing Your Recorder

Now that you've bought a new internal CD-RW drive (or perhaps an external SCSI drive), someone has got to install it. Perhaps you're nervous about digging into the insides of your computer and you don't have any techno-wizard friends to help. Naturally, no one in the computer service industry is going to try to change your mind or tell you the real story—after all, your local computer repair store probably *wants* you to drop by with your new CD recorder! They'd be more than happy to charge you $50 (or maybe more) to install it, even though the entire process takes a trained computer technician about 15 minutes.

I'm here to put an end to the installation myth once and for all: If you can read a set of step-by-step instructions and you know which end of a screwdriver to hold, you can install a standard EIDE CD recorder! Afterward, you'll feel like a million bucks because you did it yourself—and who knows, you might become even more popular among your friends. (At least those with computers!)

In this chapter, I show you how to evaluate installation requirements and how to install an internal EIDE recordable CD drive and both internal and external SCSI drives. I also help you install Adaptec's Easy CD Creator software and troubleshoot the most common problems you may run into.

I don't cover the installation or troubleshooting of USB, PCMCIA, and parallel port drives in this book, because they're all external interfaces that simply need a cable connection. However, I recommend that you read the information at the end of the chapter, where I demonstrate how to install Easy CD Creator recording software.

Determining the Minimum Requirements for EIDE and SCSI

Is your computer ready for a new EIDE or SCSI recorder? It's easy to find out, especially because you determined the interface you needed in the last chapter. If your computer doesn't meet one of these minimum requirements, then you'll have to upgrade it first before you can install your drive.

Note

You may be asking, "Isn't it important which processor I have, or how much memory?" Actually, the answer depends on the top recording speed of your new drive. If you have a Pentium II or Pentium III computer with a reasonably fast hard drive, you can comfortably record without errors at 8x. On the other hand, if you're still using an original Pentium processor, your machine probably reaches its limit at 4x recording. On the Macintosh side, a G3 or G4 machine can easily handle 8x, whereas an older PowerPC or 68040 model should stick to 4x. As for memory, if your computer has at least 32 megabytes of system RAM, you should be able to record your own discs without a problem.

EIDE Requirements

If you've decided to use an internal EIDE CD recorder, your computer needs:

- **An open EIDE connector.** As I mentioned in the last chapter, most PCs made in the last two or three years have four available EIDE device connectors (a primary master and slave, and a secondary master and slave). You'll need at least one for your new recorder.

Tip

Even though you may be able to add another EIDE device, you may still need a cable! Many PC manufacturers include a secondary connector on the motherboard, but don't actually connect a cable to it—it's up to you to do that. Luckily, an EIDE cable is cheap (usually under $5) and available from most computer stores. If you need help in locating your secondary EIDE connector, check your system manual.

- **Windows 95 or later/Mac OS 8.0 or later.** Take my word for it, you don't want to record discs on Windows 3.1, DOS, or System 7.5! These older 16-bit operating systems are slower and less efficient—which can lead to recording errors—and they don't have the built-in support for current hardware.

- **At least 700 megabytes of free drive space.** If you intend to copy discs from your hard drive, you should reserve at least 700 megabytes to hold that information. If you're going to continue using your computer while recording in the background—for example, if you'll use a word processor at the same time you record—it's also a good idea to reserve an extra 300 megabytes for your recording software and the Windows virtual memory swap file.

  Unsure of how much space you have remaining on your hard drive? If you're running Windows 95 or 98, click My Computer to open it, right-click your hard drive icon, and choose Properties. Windows displays a dialog box like the one in Figure 5.1 that includes the amount of space remaining on your hard drive. If you need additional space, check out the section "Creating Space on Your Hard Drive" in Chapter 7.

- **An open drive bay.** An internal device needs a home, and in this case you need a standard 5.25-inch drive bay with an opening to the front of your case.

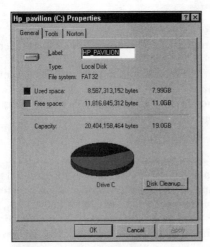

Figure 5.1 Displaying the amount of free space on a PC running Windows 98

■ **An open power connector.** Naturally, that drive isn't going to cooperate at all if you don't connect it to your system's power supply! To add a device, you need an open power connector, as shown in Figure 5.2. If you don't have an available power connector (which can happen if your machine is stuffed full with a second or third hard drive), visit your local computer store and get a power cable Y splitter, which turns one connector into two.

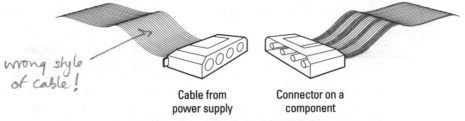

wrong style of cable!

Cable from power supply   Connector on a component

Figure 5.2 A power connector for internal PC devices

SCSI Requirements

If you've decided to use an internal or external SCSI CD recorder, your computer needs:

■ **An available SCSI connector.** You need one available device ID on your SCSI chain and at least one available connector (internal or external). If "device ID" sounds like a foreign language to you, don't worry—I go over it in detail later in this chapter.

- **Windows 95 or later/Mac OS 8.0 or later.** As I mentioned earlier, take advantage of the built-in hardware support and improved efficiency of a newer operating system, and stay away from Windows 3.1, DOS, or System 7.5.

- **At least 700 megabytes of free drive space.** Again, reserve yourself enough space to copy the contents of an entire CD image, and if you have the hard drive space to spare, consider adding additional space to your swapfile.

- **An open drive bay.** If you're installing an internal SCSI drive, you need a standard 5.25-inch drive bay with an opening to the front of your case. An external drive won't need a drive bay.

- **An available power connector.**

Preparing to Install Your Drive

You need more than just the right components and software to properly install your new drive. I recommend that you prepare yourself with the following:

- **A stable tabletop or workbench.** If you're working on top of the kitchen table, spread newspaper—*not* cloth, which can carry static—on top to protect the finish.

- **A good light source.** Remember those gooseneck lamps that you could adjust anywhere you like? That's the perfect light source for working on your computer—which is why I have one on my workbench! In a pinch, though, any good lamp that you can adjust will work fine.

- **A magnetic screwdriver.** Why magnetic? If you lose a screw inside your case, you have to turn the case upside down to retrieve the screw unless you can pick it up with your trusty screwdriver. Besides, a magnetic screwdriver "holds" the screw in place, so it's easier to start.

- **A plastic bowl or container.** Every hardware-installing computer techno-wizard needs a parts bin of some kind, so you might as well start one now. Besides, it can hold all of the screws that you remove, in case you have to reinstall them later.

- **A knowledgeable friend.** If you have a friend who knows computers and you're the least bit nervous about working on your machine, then ask for your friend's help!

- **Patience!** Last but not least, you need patience—take your time. Rushing through an installation is an invitation for mistakes and misplaced parts. If you follow my instructions and the documentation that accompanied your drive, you can do the job right the first time.

Speaking of documentation, it's *always* important to read the documentation that came with your drive! The steps I follow in the next two sections are general, and your drive may require a special setting or an extra step. In fact, the master/slave configuration step is different for just about every brand of hard drive and CD recorder made, so don't toss those instructions. Follow my instructions, but if the installation documentation for your drive differs significantly, follow it instead!

Installing an EIDE CD Recorder

Okay, it's show time: You're prepared and you've set aside a couple of hours (just in case) of uninterrupted time to spend with your computer. Grab your screwdriver, and follow these steps:

1. First, a very important warning about static: Static electricity can damage electronic components, so you must discharge it *before* touching the interior of your new recorder. To discharge static electricity, touch a metal surface, such as your computer's case or metal surrounding your work surface, often before and during the installation.

2. Shut down your computer and unplug it from the AC wall outlet.

3. Remove the screws that secure the cover to your computer and put them in your parts bowl. Take off the cover and set it aside.

4. To determine what the jumper positions you should use for your existing EIDE hard drive, your existing CD-ROM drive (if you have one), and your new CD recorder, take a look at Table 5.1. A *jumper* is a simple wire-and-plastic electrical crossover that connects pins on a circuit board (in this case, the drive's circuit board). You can move a jumper to different positions to connect different sets of pins, which in turn changes the drive's EIDE configuration. These positions should be printed on the drives, and they can also be found in your CD-R drive's documentation. You can use a pair of tweezers to pull off a jumper from one set of pins and replace it on the right pins.

Tip

Having problems finding the drive jumper settings? Even if the jumper settings aren't printed on the drives and you can't find the documentation, you can still visit the manufacturer's Web site, where you'll likely find configuration settings for your drive in the Technical Support section. You can also call the manufacturer's voice technical support department if you're still stuck.

5. Select an open drive bay for your hard drive. Remember, the bay needs to be open to the front of the case. If a plastic insert on the front of the case covers the open bay, you should be able to remove it by pushing on it from either side of the case. Some of these inserts are snapped into place, so you may have to pry the insert off with a screwdriver; if so, be careful not to gouge or scratch your case in the process.

Put CD drive on New cable—secondary IDE & jumper as Master

Put both CD drives on secondary cable

Put CD as slave on Same cable as existing CD

Existing

Table 5.1 **Jumper Configurations**		
One Hard Drive	**One Hard Drive and One CD-ROM on the Same Cable**	**One Hard Drive and One CD-ROM on Different Cables**
Set the hard drive as "multiple drive, master unit" and set your recorder as "multiple drive, slave unit."	Set your recorder as "single drive, master unit" and connect it to the secondary EIDE cable. Leave the existing drives alone.	Set your recorder as "multiple drive, slave unit" and connect it to the EIDE cable that the hard drive is using, then set the hard drive to "multiple drive, master unit." Leave your existing CD-ROM alone.

These are good first checks but should be altered when ok.

6. Once the bay is open, slide the drive into it from the front of the case, as shown in Figure 5.3. The end with the connectors should go in first, and the drive should be facing upright — there's usually printing or lettering on the front of the recorder that helps you determine "which way is up."

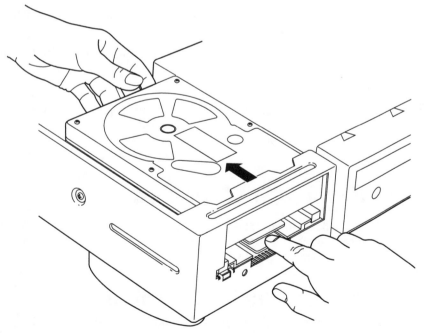

Figure 5.3 Sliding the recorder into the drive bay

7. Now slide your new drive gently back and forth in the drive bay until the screw holes in the side of the bay line up with the screw holes on the recorder. Attach the recorder to the bay with the screws supplied with the recorder. Although you should try to add all four screws, it may be harder to reach some of them—if you can attach at least two screws, the recorder will be fine.

8. Next, connect a power cable from your power supply to the recorder's power connector. Because this connector only fits one way, there's no chance of making a mistake. Press firmly—power cables can easily pull out.

9. Attach the ribbon cable coming from the computer's EIDE connector to EIDE connector on the back of the recorder. Again, this cable should only fit one way; a small notch on the cable connector must line up correctly with a matching cutout on the drive's connector. Once you're sure that the alignment is correct, press the connectors firmly together.

Tip

Ever wonder how technicians can tell which is Wire 1 on a ribbon cable? It's always marked, either with a stripe or with distinctive lettering. Because most hardware manufacturers label the pins on their connectors, this makes it easy to tell (even without the notch).

10. Check all connections to each device to make sure a cable hasn't been inadvertently unplugged.

11. Replace the cover on your computer and fasten it with the original screws from your parts bowl.

12. Plug in the power cable.

13. Turn on your computer and install any required software.

You're ready to burn!

Installing a SCSI CD Recorder

If you've decided on a SCSI recorder, you have a little more work ahead of you. Before I launch into the installation of the hardware, let's discuss two settings you have to make: termination and the SCSI device ID.

Setting SCSI Device ID Numbers

Because a SCSI device chain can include multiple devices, your SCSI adapter needs to be able to identify which device is which—this is why the unique SCSI ID number is needed. The most common variety of SCSI devices, called the SCSI-2 standard, use a range of ID numbers from 0 to 7. Typically, most manufacturers reserve ID number 7 for the adapter card itself, so you have seven ID numbers to choose from for your SCSI components; it's a good idea, however, to check your documentation to see which default ID number your SCSI adapter uses. Figure 5.4 illustrates a typical SCSI device chain with three devices and the SCSI card.

SCSI ID: 7   SCSI ID: 4   SCSI ID: 3

Figure 5.4 The device ID numbers on a typical SCSI device chain

To set your recorder's SCSI ID number, you use one of the following mechanisms:

- **A jumper.** You can set your SCSI device ID using jumpers, similar to the jumper configuration step I described for an EIDE drive. Using your trusty tweezers, remove and reposition the jumpers as indicated in the recorder manual for the SCSI device ID you need to set.

- **A thumbwheel.** Turn the thumbwheel (which looks something like an odometer on a car) on the back or the bottom of the drive until a unique number is displayed in the window.

- **Automatic setting.** If your SCSI adapter supports SCAM (SCSI Configured Automatically) and all the devices on your drive chain are SCAM-compliant, you can set the card to automatically allocate SCSI ID numbers.

Setting Termination Correctly

A SCSI device chain must be terminated on each end to indicate that there are no more devices further down the line. Without a terminator, your SCSI card continues to look for devices, and the drive won't work. (You'd think that the whole interface would be a little "smarter," but not everything is automatic in the world of computers!) Conversely, a chain that's terminated too early causes your SCSI adapter card to miss another SCSI peripheral connected farther along the cable. When your SCSI components aren't terminated correctly, your computer is unable to recognize them, and none of the devices work.

I find that examples help when introducing someone to the design of a SCSI device chain: Let's suppose that you want to add a SCSI adapter card and a SCSI CD-RW drive to your PC. As I mentioned, you have to indicate to your SCSI adapter card that there is one SCSI device on the chain, and that the chain ends with that device. Because both of these components mark an end of the SCSI chain, both need to be terminated, as shown in Figure 5.5. Note that the termination would be the same whether the drive is internal or external.

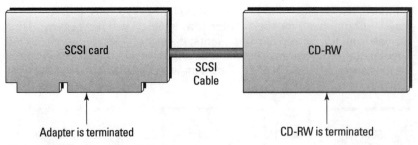

Figure 5.5 The simplest SCSI chain

That was easy—but unfortunately, things can get complex pretty quickly in the world of SCSI devices. Let's say that you have an existing SCSI adapter card and a SCSI hard drive, and you want to add an internal CD recorder. Figure 5.6 illustrates proper termination of this example SCSI chain, whereas Figure 5.7 shows a common mistake made while installing a new SCSI device into an existing chain: the adapter card is improperly terminated, and the CD recorder won't work.

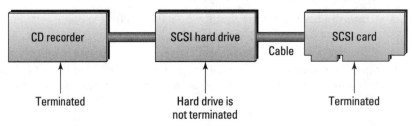

Figure 5.6 Setting proper termination for two devices and a SCSI adapter

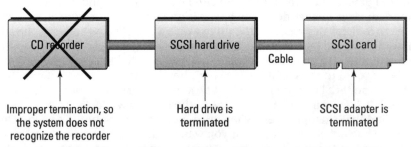

Figure 5.7 Improper termination causes problems in a device chain.

SCSI hardware manufacturers use three methods to set termination on SCSI cards and devices:

- **A resistor pack.** A resistor pack is actually just an electronic plug; however, most manufacturers require a specific type of resistor, and your SCSI recorder should come with one. To terminate a SCSI device with a resistor pack, check your manual for the location of the resistor socket and plug it in; to remove the termination, remove the resistor pack.

- **A jumper.** More jumpers; in fact, some devices use a single set of jumpers to set both the SCSI ID and the termination state! You can move the jumpers on a SCSI device to enable or disable termination. Check your recorder's documentation for the proper configuration.

- **A DIP switch.** Figure 5.8 illustrates the DIP switch, which carries a number of sliding or rocker switches that you can set with a pencil. DIP switches can be set either ON or OFF, and both termination states have their own specific arrangement of switch settings (which should be described in your documentation).

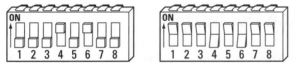

Figure 5.8 Setting a DIP switch for termination

Configuring an External SCSI Recorder

Have you decided on an external SCSI recorder? Although you won't have to worry about opening your case, you still have to set the termination and assign a unique ID number. Most SCSI adapters have an external connector like the one shown in Figure 5.9, but it may not have come with a cable. Luckily, you can pick up a standard SCSI external cable at your local computer store.

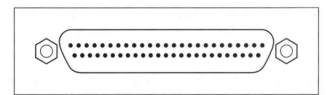

Figure 5.9 A standard SCSI-2 external SCSI port

Just because the SCSI port is on the outside of the case, you can still attach more than one external device. For example, you can add an external SCSI scanner with your CD-RW drive. Short daisy-chain cables connect these external devices.

However, adding an external CD recorder (or any external SCSI device) to an existing SCSI device chain may introduce problems. Because your SCSI adapter card is no longer one end of the chain—actually, the SCSI card is now in the middle of the SCSI chain—the card should no longer be terminated! When installing multiple external SCSI devices, you should terminate only the last external peripheral in the daisy chain, as shown in Figure 5.10.

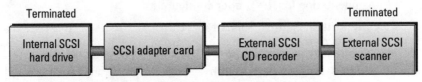

Figure 5.10 Multiple external devices, still only one terminator

Installing the Hardware

Because many SCSI CD recorders come bundled as kits with a SCSI adapter card, I cover three hardware installations in this section: installing a SCSI adapter in a PC with an existing EIDE hard drive, installing an internal SCSI recorder, and installing an external SCSI recorder.

Installing Your SCSI Card

Follow these steps to install a SCSI adapter in a PC with an existing EIDE hard drive:

1. Shut down and unplug your computer.

2. Remove the screws that attach your computer's cover and place them in your parts bowl. Take off the cover and set it aside.

3. Don't forget to ground yourself before touching any electronic circuitry! To discharge static electricity, touch a metal surface, such as your computer's case or metal surrounding your work surface, often before and during the installation.

4. Select an open adapter card slot for your SCSI card (your card's documentation should indicate which type of slot you need). Most computers made in the last two or three years use PCI adapter cards.

5. Remove the screw and the metal slot cover adjacent to the selected slot, as shown in Figure 5.11, and add them to your parts bowl.

really bad drawing — too many ISA
connectors, narrowly spaced, and
lengths badly wrong.

Figure 5.11 Opening a slot for your SCSI adapter card

6. Check your SCSI adapter for proper termination before you install it
   (this precaution helps avoid bruised knuckles later if you need to
   change the setting). As I mentioned before, your SCSI adapter needs
   to be terminated if you're installing only internal SCSI components.

7. Line up the card with the slot on the motherboard, making sure that the
   metal bracket is properly aligned with the open slot space.

8. Once you're sure that everything is aligned, apply even pressure to the
   top of the card, as shown in Figure 5.12, and push it down into the slot. If
   the card is correctly seated, the bracket should be resting tightly against
   the case.

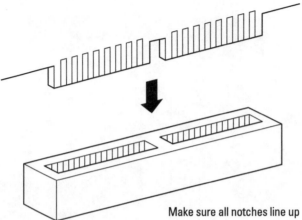

Make sure all notches line up

Figure 5.12 Seating the card in the slot — *what kind of 'slot' is this? useless diagram*

9. Add the screw and tighten down the bracket.

10. Attach the SCSI ribbon cable to the data connector on the card — this should be indicated by the documentation or instructions that come with your drive.

Adding an Internal SCSI Recorder

With a SCSI adapter card successfully installed, you're ready to add an internal SCSI recorder to your system!

Warning

Are you adding an internal SCSI CD recorder to an existing SCSI chain? Keep in mind that this change is almost certainly going to require a change in your termination on the device that's currently at the end of the SCSI device chain. If you forget to set the proper termination, your new recorder may not be recognized (or an existing SCSI device abruptly stops working)! Remember, any change to a SCSI device chain likely means a change to the current termination configuration.

To install the internal SCSI recorder:

1. If your computer is currently plugged in, unplug it and remove the cover.

2. Touch a metal surface to discharge any static electricity your body might be carrying.

3. Configure the termination and SCSI ID number on your new recorder. If the drive will be added at the end of your SCSI cable, the recorder should be terminated.

Tip

If you don't know the SCSI ID numbers for the other devices in your chain, don't worry! Your SCSI adapter card should have come with some type of diagnostic program that can display the ID numbers without your having to further disassemble your computer.

Alternatively, to display the SCSI ID number in Windows 98 or Windows 2000, right-click My Computer, select Properties, and display the properties for each of your SCSI devices in the Device Manager, as shown in Figure 5.13.

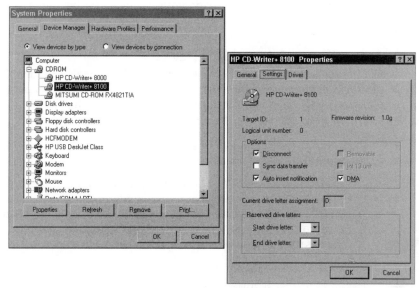

Figure 5.13 Displaying the information for a device in the Windows 98 Device Manager

4. Select an open drive bay for the new drive.

5. Slide the recorder into the bay from the front of the case, and adjust it back and forth until the screw holes in the side of the bay line up with those on the side of the drive. Use the screws that came with the recorder to secure the drive to the bay.

6. Now plug an open power cable from your power supply to the power connector on the recorder.

7. Connect the ribbon cable coming from your SCSI adapter card to the back of the drive. To make sure the connection is secure, press firmly after you align it correctly. If you're installing the first internal SCSI peripheral on your SCSI chain, use the first open device connector on the cable. If you're installing an internal SCSI peripheral on an existing SCSI device chain, use the next open connector on the cable.

8. Check all connections to each device to make sure a cable hasn't been inadvertently unplugged.

9. Replace the cover on your computer.

10. Fasten the cover with the original screws from your parts bowl.

11. Plug in the power cable.

12. Turn on your computer and install any required software.

That's it! Although a SCSI recorder installation is a little trickier than adding an EIDE drive, you can now expand your hardware far beyond a typical EIDE-only system!

Connecting an External SCSI Device

As I mentioned earlier, adding an external SCSI CD recorder probably requires a termination change on your system. In most cases, this means disabling the termination on the SCSI adapter card and enabling it on the external recorder.

To install an external CD recorder:

1. Set the correct termination and SCSI ID number for your external peripheral.

2. Locate the external SCSI port on the back of your computer. Most varieties of SCSI use a 50-pin standard connector. If you're installing a new external SCSI CD recorder onto an existing external daisy chain, plug the cable from the new drive into the secondary SCSI port on the external SCSI device that's currently last on the chain, as shown in Figure 5.14.

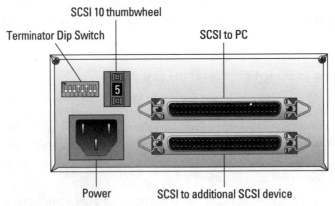

Figure 5.14 The back of a typical SCSI external device showing the secondary SCSI port

3. Align the connector on the end of your SCSI cable with the SCSI port and push the connector in firmly. Once again, someone designed this connector the right way, because the angled edges make sure that it only goes on the right way.

4. Tighten the connector by snapping the wire clips toward the center of the cable, as shown in Figure 5.15.

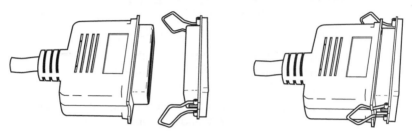

Figure 5.15 A SCSI port usually has metal clips to help hold the cable.

5. Connect the power cord from the recorder to your AC wall socket or surge protector.

6. Turn on the external hardware first! This is an important rule when starting a computer system with external SCSI devices. (Actually, that's also true for any printer as well.) Because Windows 95/98 and Windows 2000 look for these devices when they start to determine your current hardware configuration, any external devices must be powered on to be recognized.

7. Now turn on your computer and install any required software.

You're set! Time to start backing up all those files (or burning all those custom audio CDs)!

Installation Troubleshooting

I'd like to say that every single hardware installation that I've performed has gone flawlessly . . . hah! Computer hardware technicians are human too, and they're just as likely to be distracted, tired, or preoccupied as any other person. Therefore, experienced hardware hackers have spent many an hour *troubleshooting* (a fancy techno-word for "fixing") problems with new equipment. In this section, I give you possible answers for common problems that may occur as you install a CD recorder.

EIDE Installation Problems

First, let's discuss potential problems that can occur with EIDE drives.

My new recorder doesn't eject or show a power light.

- **Power cable loose or unplugged.** Even if your drive is incorrectly configured, it should still be receiving power; therefore, if the power indicator doesn't light or the drive tray doesn't eject when you press the Eject button, check the power connector.

I get power, but Windows doesn't recognize my drive.

- **Master/slave incorrectly set.** Remember, you have to correctly set the master/slave jumpers for *both* drives if your new recorder is sharing a cable with another device.

- **Data cable loose or unplugged.** Check your ribbon cable to make sure that it's firmly seated and both ends are properly connected.

I get a weird message about something called a BIOS error.

- **Incorrect BIOS configuration.** Most computers made within the last two or three years automatically detect EIDE devices and add (or remove) them from your computer's BIOS configuration. If you have an older PC, however, you may have to make this change manually. Check your system documentation for the key(s) that you need to press during the boot sequence to display your system BIOS, and add the recorder to your active EIDE device list.

SCSI Installation Problems

Because SCSI devices have more configuration settings, computer owners installing SCSI hardware for the first time are likely to encounter at least one of the problems listed here. Don't worry! They can all be easily fixed!

My new recorder doesn't eject or show a power light.

- **Power cable loose or unplugged.** Just as in the case of an EIDE drive, no power indicates a cable connection problem.

I get power, but windows doesn't recognize my drive.

- **Termination/SCSI ID incorrectly set.** If your adapter enables you to boot with an incorrect configuration, your new recorder simply won't appear. Unplug your computer, remove the cover, and review your SCSI ID and termination settings on all devices in your SCSI device chain.

- **Data cable loose or unplugged.** Another victim of a loose or overlooked cable connection.

- **External SCSI device not turned on.** If you've installed an external SCSI recorder and it's daisy-chained with another SCSI device, make sure that all external SCSI peripherals are turned on *before* you boot.

My computer just hangs . . . and boy, it locks up tight.

- **Termination/SCSI ID incorrectly set.** Unfortunately, many SCSI adapter cards aren't polite enough to show an error message if they encounter a configuration problem — instead, they simply lock up your machine. Unplug your computer, remove the cover, and review your SCSI ID and termination settings on all devices in your SCSI device chain.

Tip

If you continue to experience problems with a SCSI recorder, help is as close as your telephone or your Web browser! Don't forget to read the instructions or visit the drive manufacturer's Web site and check for technical bulletins on installation. If nothing else works (and you've read the instructions), call the company's voice technical support.

Installing Adaptec's Easy CD Creator

Finally, I'd like to demonstrate how to install the most popular CD recording software available for the Windows 95/98 and Windows 2000 platforms: Easy CD Creator from Adaptec.

Follow these steps to install Easy CD Creator 4 from the installation CD-ROM:

1. Insert the Easy CD Creator CD-ROM into your recorder or system CD-ROM drive.

2. If you have AutoRun turned on within Windows, the installation Setup program should run automatically and display the welcome screen shown in Figure 5.16 — if it doesn't, double-click My Computer and double-click the drive icon.

3. Click Next to continue at the Welcome screen.

4. If you agree to the software license, click Yes to continue.

Figure 5.16 The Easy CD Creator installation welcome screen

5. At the Setup Type screen, which is shown in Figure 5.17, most computer owners should select the Typical installation type. If you're using a laptop or you're running low on hard disk space, the Compact setting is a good choice (but keep in mind that the installation program will not install all of the features of the full package). I recommend that you use the default folder unless you have a specific reason for changing it. Once the settings are correct, click Next to continue.

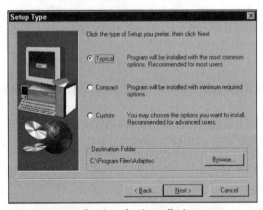

Figure 5.17 Selecting the installation type

6. At the Personalization screen shown in Figure 5.18, enter your full name, a company name, and the Tech Support ID number from your software package. Click Next to continue, and the installation program begins to copy files.

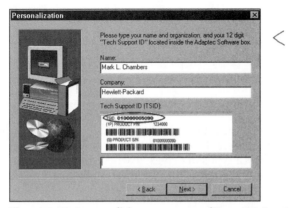

Figure 5.18 Personalizing your copy of Easy CD Creator

7. Once all the files have been successfully copied, the installation program prompts you for permission to reboot your computer (Figure 5.19). Make sure that all other applications have been closed; if a floppy disk is loaded, eject it. Finally, select Yes and click Finish to complete the installation process.

Figure 5.19 The installation program must reboot your PC to finish its job.

Tip

If you are installing multiple software applications, you may want to delay restarting your computer until all have been installed. Otherwise, you probably have to reboot after each installation.

Once your PC has rebooted, Easy CD Creator is available from your Start menu, and the DirectCD program (which I discuss in detail later in the book) is running in your taskbar.

In Review

This chapter was a hands-on guide to installing and configuring the two most popular types of CD recorders: EIDE and SCSI drives. You reviewed the installation requirements for both types of drives, learned the installation procedures, and found troubleshooting answers for potential problems. Finally, you now know how to install Adaptec's Easy CD Creator recording suite for Windows 95/98 and Windows 2000.

Recording a CD-ROM

Preparing Your Material

In earlier chapters, I discuss recordable CD hardware and software. Now it's time to talk about the compact discs themselves. Often, many computer owners who are new to recording CDs don't know that there are <u>three</u> different types of discs and several recording modes to choose from, each of which is best suited to a particular type of data or a particular application. Selecting the right type of disc and the right recording format is an important first step you should take before a single byte of data is written to that new disc!

It's also a good idea to consider the organization of your data CDs before you start recording. For example, should the files you're recording straight from your hard drive be divided into folders? Are different types of files mixed together? Should you arrange them in groups? The decisions you make while organizing your disc will help determine how easy it is to use in the future.

Finally, you should always consider the legal aspect of CD recording, especially when you're creating a disc for distribution to others. What constitutes a copyrighted program? Does a change in an image make it your property? Can you copyright your own work before you record it?

I answer all of these questions and more in this chapter as I show you how to prepare your material for recording.

Selecting a Disc Type

Here's a mistake that's probably made at least once by every owner of a brand-new CD recorder — see if you can spot the problem. Let's assume that you've decided to record your first audio CD from MP3 or WAV files that you've downloaded from Web sites. You fire up your recording software, carefully drag and drop each digital audio file to your disc layout, and start the recording. Everything proceeds normally — no error messages, no smoke pouring out of your computer's case. Yet, the recording that you've just made *won't* play in an audio CD player! What happened, and how can you prevent this from happening in the future?

The source of the problem can be found in the disc that was used. In this case, a *data* disc was used instead of an *audio* disc to record digital music! You can, in fact, listen to the music that you've recorded to a data disc, but not on a regular stereo CD player. Instead, you must load the disc in your computer's CD-ROM drive and listen to it with a program like WinAmp or the built-in Windows WAV player.

How can you prevent such a mistake from happening again? Learn which type of disc fits which application, and which type of disc is suitable for the hardware that will use it. You can create three different types of disc with your new recorder: *audio, data,* and *mixed-mode.*

Audio Discs

First, consider the digital audio disc. Music recorded for use in audio CD players should be recorded in the *Red Book* standard, which is a universally recognized recording format that determines how data is arranged on an audio disc. Other book standards exist as well, but the Red Book standard is probably used more than the others. In fact, you'll see this name within many recording programs instead of the word "audio," so you need to remember it. If a disc is recorded in anything other than the Red Book format, it will not play in an audio CD player.

Why is the Red Book standard such a necessity? Consider how many audio CD players have been manufactured over the years, and how many different factories around the world now produce audio CDs; without a standard, the manufacturer of your car audio CD player would never be able to guarantee that it could play any disc in your CD collection!

Here's another rule to keep in mind about audio CDs: You can't store any computer data on a disc recorded in the Red Book standard. Your recording software should make sure that this doesn't happen. For example, as you can see in Figure 6.1, Easy CD Creator keeps separate layouts for Red Book audio CDs and data CDs, so you won't be able to drag a binary word processing document into the audio CD layout screen.

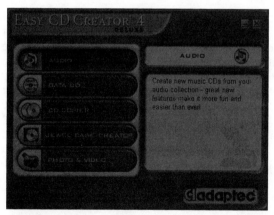

Figure 6.1 Audio and data: Easy CD Creator gives you a way to keep them separate.

Most audio recordings these days are taken from one of four audio sources:

- **MP3 digital audio.** Because of the Web, MP3 has become the most popular type of digital audio around. It supports 44 KHz CD-quality audio, and MP3 files are actually very compact compared to other types of sound files. The MP3 standard supports both stereo and mono playback.

~ 1 Mb per minute

■ **Microsoft WAV digital audio.** Although the built-in support for WAV format sound files in Windows 95/98 and Windows 2000 (Figure 6.2) guarantees that WAV files will be generally accepted, they're much, much larger than the same audio recorded in MP3 format. WAV files support stereo and mono playback at 44 KHz sampling rates.

~ 10 Mb per minute

Figure 6.2 Listening to a WAV format sound file using the Microsoft Windows WAV player

■ **AIFF digital audio.** AIFF is the digital audio format of choice on the Macintosh — it's very similar to the WAV format. AIFF files support CD-quality stereo sound, but they can be even larger in size than WAV files, so it's a good idea to get them off your hard drive and onto an audio disc as soon as possible!

■ **MIDI audio.** MIDI stands for *musical instrument digital interface.* Unlike the other sources I've mentioned, it's not really a digital format; instead, MIDI is the technology that enables many types of musical instruments to communicate with your computer. With a MIDI connection, you can play music directly into your computer, which will record it so that it can be played on any other computer with MIDI — or, alternatively, your computer can actually "play" a MIDI song on a MIDI instrument automatically! Normally, MIDI songs must be "prerecorded" on your hard drive in MP3 or WAV format before you can create a Red Book audio CD of your original music. However, some expensive, high-end programs written especially for musicians enable a MIDI song to be mastered directly to an audio CD.

MIDI files are extremely compact.   ~ 10Kb per minute

Data Discs

Most of the CD-ROMs you use on your computer are recorded as *data* discs, because they store binary computer files that you can retrieve as needed. Data discs are created according to one of two different international Book standards: the *Yellow Book,* which describes the layout of a commercially manufactured computer data CD-ROM, and the *Orange Book,* which details the physical arrangement of data on a CD-R disc.

Here's rule number one when it comes to data discs: Never try to play a data disc in an audio CD player! Believe me, the heaviest metal you've ever heard comes *nothing* close to the screaming earful you'll get if you try to play a data CD-ROM—if your player recognizes the data track on the disc at all, that is. In fact, I have heard of folks who have accidentally damaged older audio CD players by attempting to play a data disc . . . another good reason to label your recorded discs.

A data disc has the same familiar structures as your hard drive: *folders* (also called directories) are used to store both *data files* and *programs.* Programs can be run directly from a CD-ROM without copying them to your hard drive first.

Later in the book, I introduce you to the different *file systems* that run specifically on data discs for certain operating systems. A file system is a specific set of rules that govern the logical structure of a disc—for example, how files are named and how many files can be stored in a single folder. Because they're the most popular with personal computer owners, remember these three file systems:

- **Microsoft Joliet.** This file system was developed by Microsoft for Windows 95. It allows long filenames (and folder names) of up to 64 characters, and names can include multiple periods and spaces.

- **HFS.** Short for *Hierarchical File System.* This is the file system used on the Macintosh. Although it's being slowly phased out, HFS is still important in the Mac world.

- **ISO 9660.** The Big Daddy of them all, the ISO 9660 file system was the first to be recognized worldwide back in the early days of CD-ROM distribution. It was developed by a standards committee (formed by compact disc hardware manufacturers) called the High Sierra Group. The ISO 9660 file system is compatible with just about every operating system and drive on the face of the planet, so if you create an ISO 9660 disc, it should be readable on everything from Windows 95/98 and Macintosh computers to the increasingly popular Linux and BeOS operating systems.

Mixed-Mode Discs

Okay, now that I've described to you all of the differences between audio and data—as well as all the restrictions—here comes the mixed-mode disc to turn everything upside-down! A mixed-mode disc actually has both digital audio tracks and a data track on the same disc. For this reason, most of the multimedia titles are recorded as mixed-mode discs.

Figure 6.3 illustrates how this is done. The first track on the disc is recorded as computer data, and successive tracks are recorded separately as digital audio. A good example of how a mixed-mode disc is used is one of today's multimedia computer games, which will carry the game program and data files on the first track and all of the music and other sound effects as subsequent tracks of digital audio.

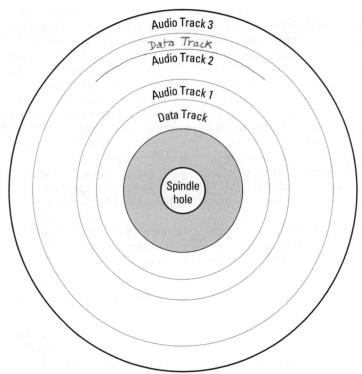

Figure 6.3 The structure of a mixed-mode disc pulls together both data and digital audio tracks.

I should note, however, that certain rules still apply to a mixed-mode disc:

■ **Don't play a mixed-mode disc in your audio CD player.** Because the first track of a typical mixed-mode disc is still computer data, you run into the same problems as you would attempting to play a "pure" data disc. Special types of mixed-mode discs called *CD-Extra* (also called *Plus* or *Enhanced*) can indeed be played on a standard audio CD player, but this is because they're recorded with the audio tracks appearing first on the disc, as shown in Figure 6.4. The additional data track on a CD-Extra disc is ignored by your audio CD player.

Tip

If you're wondering how bands like the Rolling Stones and the Squirrel Nut Zippers add computer programs, full-motion video, and lyric sheets to their audio CD releases, you now know the secret: They're using CD-Extra mixed-mode discs!

■ **Mixed-mode discs aren't completely compatible with all hardware.** Older CD-ROM drives may not be able to read either the data or the digital audio from a mixed-mode disc.

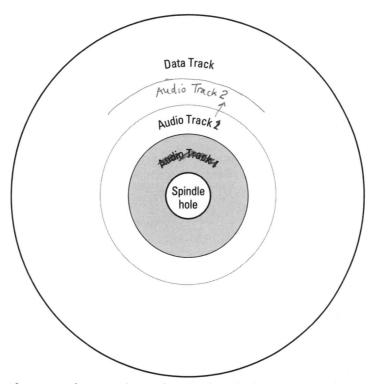

Figure 6.4 The exception to the mixed-mode disc: A CD-Extra disc can be played like an audio CD.

- **Your operating system must support mixed-mode discs to read them.** Good luck trying to read a mixed-mode CD-Extra disc under DOS or older versions of UNIX. But then again, most computer owners would argue that it's high time to forget about "ancient" operating systems like DOS and Windows 3.1, anyway. (Boy, I feel old—I started out in the days when a mouse ran around in a cage.)

Deciding Which Disc Type to Use

Choosing the right type of disc for the data you're recording is easy (now that you understand what each disc type is designed to hold)! For example, suppose that you were creating three different types of discs:

- One that will hold your data files for your income tax preparation program.

- One that will hold your favorite Abbott and Costello comedy routines— and naturally, you'll want to play them through your stereo system.

■ Finally, a third disc that will hold both your library of Web animated graphics and a number of WAV format sound effects.

To decide which type of disc to use:

1. Ask yourself, "Will this disc need to be compatible with a number of different computers, or just my computer?" If you'll be distributing the disc to a large number of people, stick with a true data or audio disc; I would recommend that you avoid recording a mixed-mode disc.

2. Consider whether or not you want to play the disc in an audio CD player. If so (and you have no need to store computer data on the same disc), then the audio type is the clear choice.

3. Decide if you *do* need to store both audio and data on the same disc. If so, you have two choices: You can record a mixed-mode CD-Extra disc, or you can simply save the audio as WAV or MP3 sound files and record them as part of the data track.

Choosing a Recording Mode

Once you've decided what type of disc you'll be creating, the next step is to select a *recording mode.* Several recording modes exist; each has its advantages and disadvantages, and some CD recorders will not be able to record all four modes.

Cross-Reference

I introduce you to each of the four modes in this section, but I cover each recording mode in more depth in Chapter 9, "Introducing Adaptec's DirectCD Step-by-Step" and in Chapter 12, "Recording Multisession CDs Step-by-Step."

Track-at-Once

Track-at-once recording mode (also called CD-ROM Mode 1) is the most basic disc recording mode — every CD recorder can burn a disc in track-at-once mode, and it should be readable on any CD-ROM drive. Figure 6.5 illustrates how track-at-once works: The laser write head writes each data and/or audio track individually, moving from the center of the disc to the outside. The drive turns off the recording laser between tracks. Unfortunately, the "empty" space between tracks will cause some audio CD players to make an audible clicking noise between songs.

This method is suitable for data discs — it's the general-purpose default for most recording programs.

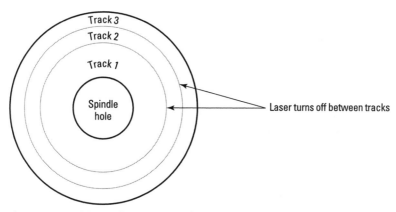

Figure 6.5 Writing a disc using track-at-once

Disc-at-Once — audio CD

In disc-at-once recording mode, the entire disc is written in a single pass, moving from the center of the disc to the outside. Although the tracks are there, they're written as part of the entire disc image. As shown in Figure 6.6, the laser is *not* turned off between tracks, making disc-at-once the best choice for audio recording.

Many lower-price and most older CD recorders can't record disc-at-once, and if you're recording more audio discs than any other type, the disc-at-once recording feature is definitely a feature to look for when buying a CD-R or CD-RW drive.

Multisession

Multisession mode (also called CD-ROM/XA Mode 2) is a breed apart. A disc recorded in multisession mode can hold multiple complete volumes, and each can be accessed separately (almost as if each volume were actually on a separate disc). Figure 6.7 gives you an idea of how a multisession disc is accessed.

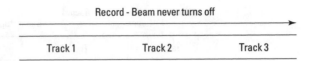

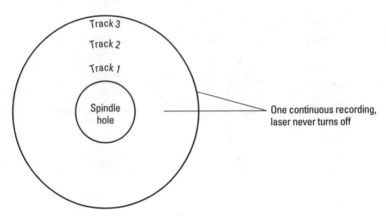

Figure 6.6 Writing a disc using disc-at-once

Although multisession is still a choice for recording data discs, it's very rarely used anymore for a number of reasons:

- **Multisession discs can't be read on some CD-ROM drives.** You'll probably learn this the hard way when you discover that your CD-ROM drive can only read the first session of a multisession disc.

- **You can't create audio discs using multisession mode.** Multisession works only for data sessions, so Red Book audio CDs are out.

- **You have to switch sessions manually.** Although most operating systems can read multisession discs, you still need to switch between sessions manually. To do this, you may need to run a separate program, like the Adaptec Session Selector, which is shown in Figure 6.8.

has it?

- **Multisession has been replaced by rewritable technology.** In the early days of CD recording (before the arrival of CD-RW and UDF/packet), multi-session was seen as a way of extending the life of a recorded CD by enabling you to add new sessions, up to the total of 650 megabytes. CD-RW enables you to record over and over again on the same disc, which is much more convenient, while UDF/Packet enables you to record new information on an existing disc without the hassles of setting up a multisession recording beforehand.

But there is a limit to the number of rewrites and UDF is only available under Windows

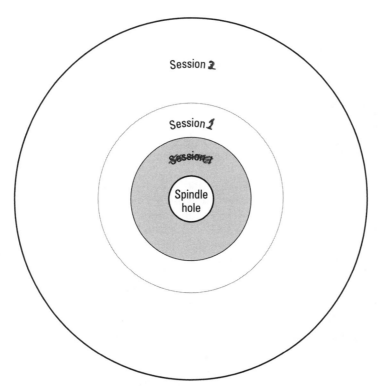

Figure 6.7 Writing a disc using multisession mode

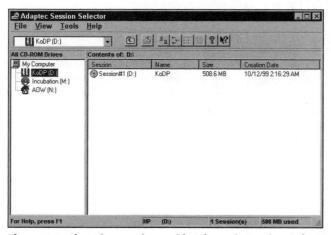

Figure 6.8 Changing sessions with Adaptec's Session Selector, which comes with Easy CD Creator

Universal Disc Format/Packet-Writing Mode

Finally, we come to *Universal Disc Format* (UDF) recording, which is also popularly called *packet-writing*. As I mention earlier in the book, with UDF there's no need to design a disc layout ahead of time—you can simply copy and move files to your CD recorder as if it was a hard drive, and you can create folders and organize your discs the same way you would a removable hard drive or a floppy disc. Adaptec's DirectCD is the perfect example of a UDF recording program.

Cross-Reference

To learn more about copying and moving files to your CD recorder using UDF recording, take a look at the section "Copying and Moving Files to Your Disc" in Chapter 9, "Introducing Adaptec's DirectCD Step-by-Step."

One of the advantages of UDF is the ability it gives you to "delete" files from a CD-R or CD-RW disc after you've recorded them. Of course, you can't really delete a file from a CD-R disc, but UDF does enable you to update the disc's directory information so that the files you've deleted are no longer accessible—essentially deleting them—but you won't recover any of that space from the disc.

UDF does have two disadvantages:

- **It can't create Red Book audio discs.** You'll have to use track-at-once or disc-at-once mode to record your favorite compilation CD with those rockin' hits from the 70s.

- **Most other operating systems don't support it.** Count on the discs that you create with UDF to be readable only on computers running Windows 95/98 and Windows 2000.   why?

Organizing Your Files

Now that I've introduced you to all of this information on selecting disc types and recording modes, you're not just going to slap files on a disc without thinking ahead, are you? Remember, UDF is the exception when it comes to recording—if you're using any other mode, you're locked in to the file organization that you build as you create your disc layout. At the time you record your information, you're probably familiar with each and every file that you're recording. But what about the moment a couple of years in the future, when you're searching that archival CD-ROM for a single file and you have no earthly idea what you named it?

That's where logical organization comes in! Here are the guidelines I follow after years of hard-earned experience:

- **Use subdirectories!** I can't stress this enough: If you're recording a data disc, *do not* pile all of your files into the root directory! It'll be practically impossible for you to find anything in the chaos that results — and besides, depending on the limitations of the file system that you're using, you may actually run out of file slots. Instead, create new folders in the root directory of your CD layout and give them logical names.

- **Use long filenames, if possible.** Speaking of logical filenames, Easy CD Creator doesn't use the Microsoft Joliet file system as a default — take advantage of the long filenames that this system provides! After all, which folder name will be easier to understand in three years: "PICACKOV" or "Pictures of Akron, Ohio From Overhead"?

- **Arrange files by probable search criteria.** Suppose you've got an entire disc of images you want to organize before you record them, such as Windows bitmap files, a large number of JPEG pictures, and even a few older GIF files to store. Are you really doing yourself a favor by creating three directories called "Bitmaps," "JPGs," and "GIFs"? How will you find a picture of a bowling ball on a disc like that? Instead, create directories like "Sports," "Animals," and "Cars." (In fact, if you have any clip-art CD-ROMs in your collection, think about how they organize their library of files — by subject!)

- **Use a catalog program whenever possible.** Programs like Paint Shop Pro (Figure 6.9) can create browse files that you can save within a directory that contain thumbnail pictures of every image in the directory. This approach is a fast and painless, and it makes it remarkably easy to find something. Other programs like this exist for sound files, video clips, and even word processing documents. I definitely recommend that you use one of these catalog programs if possible.

Tip

Once you're finished organizing your files, it's a good idea to run your anti-virus scanner and check them for possible viral infection. Passing an infected CD-ROM to someone else is not generally considered a friendly gesture.

Using Copyrighted Material

Talk about a minefield — whenever the legalities of recording your own CD-ROMs are concerned, it's best to tread carefully and act on the conservative side if your discs will contain any material that might be copyrighted.

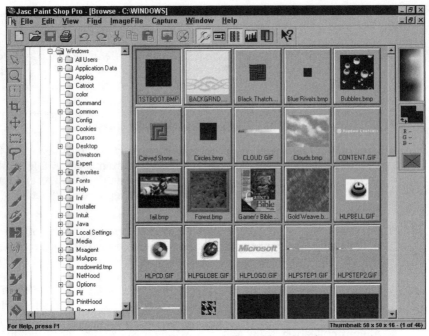

Figure 6.9 Browsing an entire directory of files with Paint Shop Pro

Before I go any farther, I'll state that I am not a lawyer, and the generalizations that I make in this chapter are just that: general warnings, guidelines, and information! For definitive legal help in answering your copyright questions, you must call on the knowledge of a copyright lawyer!

With that said, here are the tips that I can provide to anyone who's recording:

■ **Changing media changes nothing.** If you scan an original photograph and record the image on a disc, that image isn't suddenly transformed into your original work. (Wouldn't that be a neat trick!) You need permission from the author to use the work. Of course, this applies to any copyrighted document, not just images.

■ **Participants have copyrights too!** If you've taken a picture of another individual or recorded their voice as part of a song, you should obtain their permission in writing to use their image or voice before claiming a copyright on the work.

■ **Backups are allowed.** Are you recording a CD-ROM to back up your system, including your commercial software? Most companies allow you to back up their programs as long as you don't distribute the disc. The backup is for your personal use on the original machine.

■ **A copyright stands no matter how you received the work.** Okay, I know that you may have downloaded that image from another Web site, or found it on an Internet newsgroup—however, if it's copyrighted, it doesn't matter how you obtained it, you need to contact the author for permission to use it.

■ **"But it didn't have a copyright mark!"** Sorry, that's no excuse. Copyright is granted immediately upon creation of an original work, and a copyright notice does not have to appear visibly on the work.

■ **There's no such thing as "blanket" permission.** You must obtain permission to copy any original copyrighted work on an individual basis—it's a requirement even if the author has granted you permission for other similar works (like pictures in a series) in the past.

■ **Altering the work doesn't change the copyright.** You won't "claim" the copyright on an editorial cartoon you found on the Web by adding a forked tail to a politician (although many would agree that it's a change for the better). If the work wasn't yours originally, then changing it doesn't affect its status at all.

Note

Many computer and audio component manufacturers are currently promoting *CD-DA* audio CDs—you can use a blank CD-DA disc to make a legal recording of your CD collection, or make a compilation CD of MP3 files. If your audio CD recording software requires a CD-DA disc, you'll need to buy these special discs for audio CD recording (which are more expensive, because a portion of their cost is paid as a royalty) instead of standard CD-R blank discs.

Would you like to add your copyright to your original work? I strongly suggest that you do so before distributing it. The process for a program, an image, or a document is very simple:

1. Load the document into an editor so that you can make your changes.

2. Add the following line where it will be visible to others:

```
Copyright (c) [year] by [name], All Rights Reserved.
```

where [year] is the year that you created the work and [name] is your name or the name of your company. Figure 6.10 illustrates my copyright line on an original image that I've loaded into Paint Shop Pro.

3. Save the completed work.

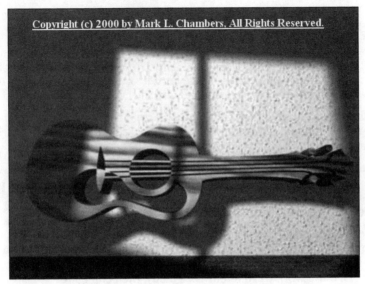

Figure 6.10 Copyrighting an original image

In Review

This chapter led you through the decisions that you have to make before recording any disc, including the type of disc and the format you should specify, the organization of the disc, and the legal questions that you may have to settle before you can distribute the finished disc.

Preparing Your Computer

IN THIS CHAPTER

- Preparing the computer for efficient CD recording

- Improving hard drive performance

- Eliminating software and network conflicts

- Optimizing operating system performance

- Recording over a network

Here's a common scenario: Some computer owners install a CD recorder and recording software, and then immediately try to create their first disc. Although everything went fine during the installation process, that first attempt turns out a useless coaster! Why does a new computer with a fast hard drive and the latest processor still encounter errors while recording?

Often, the secret lies in the preparation of your system—remember, CD recording requires precise timing and efficient data transfer from your hard drive to your recorder. The slightest decrease in performance can interrupt the flow of data, and the result is a ruined disc. The time you spend improving the performance of your system helps ensure that recording errors are reduced to a minimum (or eliminated entirely). Before you attempt your first recording, therefore, you should optimize your computer system for the best results.

In this chapter, I demonstrate how you can fine-tune Windows 98 or Mac OS to create an ideal environment for CD recording—after all, why waste a perfectly good blank disc?

Making General Preparations for Recording

Although Windows 98 and Mac OS 9 look very different on the surface, they have a surprising number of similarities. For example:

- Both Windows 98 and Mac OS are *multitasking* operating systems, meaning that more than one program or application can run on your computer at once.

- Both operating systems also provide for *program scheduling,* so that an application can launch on a regular schedule automatically.

- Both offer you the ability to communicate with other users over a network.

These are neat features, and I use them often on my own computers—unless, of course, I'm recording a CD! During a recording session, you actually want to temporarily eliminate or disable features like these to maximize the performance of your recording application. Other preparations involve optimizing your hardware—particularly your hard drive, which must be free of errors and efficiently organized.

In this section, I explain the general preparations that you should take before beginning any recording session (no matter which operating system you're using).

Tip

Some of these general recording preparations also deliver additional benefits for your other programs: faster performance throughout your entire system! I note these preparations as I demonstrate them—it's a good idea to optimize your system on a regular basis, even if you're not recording.

Creating Space on Your Hard Drive

I bought my first computer hard drive back in the days of 8-bit computers — it was a 15-megabyte external "hard disk system" especially made for my TRS-80 Model 4, and it was the size of a modern minitower PC case, complete with fan. Believe it or not, I paid well over $1,000 for that hard drive in 1984 . . . and yes, I still keep it as a memento of the pioneer days of the personal computer. (It makes a great monitor stand, too.)

Of course, today's computers come equipped with several gigabytes of hard drive space as standard equipment. However, the size of today's operating systems (and applications like multimedia games and office suites) can reduce the free space on a 20-gigabyte hard drive to less than my 15-megabyte antique!

You should reduce unnecessary clutter on your hard drive before you record because

- Many recording applications require additional space for temporary files; these files are deleted once the recording has finished.

- If you're recording from a disc image file, you need up to 750 megabytes of free space to hold the image.

- If you're running Windows, your recording application may require additional space for *virtual memory* — a buzzword that refers to the hard drive space used for the temporary storage of data that won't fit in your system RAM, as shown in Figure 7.1. As I mention later in the chapter, Macintosh owners may decide to disable virtual memory altogether.

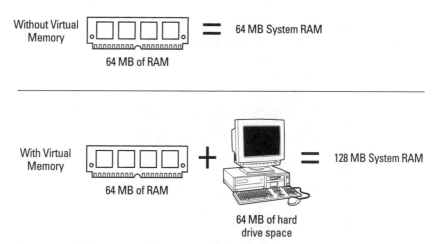

Figure 7.1 Windows can use space on your hard drive as virtual memory.

How can you tell what's unnecessary and what you can safely delete from your hard drive? In most cases, you can safely delete these types of files:

■ **Files stored in your Trash or Recycle Bin.** It's a good idea to release the space reserved for files you've deleted. Under Windows, right-click the Recycle Bin icon and select Empty Recycle Bin. Under Mac OS, click the Special menu and choose Empty Trash.

■ **Windows temporary files.** Windows 95 and Windows 98 create temporary files in the \WINDOWS\TEMP directory, and you can delete these temporary files using Explorer — close down any programs that may be running first. (Note that some temporary files may be locked if they've been created since you started your PC, so Windows won't enable you to delete them.)

■ **Game demos, shareware, and sample files.** I've never seen a PC or Mac yet that didn't have at least one or two forgotten game demos or unnecessary applications taking up space — you know, those programs that you tried once and decided not to use! Also, if an application has example files or sample documents that you know you won't need, you may be able to trim them — check the program's documentation or README file for details.

■ **Browser cache files.** Your browser may be eating up dozens of megabytes without your knowledge! In order to speed up the display of Web pages, a browser typically stores images and sound files in a *cache* — when you reload a Web page, these files can be quickly retrieved from the cache (instead of downloading them all over again from the Web site). Both Internet Explorer (Figure 7.2) and Netscape Navigator (Figure 7.3) enable you to purge their cache directories with a single click.

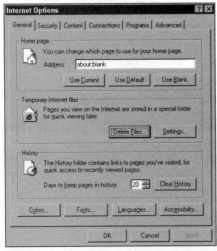

Figure 7.2 Eliminating cache files in Internet Explorer

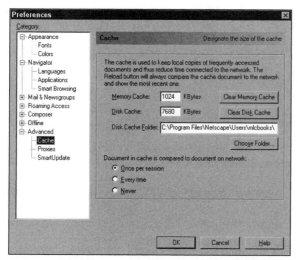

Figure 7.3 Purging the cache in Netscape Navigator

Scanning Your Hard Drive for Errors

Another potential recording problem — especially with older computers — is a hard drive with data errors. Remember, a hard drive doesn't automatically announce that it's carrying corrupted files, or that the magnetic surface of the drive is physically damaged; it's up to you to properly maintain your drive by scanning it for errors on a regular basis!

Two general types of hard drive errors can slow performance or corrupt data:

■ **Logical errors.** Errors such as lost clusters, cross-linked files, and inaccurate free space calculations arise from lockups, incorrect shutdown, and program bugs. These errors can occur even if your drive is running perfectly. On the positive side, you can generally fix these errors with little or no loss of data.

Warning

If you're running Windows 95, you should always (repeat, *always*) check your hard drive for errors immediately after an improper shutdown! This rule includes program lockups and power outages too. If you're running Windows 98 or Mac OS 9, you'll be glad to know that both Microsoft and Apple have wisely included automatic disk scanning after an improper shutdown. I like it when the architects of Silicon Valley agree with me!

■ **Physical errors.** No silver lining here: a physical error indicates that the magnetic platters inside your drive are damaged, and the problem is not likely to be something you can fix. In the archaic days of the MFM hard drive (I'm talking 1985 here), physical errors were more common than on today's IDE and SCSI drives . . . but even a modern drive can crash.

"OK, Mark, how do I detect and fix these errors before I record?" Luckily, computers running both Windows and Mac OS are already equipped with the tools you need.

Scanning under Windows 98

Windows 98 comes equipped with a program called ScanDisk that can detect and fix just about any hard drive error you're likely to meet. To run ScanDisk, follow these steps:

1. Click the Start button and choose Programs ⇨ Accessories ⇨ System Tools ⇨ ScanDisk.

2. The ScanDisk dialog box shown in Figure 7.4 appears. Click the hard drive you want to scan.

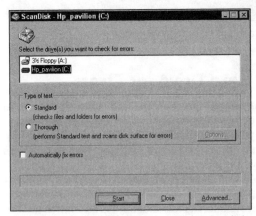

Figure 7.4 Running ScanDisk to check for disk errors under Windows 98

3. I recommend that you perform a Thorough scan at least once a month—ScanDisk checks each sector of your hard drive for physical errors. The downside to a Thorough scan is that it takes an eternity compared to a Standard scan! Use the Standard test type, therefore, if less than a month has gone by since your last Thorough scan.

Tip

Unless you're a very trusting person, it's a good idea to leave the Automatically fix errors check box disabled. This option enables you to see what's wrong before ScanDisk takes action to fix an error—ScanDisk prompts you for confirmation before making any repairs.

4. Click Start to begin the scanning process.

5. Once ScanDisk has successfully checked your drive and fixed any errors it finds, the program displays a results screen (Figure 7.5) that provides you with statistics on drive usage and total disk space (along with the number of physical errors found, if any, as bad sectors).

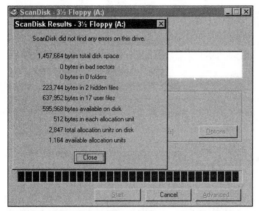

Figure 7.5 The results of a typical ScanDisk run

6. Click Close to return to the ScanDisk dialog box, and click Close again to return to Windows.

Scanning under Mac OS 9

The Mac OS counterpart to ScanDisk is called Disk First Aid. To run Disk First Aid, follow these steps:

1. Open your hard drive and open the Utility folder, then double-click the Disk First Aid icon to run it.

2. The program dialog box shown in Figure 7.6 appears. Click the hard drive you want to scan.

3. Click Verify to begin the scan; Disk First Aid displays an updated log as it checks your drive.

4. If errors are reported on the drive, click Repair to start the repair process. If you're repairing your startup hard drive, note that Mac OS likely needs to shut down all running applications to fix errors.

5. When Disk First Aid has awarded your drive a clean bill of health, click File and select Quit to close the program and return to the Mac OS desktop.

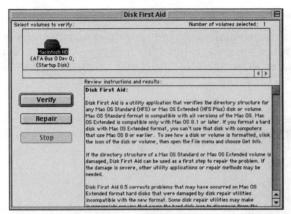

Figure 7.6 Using Disk First Aid on my Macintosh to check for hard drive errors

Disabling Scheduled Programs

It's unfortunate, but true: not every Windows or Mac OS program is "well behaved." In fact, some are downright obnoxious . . . for example, a misbehaving program may prompt you for input without allowing other programs running simultaneously to continue in the background (effectively halting your entire system). As you can imagine, such an interruption during a CD recording session likely spells doom for the unlucky disc — once again, you groan at the sound of another ruined coaster hitting the bottom of your trash can.

For this reason, it's important to disable programs that may kick in during a recording session, as well as other programs that may be running in the background. The rule of thumb is simple: *If a program isn't necessary to your operating system or your CD recording software, disable or exit that program before you launch your recording software!*

These programs can include:

- **Antivirus programs.** If you need to scan the files that you're recording, run your antivirus scanner beforehand as a separate step, then shut it down before recording.

- **Disk and system monitoring software.** Yes, I know . . . I made a big deal about scanning your drive for errors in the previous section, but that procedure should definitely happen *before* you start recording! Many system monitoring programs are infamous for their capacity to slow down your system and overwork your hard drive (neither of which is recommended during a CD burn).

- **Screen savers.** Pretty to look at, but they can turn a fast Pentium III or Motorola G3 processor into a paperweight — especially multimedia screensavers that feature digital video or animation. Under Windows 98, right-click the desktop and choose Properties, then set your screen saver choice to None. On the Mac, run the screen saver launcher program and disable it, or set it so that it won't kick in for several hours.

■ **Fax programs.** Fax programs can be performance-intensive, so be sure to disable your fax program's receive and scheduled send functions before you record.

On a Windows system, you can usually disable or exit an unnecessary program by right-clicking its taskbar icon and selecting Quit or Disable from the pop-up menu, as shown in Figure 7.7.

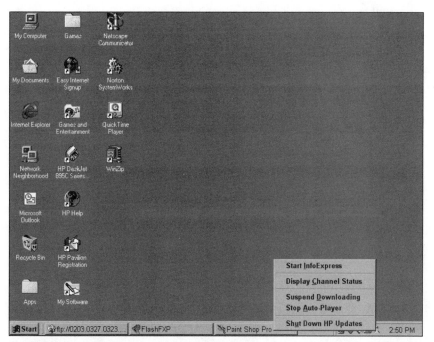

Figure 7.7 Sweeping your system of unnecessary programs is easy from the taskbar.

If you're running Windows, it's also a good idea to turn off the Task Scheduler (Figure 7.8), which can automatically launch programs without warning during a recording session. Right-click the Scheduler icon in the taskbar, and select Pause from the pop-up menu. (Don't forget to select Continue Task Scheduler after you've finished recording!)

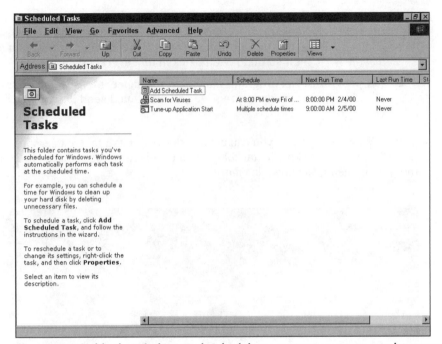

Figure 7.8 Disable the Windows Task Scheduler to prevent an unexpected appearance during a recording session.

If you're running Mac OS, use the Applications menu (shown in Figure 7.9) to switch to other programs that are running—then select the Quit menu item from the File menu of each to shut them down.

Figure 7.9 Click the Mac OS Applications menu to switch to the programs you want to quit.

Disabling Power-Saving Mode

Today's "green" computers do everything they can to conserve power—this is a good thing, unless (you guessed it) you're recording a CD. After a certain period of inactivity, your computer may spin down its hard drives to save power; the delay while they spin up again can wreak havoc with CD recording. Unfortunately, some computers do not recognize the disk access during a recording session as "activity"—therefore, it pays to disable power-saving mode before recording.

In Windows 98, you can turn off power-saving mode from the Control Panel. Follow these steps:

1. Click the Start button and choose Settings ⇨ Control Panel.

2. Run the Power Management application (Figure 7.10).

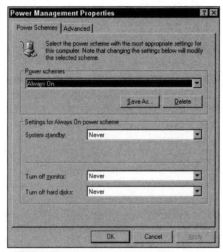

Figure 7.10 Keep that data coming by turning off the hard drive's power conservation mode.

3. Choose the Always On power scheme.

4. Set the hard disk value to Never.

5. Click OK to save your changes.

Under Mac OS, follow these steps:

1. Click the Apple menu and choose Control Panels.

2. Click Energy Saver to display the panel shown in Figure 7.11.

3. Click the Separate timing for hard disk sleep check box to enable it.

4. Move the slider to the Never setting.

5. Click the Close box in the upper-left corner to save your changes.

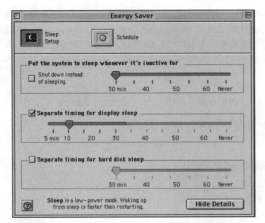

Figure 7.11 A good Macintosh hard drive never sleeps.

Disabling Network Access

Is your computer connected to a LAN? If so, that network connection is yet another potential disaster waiting to happen during a CD recording session. Why? For three good reasons:

- **File sharing can bog down your computer.** If another network user attempts to access your computer's files or printer, the performance lag can easily be enough to cause buffer underrun errors (especially on an older computer).

- **A network crash can lock your computer.** When (not if, but when) the network locks, so does your computer, and a lockup is fatal when recording CDs.

- **Network messages and communications can disrupt recording.** If a fellow network user sends a network message (either global or directly addressed to you), some network clients halt all the programs that are running to display it.

It's easy to prevent these catastrophes during a burn: simply boot your computer without logging in to the network (typically, this is done by clicking Cancel at the login screen). After you've finished recording, reboot your computer and log in normally.

Defragmenting Your Hard Drive

If you've never defragmented your hard drive, you're in for a treat — you can boost performance on any computer by taking care of this simple task, and the older the computer, the more defragmenting helps!

First, a quick explanation of fragmentation is in order. When you first began writing files to your computer's hard drive, they were written *contiguously*—all in the same area, and unbroken from beginning to end. Over time, however, your drive has filled up, and your operating system must save new files in the space freed when you delete files. Therefore, your operating system is presented with a problem: larger files can no longer be saved contiguously.

Both Windows and Mac OS solve this problem in the same manner: A file is broken up into smaller pieces that fit into those "holes" left by deleted files, and it is saved in pieces (or segments) on your drive. The segment locations are saved, so your drive knows where all the parts of a particular file are stored. When a program wants to read that file, the operating system automatically combines all the smaller segments of the file back into their original order, and then it sends the restored file to the program. It's a pretty neat process, and invisible to both you and the programs you run.

But the process isn't perfect, and Figure 7.12 illustrates why—it takes more time for your computer's operating system to reassemble the file, and the delay grows if there are a large number of segments that are spread out all over your drive. This is the ongoing process of *fragmentation,* and it gets worse over time: Files become more and more fragmented, and they take longer and longer to reassemble, which translates into slower disk performance. And, as I've already mentioned several times, disk performance is critical when you're recording at higher speeds.

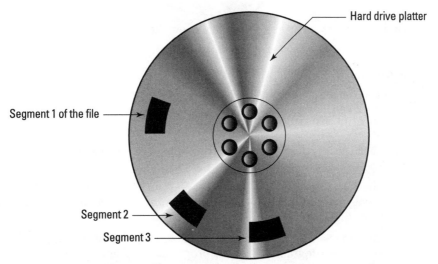

Figure 7.12 A typical file scattered in segments across the surface of a hard drive

To solve this problem and optimize your drive, you need a *defragmenter:* a utility program that reads in the files on your drive and rewrites them in contiguous form, one after another. Figure 7.13 shows that same file after a defragmenter has done its work—note that the same file is now contiguous, so it takes far less time (in computer terms, anyway) for your operating system to read it and send it to your CD recorder.

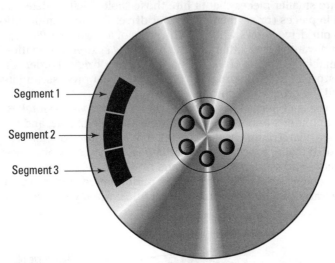

Figure 7.13 After we've run a defragmenter, our file is contiguous and easier to read!

Defragmenting under Windows 98

Thanks to the good folks at Redmond, you won't need to buy a defragmenter—Windows 98 includes Disk Defragmenter, which you should run at least once a month. To run Defragmenter, follow these steps:

1. Click the Start button and choose Programs ⇨ Accessories ⇨ System Tools ⇨ Disk Defragmenter.

2. The Select Drive dialog box shown in Figure 7.14 appears. Click the hard drive you want to scan—if you have more than one drive, choose the drive that holds the files you'll be recording.

3. Click the Settings button and make sure that you've enabled the Rearrange program files so my programs start faster check box. Click OK to exit the Settings dialog box.

4. Click OK to begin defragmenting your drive. If you like, you can click Show Details to display a graphical status screen as Defragmenter does its thing.

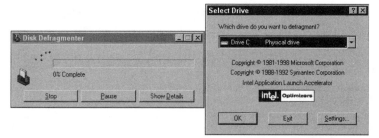

Figure 7.14 Selecting a drive to defragment under Windows 98

Defragmenting under Mac OS 9

Sadly, Mac OS 9 still lacks a defragmenter as standard equipment; however, there are many fine commercial utilities that can do the job. My favorite is Speed Disk, a part of the Norton Utilities package for the Macintosh (which also includes Disk Doctor, a great disk-scanning program, as well). Figure 7.15 shows Speed Disk at work defragmenting my drive under Mac OS 9.

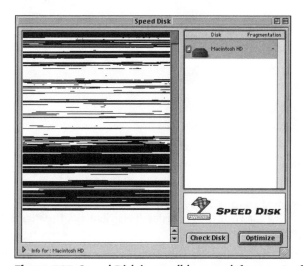

Figure 7.15 Speed Disk is a well-known defragmenter for Mac OS.

Preparing a PC under Windows 98

If you run Windows—and you'd like a faster machine—then this is the place to be! In this section, I discuss a number of tips and tricks you can use to squeeze the best possible performance from your system (with high-speed CD recording in mind, of course).

Optimizing Your Hard Drive Performance

By default, Windows 98 is not optimally configured for recording CDs. In this section, I show you how to fine-tune several Windows settings to help turn your PC into a stable recording platform.

First, you should make sure that your CD recorder's hardware configuration is set correctly. Follow these steps:

1. Right-click the My Computer icon and select Properties from the pop-up menu.

2. Click the Device Manager tab to display the panel shown in Figure 7.16.

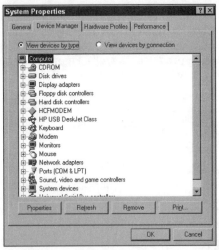

Figure 7.16 Displaying the Device Manager in Windows 98

3. Click the plus sign next to the CDROM entry to expand the list, and double-click the entry for your CD recorder. This displays the Properties dialog box for your CD recorder.

4. Click the Settings tab to display the panel shown in Figure 7.17. In this case, these settings control my Hewlett-Packard 8100-series CD recorder.

5. Make sure that the Disconnect check box is enabled, whereas the Auto insert notification check box should be disabled.

6. If the DMA check box is available, make sure that it's enabled. (Not all drives support DMA, but if yours does, it's a feature you definitely appreciate.) The other settings on this panel should be left as is.

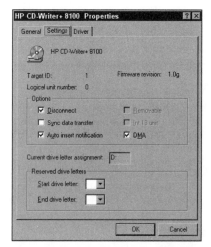

Figure 7.17 Standard hardware settings for a CD recorder

Tip

Note that the firmware revision for your CD recorder is displayed on this panel —
it's a good idea to write the revision number down, so that you can check later to
determine if a newer firmware revision is available from the manufacturer.

7. Click OK to save your changes.

Optimizing Your CD-ROM Performance

As you do with your hard drive, you can boost the performance of your CD-ROM
drive by changing settings within Windows 98. Most recording programs enable
you to copy from a CD-ROM drive directly to your CD recorder, so improved
CD-ROM performance results in fewer errors when copying directly from drive
to drive.

To optimize the performance of your CD-ROM drive:

1. Before you leave the System Properties dialog box, click the Performance
   tab and click the File System button to display the panel shown in
   Figure 7.18.

2. Set the Typical role of this machine to Network server, which provides
   faster disk performance, and set the Read-ahead optimization to Full if
   it's not already at the maximum.

3. Next, click the CD-ROM tab to display the settings in Figure 7.19. The
   Supplemental cache size should be set to the largest possible, and set
   the access pattern to Quad-speed or higher.

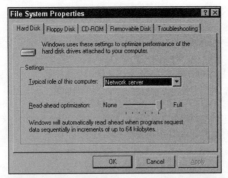

Figure 7.18 Displaying the File System Properties dialog box

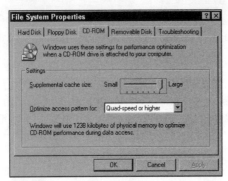

Figure 7.19 Setting CD-ROM performance settings under Windows 98

4. You're done! Click OK to exit the File System Properties dialog box, and then click OK again to exit the System Properties dialog box. If you changed any settings during this procedure, you probably have to reboot.

Preparing a Macintosh under Mac OS 9

The Macintosh also requires a few setting changes before you begin recording, and the steps in this section help you to make them. Note that these instructions apply only to Mac OS version 8.5 and higher—if you have version 8.0 or earlier, I strongly recommend that you upgrade if possible.

Allocating Memory to Your Recording Application

Like other Macintosh applications you may use to edit large desktop publishing, graphics, or multimedia files, your Macintosh CD recording software probably deserves additional RAM. This extra memory is used as "work space" in memory, including the buffer that stores data before it's sent to the drive for recording. Even if your recording application doesn't advise you that it's running out of memory, it's still a good idea to allocate additional system RAM.

Follow these steps to increase the memory allocation for your recording program:

1. Shut down your recording program and return to the Finder and your desktop.

2. Click the recording program's icon once to highlight it, then click the File menu family and choose the Get Info item.

3. Click the Show drop-down list and choose Memory, as shown in Figure 7.20.

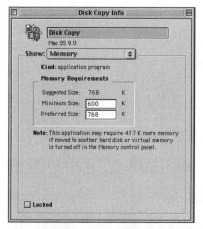

Figure 7.20 You can allocate additional memory from the Disk Copy Info dialog box.

4. Click in the Preferred Size box and enter a higher amount of RAM.

Tip

How much memory should you add? If the documentation that accompanied your recording software doesn't name a figure, I would recommend adding at least 2,048K (or 2 megabytes) of additional RAM to the Preferred Size box.

5. Click the Close box to close the dialog box and save your changes.

Disabling Virtual Memory

Both Windows and Mac OS can use some of the area on your hard drive as *virtual memory*—this is the only way that many applications can load very large documents. Virtual memory is also a factor in *multitasking,* where the operating system can run multiple programs simultaneously.

However, virtual memory is a little less efficient in Mac OS than it is under Windows, so it's actually beneficial to turn off virtual memory when you're recording discs! If you're running an older PowerPC with at least 64 megabytes of system RAM and Mac OS 8 or better, your entire system runs significantly faster (especially because hard drive performance is so important for a successful recording).

1. Click the Apple menu and choose Control Panels.

2. Run the Memory Control Panel, which is shown in Figure 7.21.

3. Click the Off button in the Virtual Memory portion of the dialog box.

4. Click the Close box to close the dialog box and save your changes.

5. Restart your Mac.

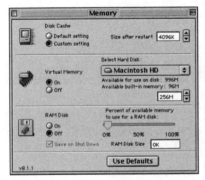

Figure 7.21 Use the Mac OS 9 Memory Control Panel to turn off virtual memory and expand your disk cache.

Expanding Your Disk Cache

Because disk performance is critical during the recording process, it's a good idea to expand the size of your disk cache if your Mac has at least 64 megabytes of system RAM. This disk cache holds data that's accessed often and helps improve the efficiency of your hard drive's read and write operations, which leads to better disk performance. Follow these steps to expand the disk cache in Mac OS 9:

1. Click the Apple menu and choose Control Panels.

2. Run the Memory Control Panel.

3. Click the Custom setting button in the Disk Cache portion of the dialog box.

4. At the confirmation prompt, click Custom to continue.

5. Click the arrows to select the size of the disk cache.

Tip

For Macs with at least 64 megabytes of system RAM, a cache size of 4,096 is a good choice—but if you've got an abundance of system RAM (for example, 128 megabytes or more), I recommend a cache size of 6,048.

6. Click the Close box to close the dialog box and save your changes.

7. Restart your Mac.

Should I Record over a Network?

Now it's time to address an issue that most CD recorder owners face in an office environment: the dreaded "Can I record some of the stuff from my workstation on your drive? I can record it directly over the network."

For most office applications, the average 10/100 Ethernet network is fast and furious—for example, a shared accounting package or a productivity suite like Microsoft Office runs fine. As I mentioned earlier in this chapter, however, networks and CD recording don't mix. Further, I recommend that you avoid attempting to read files directly from a remote network drive to your CD recorder (especially when you're recording at 4x or faster). Besides the reasons I listed earlier, network recording involves two additional risks:

■ **Network speeds vary.** Network speeds depend on the number of users logged in and the applications they're using. Although it may be able to keep up normally, your office LAN may be too busy and sluggish at times to keep up with the peak demands of your CD recorder.

■ **Network restrictions can be costly.** If your network pauses because you've mistakenly tried to record a file that's outside your range of access permissions, you can add another coaster to your collection.

So how can you record data from a remote computer? Copy the files to your hard drive first, *before* you begin recording! If you don't have enough space on your local hard drive to hold all of the information and you have to use a network connection as your source, keep the following points in mind:

- **Use a packet writing program such as Adaptec's DirectCD.** Packet writing (which enables you to simply drag and drop files to your CD recorder using Windows Explorer) is far less sensitive to timing delays than track-at-once or disc-at-once recording.

- **Record during low-traffic periods.** Wait until after others have left the office before you begin your recording, so that the network can provide faster data transfer and a lower risk of interruption.

In Review

In this chapter you learned both general and specific preparations that you can make (both before your first recording and before each subsequent recording session). You can now check your hard drive for errors and increase your available hard drive space, and you know how to fine-tune your entire system for the fastest possible performance. In Chapter 8, "Introducing Easy CD Creator Step-by-Step," you learn the basics of creating your own CDs with the very popular Easy CD Creator from Adaptec.

CHAPTER

8

Introducing Easy CD Creator Step-by-Step

IN THIS CHAPTER

- Using Easy CD Creator to record data and audio CD-ROMs

- Adjusting CD layout properties for data and audio recordings

- Configuring and testing your system for optimal performance

- Finding files on your system

Adaptec's Easy CD Creator is probably the best-known CD recording software suite on the shelves these days, and for good reason: It can handle just about any recording chore, including advanced recording tasks like creating bootable CD-ROMs, video CDs, and photo CDs. This great program makes it easy to organize data and audio CDs, and it follows up the recording process with custom jewel case liners and CD labels.

In this chapter, I cover the basics, including how to configure Easy CD Creator to produce different types of discs. In fact, if you're creating a simple data CD-ROM or a standard Red Book audio CD — the two most common recording chores — you should find everything that you need to successfully record in this chapter.

Cross-Reference

You can take advantage of the features of Easy CD Creator that I've mentioned here with the step-by-step projects in Chapter 13, "Doing Basic Recording," and Chapter 14, "Practicing Advanced Recording."

Using Easy CD Creator

One of the advantages of Easy CD Creator is the unified appearance of most of the menu system and user interface — you can record many types of discs using the same layout tools, and once you've recorded a basic data CD-ROM and an audio CD, you'll become more familiar with the program's look and feel. In this section, I demonstrate the basic steps that you take — the "building blocks" of more advanced disc projects that you create later in the book.

Recording a Data CD-ROM

audio?

Most computer owners buy a CD recorder to make their own data discs, and Easy CD Creator automates the process as much as possible. To record a simple data disc with files from your PC's hard drive:

1. Load a blank CD-R or CD-RW disc into your drive. Easy CD Creator automatically displays the Create CD Wizard welcome screen shown in Figure 8.1.

Tip

You can also run the Create CD Wizard from the Windows 98 Start menu. Click Start and choose Programs ➪ Adaptec Easy CD Creator 4 ➪ Create CD. To run the actual Easy CD Creator program from the Windows 98 Start menu, click Start and choose Programs ➪ Adaptec Easy CD Creator 4 ➪ Features ➪ Easy CD Creator.

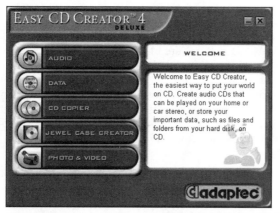

Figure 8.1 The opening screen from the Create CD Wizard

2. Click Data to display the different types of data discs you can record.

3. Click Data CD. Easy CD Creator loads and displays the Data CD Layout screen shown in Figure 8.2.

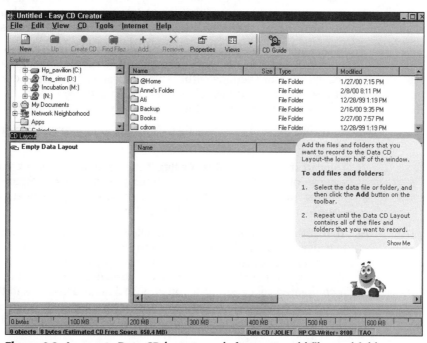

Figure 8.2 An empty Data CD layout, ready for you to add files and folders

Tip

If you need additional help while setting up your recording, you can refer to the animated CD-ROM assistant. If you tire of the assistant, you can get rid of him by right-clicking him and choosing Hide from the pop-up menu!

4. Within the Explorer display at the top right of the Layout window, navigate through your hard drive until you find the files and folders to record. Click the icon for the file or folder you want to add to your data CD to highlight it. To highlight multiple files and folders, hold down the Ctrl key while you click each icon.

5. Click Add in the toolbar to copy the files, as shown in Figure 8.3.

Tip

You can also add files and folders to your layout by clicking the selected icons and dragging them to the CD layout tree display in the lower-left portion of the window.

6. Repeat steps 4 and 5 until you've added all the files you want to the layout. Note the bar marked in megabytes at the bottom of the window; it indicates approximately how much of the disc is used by the files you've added. The disc is completely filled when the bar reaches the end — for a standard disc, this should be about 650 megabytes.

7. At this point, you're ready to record your disc — you can also make adjustments to the contents, format, and structure of your disc, which I cover in other sections within this chapter. For now, let's create a disc with the default settings. Click the Create CD button on the toolbar to display the CD Creation Setup dialog box shown in Figure 8.4.

8. To record one copy of your disc using the default recording speed, click OK.

9. You can start the actual recording if the default settings are correct — or, you can display the advanced settings screen shown in Figure 8.5 by clicking Advanced. (I describe these advanced settings next, but if you want to start recording now, skip to step 15.)

10. To test the recording process first, click either Test or Test and Create. Because no data is actually written to the disc, this can save you from wasting a blank disc if the recording aborts with errors. If you choose Test, Easy CD Creator performs a test recording and reports whether it completed successfully. If you choose Test and Create and the test recording completes successfully, the program automatically records the disc afterward.

Find the files you want to record here

Click here to add files to the CD

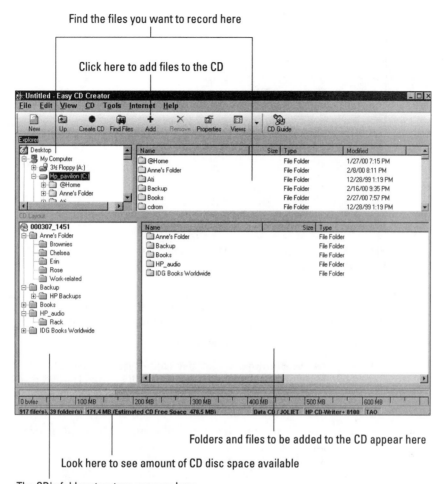

Folders and files to be added to the CD appear here

Look here to see amount of CD disc space available

The CD's folder structure appears here

Figure 8.3 Adding files to a Data CD layout

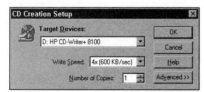

Figure 8.4 The CD Creation Setup dialog box

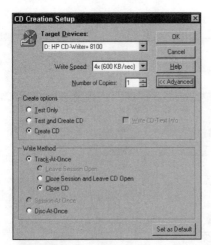

Figure 8.5 The advanced settings available within the CD
Creation Setup dialog box

11. To make multiple copies of the data disc, click the arrows next to the
    Number of copies field and specify how many copies you need.

12. To record in track-at-once mode, select a session type:

    - **Leave the session open.** The disc cannot be read in a standard
      CD-ROM drive — only the CD recorder will be able to read the
      data. Data can be added later without creating another session.
      This feature may not be available for your CD recorder.

    - **Close the session and leave the disc open.** This option creates a
      disc that any CD-ROM drive can read, and the disc can be written
      to again — however, you must record additional data later in a new
      session, creating a multisession disc. Some CD-ROM drives can't
      read multisession discs.

    - **Close the CD.** This permanently finalizes the CD so that it can't be
      written to again in the future.

13. To record in Disc-at-Once mode, click the desired option. Your recorder
    may not support these modes.

Cross-Reference

For a complete discussion of Disc-at-Once mode, see Chapter 6, "Preparing
Your Material."

Tip

Disc-at-Once mode isn't really necessary when creating a data CD—it's not as compatible with all brands of read-only CD-ROM drives as a Track-at-Once recording. Also, as I mentioned earlier, many drives can't create discs in this alternative mode. However, if you're creating a master disc to send to a commercial CD manufacturer for duplication, Disc-at-Once may be required. If your drive can't record in Disc-at-Once mode, you have to take the data to another computer with a drive that supports it.

14. To save these settings as the defaults for future recordings, click Save as Default.

15. Click OK to begin recording.

16. Easy CD Creator displays the CD Creation Process dialog box shown in Figure 8.6—if you need to load a blank disc, the program automatically ejects the disc and prompts you.

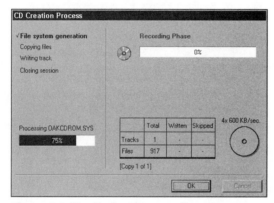

Figure 8.6 Monitoring the recording process

17. You can follow the progress of your recording from the CD Creation Process display.

Recording an Audio CD

Audio discs can be created by reading tracks from existing audio CDs or by recording tracks from audio files on your hard drive. To record a Red Book audio CD:

1. Run the Create CD Wizard from the Windows 98 Start menu.

2. Click Audio and select Audio Disc.

3. Easy CD Creator displays the Audio Layout screen shown in Figure 8.7. Using the Explorer display at the top of the window, navigate through your system and locate the audio files you want to record. To copy tracks from an existing audio CD, load the disc into a CD-ROM drive or your CD recorder, and then select that drive to display the tracks as "files." You can load multiple audio CDs if necessary, one after the other.

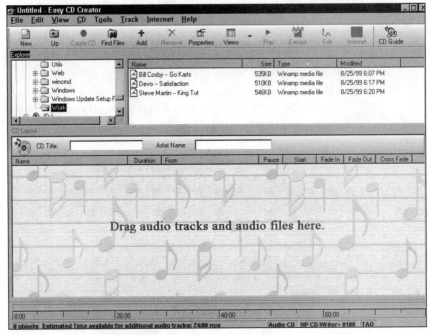

Figure 8.7 The Easy CD Creator Audio Layout screen

4. Click the audio files to highlight them. Remember, Easy CD Creator automatically converts tracks from audio CDs, WAV, and MP3 files to digital audio files on your hard drive before recording them. To select multiple files, hold down the Ctrl key while you click.

5. Click Add in the toolbar to copy the files, as shown in Figure 8.8.

Tip

As in the Data CD layout, you can drag and drop audio tracks to the CD layout tree display in the lower-left portion of the window instead of using the Add button.

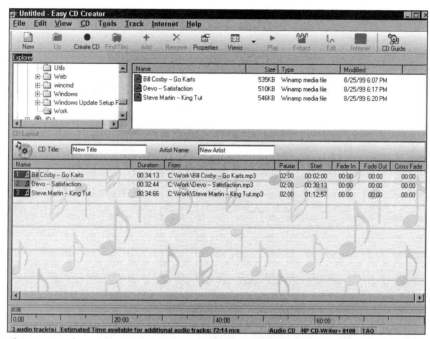

Figure 8.8 The audio tracks you've selected are displayed in the Layout window.

6. Repeat steps 4 and 5 until you've added all the tracks you want to your
   CD playlist. The Estimated Time bar at the bottom of the screen indicates
   how much time the tracks take up, and how much of the disc's capacity
   remains to be filled. A standard CD-R disc recorded as a Red Book audio
   disc can hold a maximum of 74 minutes of music.

7. If you like, you can rearrange the tracks on your audio CDs before the
   recording process begins. To move a track to a new position in the list,
   click the track entry to highlight it and drag it to the new location.
   Release the mouse button to reorder the tracks.

8. Click within the CD Title field and type the name of the audio CD. If you
   like, you can also enter the artist's or band's name in the Artist Name
   field. To enter or change the name of a track, click the track name and
   enter it into the editing box that appears.

Tip

To listen to one of your audio tracks, double-click the track entry. Easy CD Creator
displays an audio player similar to a CD player. To close the preview audio player,
click the Close Window button at the top right of the dialog box.

9. When you've entered all the information and all the audio tracks, it's time to record—click the Create CD Toolbar button. If you've selected tracks from an existing audio CD, Easy CD Creator prompts you to load the audio CD so that the track can be temporarily copied to your hard drive (of course, this won't be the case if you're recording MP3 or WAV files). After all the tracks are on your hard drive, Easy CD Creator displays the CD Creation Setup dialog box shown in Figure 8.9.

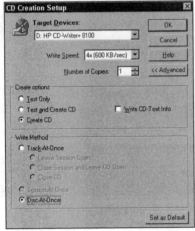

Figure 8.9 Specifying recording settings for an audio CD

10. Choose Create CD.

11. To make multiple copies of the audio CD, click the arrows next to the Number of copies field and specify how many copies you need.

12. If your recorder supports Disc-at-Once, select it. Otherwise, choose Track-at-Once mode and close the CD.

13. Click OK to begin recording.

14. Easy CD Creator displays the CD Creation Process dialog box. If you need to load a blank disc, the program automatically ejects the tray and prompts you.

Copying One CD to Another

Need to make an exact copy of an existing disc? You won't even have to run Easy CD Creator! Instead, you can use a separate program called CD Copier. If you have a CD-ROM drive in your computer as well as a CD recorder, you can even copy directly from one drive to the other.

To copy data from one CD to another:

1. Click Start and choose Programs ⇨ Adaptec Easy CD Creator 4 ⇨ Features ⇨ CD Copier. The program loads and displays the screen shown in Figure 8.10.

Note

Because CD Copier reads the drives in your system each time you run it, the drive letters and descriptions that you see will be different from the illustrations in this section.

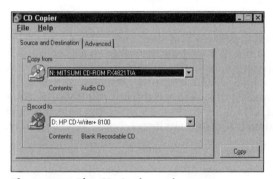

Figure 8.10 The CD Copier main screen

2. Click the "Copy from" drop-down list box and choose the source drive that contains the disc from which you want to copy data or audio files. Note that this drive can be either your recorder or another CD-ROM drive or CD recorder in your system. If you choose a source drive different from your CD recorder, the program may have to test your drive (which is an automatic process) to determine whether it can read data and extract audio properly. (I go over this hardware testing in more detail later in this chapter.)

Tip

If the source drive you've chosen doesn't read data or extract audio properly (which Easy CD Creator can determine), use your CD recorder as the source drive. You have to swap discs and the copy process takes longer, but virtually all CD recorders meet the requirements for the source drive. (That's another feature to check for in the specifications for a CD-ROM or CD-RW drive while shopping!)

3. Click the "Record to" drop-down list box and choose the target CD recorder that will create the copy.

4. Click the Advanced tab to display the advanced CD Copier features shown in Figure 8.11.

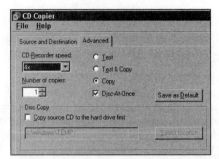

Figure 8.11 Changing advanced settings in CD Copier

5. To test the recording process first, click either Test or Test & Copy. (In this case, *testing* refers not to the hardware, but to an actual simulated recording that can help determine whether your drive can successfully create a certain disc.) Because no data is actually written to the disc, this step can save you from wasting a blank disc if the recording aborts with errors. If you choose Test, CD Copier performs a simulated recording and reports whether it completed successfully. If you choose Test & Copy and the test recording completes successfully, the program automatically copies the disc afterward.

Warning

Many commercial software programs are shipped on copy-protected CD-ROMs, which cannot be duplicated using CD Copier and will abort with errors. Remember, copyrighted software should not be duplicated (even if the disc isn't copy-protected)!

6. To make multiple copies of the source disc, click the arrows next to the Number of copies field and specify how many copies you need. If you are making three or more duplicates, it's a good idea to enable the "Copy source CD to the hard drive first" check box so that the data will be read from the hard drive after the first copy is done. This saves CD Copier the trouble of rereading the source disc for each copy.

7. If you're copying an audio CD, enable the Disc-at-Once check box if possible. Not all CD recorders support this feature, so it may be grayed out.

8. To save these settings as the defaults for future recordings, click Save as Default.

9. Click Copy to begin the process.

10. If you're using the same CD recorder as both the source and target drives, load the blank disc when prompted by the program.

Creating a Bootable CD-ROM

Most computer owners probably have never recorded a bootable CD-ROM. These very specialized discs contain the operating system and support files necessary to boot a computer without a hard drive. Bootable CD-ROMs are recorded in the _El Torito_ format. (Yes, that's actually the name of the standard!) Support for these discs used to be very rare in the days of 486 and original Pentium motherboards, but today many PCs can use a bootable CD-ROM created with Easy CD Creator. A bootable disc can hold far more data than a bootable floppy — even an entire operating system like DOS, which can then in turn be used to install Windows from files stored on the same disc! (In fact, Windows 98 and 2000 can be installed from a bootable disc on many PCs.) Many versions of Linux can also be installed from a bootable disc.

In practice, booting a computer from a CD-ROM is much like booting it from a floppy disk. In fact, creating a "master" floppy disk is required to create a bootable CD-ROM. To record a bootable CD:

1. Create a bootable floppy disk that contains all of the necessary system files (files that read during the boot process). In the case of Windows, you need to format a system disk: Insert a floppy disk into your floppy disk drive, open the Add/Remove Programs dialog box (Start ➪ Settings ➪ Add/Remove Programs) click the Startup Disk tab, and click Create Disk.

Note

Because the system files can't occupy more than the capacity of a single floppy disk, computer owners running Windows 95/98 or Windows 2000 are limited to DOS as the operating system for a bootable CD-ROM. (Note that this space limit applies *only* to the system files used to load DOS – naturally, your bootable disc can store additional files, up to the maximum capacity of the disc.) Make sure that AUTOEXEC.BAT and CONFIG.SYS files are included if you want to automatically configure your system during the boot process.

2. Click Start and choose Programs ➪ Adaptec Easy CD Creator 4 ➪ Features ➪ Easy CD Creator to load the program.

3. Click File and select the New CD Layout menu item, and then choose Bootable CD.

4. Load a blank CD into your recorder.

5. Easy CD Creator displays the prompt shown in Figure 8.12. Load your bootable floppy and click OK.

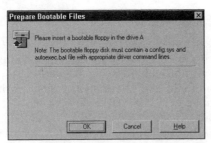

Figure 8.12 This message prompts you to load a boot floppy to create a bootable CD-ROM.

6. The files are read from the floppy disk and stored in two special files within your CD layout: BOOTCAT.BIN and BOOTIMG.BIN.

7. From this point on, the recording process is the same as for a standard data CD-ROM. Add any remaining files to your layout normally (for example, you could include all of the hardware drivers required by Windows for your computer) and click Create CD to record the disc.

Note

Remember, a bootable CD-ROM must be supported by your computer's BIOS, or it won't work. To determine if your computer can use a bootable CD-ROM, check your computer's manual or contact the manufacturer of your PC.

Using Disc Images

What's a *disc image*? It's all of the information necessary to create a CD. But instead of recording that data to a CD-R or CD-RW, you save it as a file on your hard drive for later use. You may decide to create a disc image instead of actually recording a disc itself for a number of reasons:

■ **It's convenient.** A disc image is ideal for those who have to record the same disc from time to time but don't want to create a batch of several copies. For example, if you must record a disc for each new employee within your company, you could store the disc as an image and record a single copy whenever a new employee is hired. If the disc changes, you won't waste additional discs that were recorded but never used.

■ **It's safe.** If you record a disc from a disc image, you can be sure that none of the files were altered or updated by mistake—the disc image remains stable. This fact comes in very handy for PC owners who are incrementally updating or storing information, such as archiving yearly tax records created with a tax preparation program.

■ **It's fast.** If you have a 4x or faster CD recorder, but you are using an older 486 or original Pentium-based computer with a slow hard drive or limited random access memory (RAM), you may experience recording errors. (This is especially true if you're recording a large number of small files on a disc.) If you record that data as an image first, it's much easier for your system to create a disc. Because an image is a single continuous file, your hard drive doesn't have to read all those smaller files and send them to your CD recorder.

■ **No recorder is necessary!** If you share an external CD recorder with others, you can record a disc image to your hard drive even if the recorder is being used on someone else's computer. When it's your turn to use the drive, just record the disc from the image.

Tip

Before you decide to make a disc image, be sure that you have at least 800 megabytes of free space on your hard drive. This amount provides the 700 megabytes you need to record the image with some left over, so you won't jeopardize the free space for temporary and swap files that Windows needs to operate properly.

Saving a Disc Image

To save a disc image to your hard drive:

1. Click Start and choose Programs ➪ Adaptec Easy CD Creator 4 ➪ Features ➪ Easy CD Creator to load the program.

2. Click File and select New CD Layout ➪ Data CD.

3. Build your CD layout as you normally would.

4. From the File menu, choose the Create CD Image menu item. Easy CD Creator displays the Select Image File dialog box shown in Figure 8.13.

Figure 8.13 Entering a filename for a new disc image

5. Navigate to the location on your drive where you want to store the disc image, and type a filename (note that the extension .CIF is automatically added by Easy CD Creator).

6. Click Save.

7. Easy CD Creator "records" the image to the hard drive.

Recording a CD from a Disc Image

To record a disc from a disc image on your hard drive:

1. Click Start and choose Programs ➪ Adaptec Easy CD Creator 4 ➪ Features ➪ Easy CD Creator to load the program.

2. Click File and select the Create CD from CD Image menu item.

3. Easy CD Creator displays the Select Image File dialog box.

4. Locate the disc image you want to record on your hard drive. Highlight it and click Open.

5. Easy CD Creator displays the same CD Creation Setup dialog box you would see if you were recording from a layout. Make any required setting changes and click OK. (For more information on these settings, see the section "Recording a Data CD-ROM" earlier in this chapter.) Click OK.

6. Easy CD Creator prompts you to load a blank disc, and the recording process completes as usual.

Adjusting CD Layout Properties

As I mention in earlier chapters, your CD recorder can create different types of discs for different applications. Although Easy CD Creator's Create CD Wizard automates much of this configuration, you can make many changes manually. Changing CD layout properties can determine the file system your disc uses, as well as provide extra information and data that's specific to the type of disc you're creating—for example, adding a UPC number to an audio CD you're recording so that it can be automatically cataloged by your computer's CD player program. You can also optimize the recorded data or enable automatic verification of the files on the disc from this dialog box.

Cross-Reference

Because the options available within the CD Layout Properties dialog box change with the type of disc you're creating, I cover the properties for both data CD and audio CD layouts (the two most common) in this section. Descriptions of the properties for bootable, mixed-mode, and CD Extra discs appear in Chapter 12, "Recording Multisession CDs Step-by-Step" and Chapter 14, "Practicing Advanced Recording."

Data CD Layout Properties

To change the properties for a data CD layout:

1. Click Start and choose Programs ⇨ Adaptec Easy CD Creator 4 ⇨ Features ⇨ Easy CD Creator to load the program.

2. If Easy CD Creator hasn't loaded a new data CD layout, click File and select New CD Layout ⇨ Data CD.

3. Click the File menu and choose the CD Layout Properties menu item to display the dialog box shown in Figure 8.14.

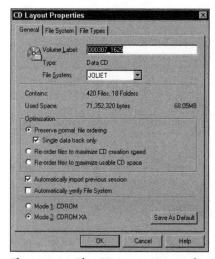

Figure 8.14 The CD Layout Properties General tab

4. Under the General tab, you can change these options:

   - **Volume Label.** A default volume label is automatically generated; if you want to use your own, highlight the text in this field and type the new label.

   - **File System.** If you're recording a disc for use under Windows 95/98, Windows 2000, or Windows NT, I recommend you choose the Joliet file system developed by Microsoft (which supports long filenames with embedded spaces). If you're creating a disc for use on another operating system, you can practically guarantee compatibility if you choose the internationally recognized ISO 9660 file system, which adheres closely to standard DOS naming conventions and can be read on just about any platform.

- **Optimization.** Under most circumstances, the normal file ordering is the best selection, and a single data track is preferable (the disc loads and runs faster). However, if you want to reorder the files to reduce the time it takes to record or maximize the amount of free space on the disc, you can choose either option.

- **Automatically import previous session.** If you're adding another session to a multisession disc that you recorded earlier, Easy CD Creator automatically includes the information from the previous session if you enable the Automatically import previous session check box.

- **Automatically verify File System.** Enable the Automatically verify File System check box if you want Easy CD Creator to check the completed recording by comparing files on the recorded disc with the original files.

- **Mode 1/Mode 2.** In most cases, choose Mode 1, because it's more widely compatible. However, if you want to create a multisession CD-ROM or a CD Extra CD-ROM, select Mode 2.

5. Click Save as Default to save your settings as the default for a Data CD.

6. Under the File System tab shown in Figure 8.15, you can change these options:

- **Publisher Name.** Enter your name or the name of your organization (up to 128 characters) here. (This is an optional field.)

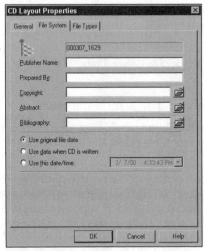

Figure 8.15 The CD Layout Properties File System tab

- **Prepared By.** Type the name of the disc's creator here. (This is an optional field.)

- **Copyright.** Enter the copyright text that applies to the material on this disc, or click the Browse icon to select a text file. (This is an optional field.)

- **Abstract.** Enter the content description for this disc, or click the Browse icon to select a text file. (This is an optional field.)

- **Bibliography.** Enter the bibliographical reference for this disc, or click the Browse icon to select a text file. (This is an optional field.)

- **Date/Time Stamp.** Select the file date and time stamping criteria you want to apply to the files on this disc. If you select Use this date/time, you can click the drop-down list box and select a specific date and time from the calendar display that appears.

7. Under the File Types tab shown in Figure 8.16, you can change these options:

- **Add all files/Exclude file types.** Generally, you want to use Add all Files to avoid excluding any files from your layout by accident. However, if you're using Easy CD Creator to back up a directory (or you want to "filter" certain files from your disc layout), choose "Do not add files of the following Types," click in the list below, and enter the three-character filename extensions that you don't want to record.

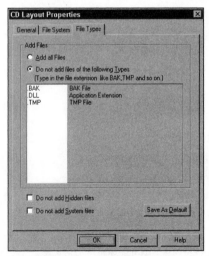

Figure 8.16 The CD Layout Properties File Types tab

- **Do not add Hidden files.** Enable this field if you want to exclude *hidden* files (which normally aren't shown in Windows Explorer or by a DOS DIR command) from the CD layout.

- **Do not add System files.** Enable this field to exclude Windows system files from your data CD layout.

8. Click Save as Default to save your settings as the default for a data CD.

9. Click OK to exit the Easy CD Creator CD Layout Properties dialog box and save your changes.

Audio CD Layout Properties

To change the properties for an audio CD layout:

1. Click Start and choose Programs ⇨ Adaptec Easy CD Creator 4 ⇨ Features ⇨ Easy CD Creator to load the program.

2. If Easy CD Creator hasn't loaded a new audio CD layout, click File and select New CD Layout ⇨ Audio CD.

3. Click the File menu and choose the CD Layout Properties menu item to display the dialog box shown in Figure 8.17.

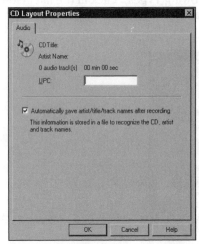

Figure 8.17 The CD Layout Properties Audio tab

4. You can change only two options for an audio CD:

- **UPC.** Every commercially produced audio CD has a *Universal Product Code* number, and many computer audio CD player programs and audio CD cataloging programs use this code to identify the disc and recall the artist, title, and track information. If you have a UPC number for this disc, you can enter it here.

Where is this stored on the CD? Tell us!

- **Automatically save artist/title/track names after recording.** Enable this field if you would like Easy CD Creator to save the information you've entered for later display (either when you load the disc to copy audio from it, or if you play tracks from it within the program). This can be a real timesaver, so I recommend it!

5. To exit the Easy CD Creator CD Layout Properties dialog box and save your changes, click OK.

Configuring and Testing Your System

Earlier in this chapter, I mentioned certain hardware tests that Easy CD Creator may perform automatically when you first use the program with a CD-ROM or CD-RW drive. You can also perform these tests manually if you like — in this section, I show you how you can use the test results to help configure the options within Easy CD Creator to help reduce errors. I also show you how to set your own preferences within the program.

Running the System Tests

As I stress earlier in the book, it's important to fine-tune your PC so that it can deliver the fastest error-free recordings; even today's Pentium III- and Athlon-based systems running Windows can run into problems if you're recording as a background task, or if your drive supports 8x write speeds. Easy CD Creator provides a battery of System Tests that you can run to help determine the optimum settings for your specific hardware — you can check the performance of each hard drive, CD recorder, and read-only CD-ROM drive.

To run the System Tests:

1. Click Start and choose Programs ⇨ Adaptec Easy CD Creator 4 ⇨ Features ⇨ Easy CD Creator to load the program.

2. Click the Tools menu and choose the System Tests menu item to display the dialog box shown in Figure 8.18.

Tip

Although it's not a requirement, I recommend that you run Defrag on a hard drive before you test it. A defragmented hard drive performs somewhat better than a fragmented drive, and this difference can affect the transfer rate reported by the System Tests.

Figure 8.18 Use the System Tests dialog box to determine optimum hardware settings.

3. Click one of the drives in the Devices listing at the left to select it. The tests presented vary depending upon whether you've chosen a hard drive, a CD recorder, or a read-only CD-ROM drive. (Because the CD Recorder tests encompass all of the possible choices, I use it for this discussion.)

4. If this is your first time to run the System Tests, I recommend that you click all three check boxes to enable them. The full battery of tests includes:

   - **Data Transfer Rate**. This test determines the average transfer rate for the selected drive, both in kilobytes per second and as an x factor (the rate that a drive can transfer data as a multiple of the original first-generation single-speed CD-ROM drives). Note that this value represents only the rate at which data is read from the drive.

   - **Audio Extraction Speed.** This test returns the average transfer rate when extracting digital audio with the selected drive (once again, displayed as both KB/second and an x factor). You use this feature when you record tracks from an existing audio CD — naturally, the faster the drive at extracting audio, the faster those tracks can be copied to your hard drive.

Tip

If you have an older read-only CD-ROM drive, it may not be able to perform digital audio extraction at all. Because almost all recorders can extract digital audio, use your CD recorder for this task instead.

- **Recording Test.** Although your CD recorder may support 4x recording, can your computer keep up the pace? This test evaluates your entire system and determines at which speeds you can safely record without errors.

5. Once you've chosen the tests you want to perform, click Test to begin the process.

6. Depending on the tests you've selected and the type of drive you're testing, Easy CD Creator may prompt you for:

- **Another disc that contains files.** If you're testing the data transfer rate for a CD-ROM drive or CD recorder, Easy CD Creator may prompt you for discs to read — one that contains a number of small files and another with at least one larger file (up to six megabytes). These files are used for benchmarking (the process of determining how fast the data can be read from the drive).

- **An audio CD.** You need an audio CD to test the transfer rate for digital audio extraction.

- **A blank CD-R or CD-RW.** The recording test needs a blank disc. Note, however, that data will not actually be written to the disc.

7. Once the testing is complete, Easy CD Creator displays a dialog box like the one shown in Figure 8.19. The data from the last test is always displayed here, so you don't have to write down the findings.

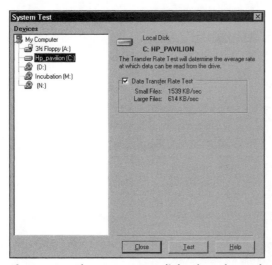

Figure 8.19 The System Test dialog box shows the test findings.

8. Click Close to exit the System Tests dialog box.

Okay, you've tested each drive on my system. What do you do with the resulting figures? You can use these results to:

■ **Determine which CD-ROM drive or recorder on your system to use for reading different types of data.** If you have more than one CD-ROM or CD recorder on your system, you'll naturally want to use the fastest drive for extracting digital audio and for copying discs drive-to-drive. (Remember, they may not be the same drive!)

■ **Determine which hard drive should store your CD images and temporary files.** Again, the fastest drive is the best. I tell you more about the temporary files used in Easy CD Creator in the next section.

Configuring Easy CD Creator Options

You can set a number of global general options within Easy CD Creator that apply to most or all of the discs that you record. For example, these options help you customize the program's operation to match your Internet connection and the amount of hard drive space available on your system. To open the Easy CD Creator Options dialog box:

1. Click Start and choose Programs ⇨ Adaptec Easy CD Creator 4 ⇨ Features ⇨ Easy CD Creator to load the program.

2. Click the Tools menu and choose the Options menu item to display the dialog box shown in Figure 8.20.

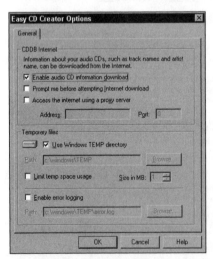

Figure 8.20 The Easy CD Creator Options dialog box

You can use the Options dialog box to configure Easy CD Creator in a number of ways:

■ **CDDB Internet.** If your computer is connected to the Internet, you can use the CDDB (*Compact Disc Data Base*) option to automatically download the track, title, and artist information for an audio CD. This information carries over if you copy tracks from that audio CD to a new audio CD that you're recording. Click "Enable audio CD information download" to turn this function on. If you enable the Internet download of CDDB data check box, you can specify whether Easy CD Creator should:

- **Prompt you for permission before attempting the download.** If you'd rather not allow Easy CD Creator to automatically connect to the Internet to download the data for a disc, enable this check box.

- **Use a proxy server for the Internet connection.** If you're using a LAN, cable modem, or DSL connection to the Internet that runs through a proxy server (a "firewall" computer that helps maintain security for an Internet service provider or a company's Internet connection), you should enable the "Access the Internet using a proxy server" check box and enter the Address and Port number for your proxy server. (If you're unsure about these values, call your Internet service provider.)

■ **Temporary Files.** Next, you can specify the location and the maximum size of the temporary files created by Easy CD Creator during the recording process. These files are deleted immediately after the recording finishes.

- **Windows TEMP directory.** By default, the program uses the Windows TEMP directory, and this location is usually a good choice. If, however, you have another hard drive on your system that has a faster data transfer rate than the drive on which Windows is located, you can click Browse and select a directory on that drive for better performance.

- **Limit temp space.** If your hard drive is running low on free space, you can enable the Limit temp space usage check box and specify a maximum size in megabytes for the temporary files. However, *I do not recommend that you do this*, because it may cause recording errors if you're recording a large amount of data and Easy CD Creator runs out of temporary file space.

- **Enable error logging.** Finally, you can enable error logging. The log contains a listing of error messages returned by the program during recording. You can use this log to help determine what's causing the problem. By default, error logging is turned off; if you turn it on, you can click Browse to specify a location at which the error log should be saved.

When you have made your changes, click Close to save your changes and exit the Easy CD Creator Options dialog box.

Finding Files on Your System

Have you ever looked for a needle in a haystack? Try locating a single file among twenty directories, each of which contains 500 files! To help you locate individual files on your system to add to your layout, Easy CD Creator includes the same Find File function offered within Windows. To locate that pesky file:

1. From within the CD Layout window, click Find Files on the program's toolbar. Easy CD Creator displays the Find dialog box shown in Figure 8.21.

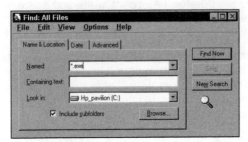

Figure 8.21 Easy CD Creator makes it easy to find a file on your hard drive to add to your CD layout.

2. If you know the filename (or a portion of the filename), enter the text in the Named field. To enter the first or last part of a name, use the wildcard symbol, as in *.dat or searchforme.* (for more information on searching in Windows, refer to the Windows Help system). If you'd like to search for a specific text string within a file, enter it in the Containing text field.

3. Click the Look in drop-down list box (or click Browse) and choose the drive or location to search. If you'd like to search the folders below the location you select, enable the Include subfolders check box.

4. Click Find Now to display the files that match your criteria.

You can also perform searches based on the file's time and date stamp (click the Date tab) or searches based on the size of the file (click the Advanced tab).

In Review

In this chapter, you became familiar with the basics of Easy CD Creator, including how to record data and audio CDs and bootable CDs. You learned how to duplicate an existing disc using CD Copier. You tested your system hardware and used that data to make adjustments to the recording options within the program. Finally, you learned how to modify your discs by changing the properties of a CD layout, including optimization, disc information, and Joliet and ISO 9660 file systems.

CHAPTER
9

Introducing
Adaptec's DirectCD
Step-by-Step

As I mention earlier in the book, UDF recording (Universal Disc Format, also called *packet-writing*) has become one of the most popular applications for a CD recorder over the last three years. With UDF, you can copy files to a disc (and delete them) as you would save files to a floppy disk or hard drive — UDF supports drag-and-drop, Windows Explorer, and any other application that saves files transparently, so you don't have to worry about creating a layout or recording a session.

When UDF is coupled with rewritable CDs, things get even better . . . your CD-RW drive becomes what many computer owners consider the "perfect" removable media drive. Although there are other removable-storage devices that deliver more space, 650 megabytes is still a lot of elbow room, and the common availability of MultiRead drives on today's PCs makes a UDF disc a practical choice for carrying data on your next business trip.

The best-known UDF program by far is Adaptec's DirectCD, which you can purchase separately from Easy CD Creator. However, CD-RW drives from Hewlett-Packard and other manufacturers usually include DirectCD with their drives, so you may have already installed it when you set up your drive.

Recording CDs with Adaptec's Direct CD

In this step-by-step tutorial, I show you all you need to know to use your CD-R or CD-RW drive with DirectCD.

Installing DirectCD

If you haven't already done so, install DirectCD by following these steps:

1. Insert Disk 1 into your floppy drive. If your copy of DirectCD came on a CD-ROM, place the CD in your CD drive and close the door.

2. Click the My Computer icon on your desktop and then double-click the A: drive. If you are installing from a CD-ROM, double-click the CD-ROM drive and open the folder called "Disk 1."

3. Run the Setup program, which displays the welcome screen shown in Figure 9.1. Click Next to continue.

4. Click Yes to continue if you agree to the software license.

5. Next, the Setup program asks if you'd like to install the CD-RW utilities (Figure 9.2). If your CD recorder is a CD-RW drive, click Yes, and then click Next to continue. If your CD recorder is a CD-R drive, you won't need these programs, so click No and then click Next to continue.

? InCD

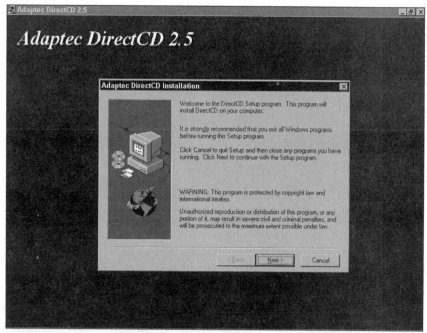

Figure 9.1 The DirectCD installation welcome screen

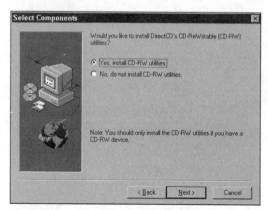

Figure 9.2 DirectCD can be installed with utilities especially made for CD-RW drives.

6. The next screen, which is shown in Figure 9.3, prompts you for the location on your hard drive where you'd like to install DirectCD. Personally, I always use the default directory, because it may make the installation of patches and upgrades easier in the future. To keep the default directory, click Next; to choose an alternate directory, click Browse and select the directory into which you prefer the program be installed.

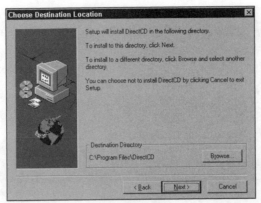

Figure 9.3 Specifying a location where DirectCD will be installed

7. The Setup program will begin copying files to the target directory, as shown in Figure 9.4.

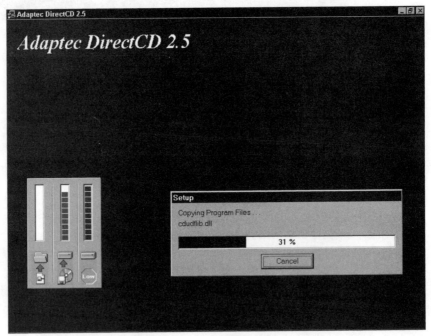

Figure 9.4 Copying DirectCD files to your hard drive

8. Once all the files have been successfully copied, the installation program will prompt you for permission to reboot your computer (Figure 9.5). Make sure that all other applications have been closed. If you're installing from floppy disk, make sure that you eject it before continuing. Select Yes and click Finish to complete the installation process.

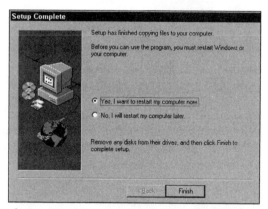

Figure 9.5 Before you can run DirectCD, the Setup program must reboot your PC.

Once your PC has rebooted, you see the DirectCD banner appear during the Windows boot process. DirectCD is available from your Start menu, and it runs in your taskbar.

Formatting a DirectCD Disc

The first step in using DirectCD is formatting a disc to prepare it for recording (much like you'd format a floppy disk). To format a CD:

1. Load a blank CD-R or CD-RW disc into your recorder.

2. DirectCD automatically displays the Welcome screen shown in Figure 9.6. Click Next to continue.

Note

If you've also installed Easy CD Creator, the disc type selection dialog box appears first. Click Data and then click DirectCD to display the Welcome screen. You can also right-click the DirectCD icon in the taskbar and select Format from the pop-up menu.

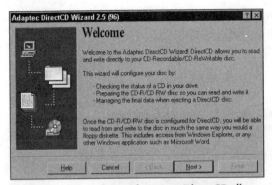

Figure 9.6 Preparing to format a DirectCD disc

3. If you have multiple CD recorders on your system, use the Drive Information screen (Figure 9.7) to pick the drive you want to use to format the disc, and click Next to continue.

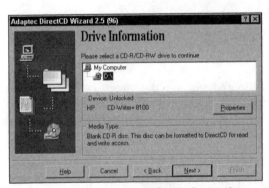

Figure 9.7 Selecting a recorder for formatting

4. Before beginning the formatting process, DirectCD displays a screen prompting you for confirmation. Click Next to confirm and continue.

5. Next, enter a descriptive Volume name for this disc on the Name Your Disc screen shown in Figure 9.8. The name will be displayed in Windows applications, under My Computer, and in Explorer just like a hard drive or floppy drive name. You can use up to 11 characters. Once you've entered a name, click Finish to start the formatting.

6. DirectCD displays the progress dialog box shown in Figure 9.9 while the disc is formatting.

Figure 9.8 Naming a new DirectCD disc

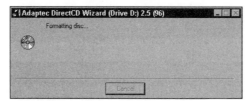

Figure 9.9 The format step in progress

7. Once the formatting process has completed, you see the Disc Ready
   dialog box, as shown in Figure 9.10, and your new disc is ready to use.
   (Note that you can disable this notification message for the future by
   disabling the check box at the bottom of the dialog box.) Click OK, and
   you're ready to record!

Figure 9.10 Your DirectCD disc is formatted and ready for recording!

As you can see in Figure 9.11, my new DirectCD disc (aptly named "Mark's Disc") is now available within My Computer. Although the drive icon looks just like a typical read-only CD-ROM icon, you can copy and move files and folders to it.

New CD icon

Figure 9.11 My DirectCD as it appears in Windows 98

By the way, if you check the DirectCD icon in the taskbar, notice that it now has a tiny red lock. This indicates that you've loaded a DirectCD disc, and the disc can't be ejected like a standard read-only CD-ROM disc. If you rest your mouse pointer on top of the DirectCD icon, it will also display a message that it's locked. (I cover more on how to properly eject a DirectCD disc later in this chapter.)

Copying and Moving Files to Your Disc

This is probably the shortest section in the entire book, and for good reason: DirectCD operates entirely in the background—nearly invisible—while you use your new CD-R or CD-RW disc. You can read, copy, and move files to your DirectCD disc using the same standard Windows menu commands, keyboard shortcuts, and drag-and-drop mouse operations that you're already using. Your applications can open and save data to documents on a DirectCD disc, just as they would with a hard drive. Even if you use Windows Explorer or another file management program, there are no settings to change or adjustments to make to use a DirectCD disc — it's all taken care of by the program, and that's all there is to it!

For example, if you have a file saved on your Windows desktop, follow these steps to copy it to your DirectCD disc:

1. Double-click My Computer to open it and display your drive icons.

2. To copy the file into a folder on your DirectCD disc, double-click the icon for your CD recorder and double-click the desired folder to open it.

3. Click the file you want to copy and continue to hold down the mouse button.

4. Drag the file to the folder window to copy it.

Checking Free Space

If you like, you can check on the amount of free space remaining on a DirectCD disc in the same way that you can check a hard drive.

If you're using the default Windows 95/98 or Windows 2000 folder options, you can get a quick idea of the free space remaining by highlighting the drive icon within My Computer. As you can see in Figure 9.12, the approximate space used and the approximate space remaining are both displayed on the left side of the window.

To get an exact count of the number of bytes available using Windows 95/98 or Windows 2000:

1. Double-click the My Computer icon on your desktop to open it.

2. Right-click the DirectCD drive icon to display the pop-up menu and click Properties.

   Windows displays the Properties dialog box shown in Figure 9.13, which lists the bytes free.

Tip

Need to change the volume label on a DirectCD disc? You can do that from the Properties dialog box as well!

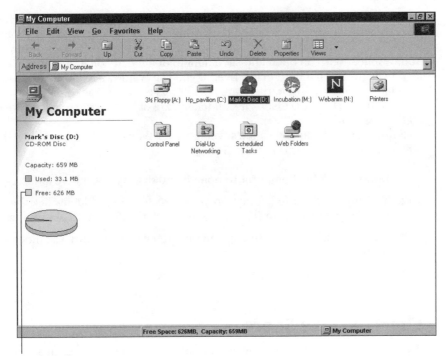

Available disc space

Figure 9.12 Windows 98 displays the approximate free space from the My Computer window.

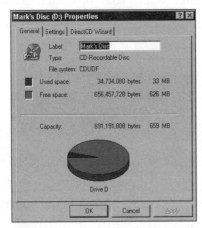

Figure 9.13 Displaying the properties for a DirectCD disc

Ejecting a Disc

Before you can use a DirectCD disc in another PC running Windows 95/98 or Windows 2000, you must properly eject it. This step enables DirectCD to *fix* the disc by updating the directory information so that another drive can access the files. To eject a disc:

1. Right-click the DirectCD icon in the toolbar to display the pop-up menu, and then click Eject. You can also press the Eject button on the front of the drive to begin the process.

2. DirectCD automatically displays the Eject Disc screen shown in Figure 9.14. You have two choices, and the choice you make is determined by the reason you're ejecting the disc:

   - If you have more data to record later and you simply need the drive, you should choose the Leave the disc as it is option. This option will quickly eject the disc without fixing it, so it will not be readable on a standard CD-ROM drive. Later, when you're ready to write to the disc again, you can reload it.

   - If you've filled the entire disc or you'd like to access the files you've recorded on another PC running Windows, you have to choose the Organize the disc option. This step takes more time, because DirectCD has to fix the disc. You can also choose whether to leave the disc open, so that you can make it writable again in the future, or whether to permanently protect the disc so that it can't be written to again.

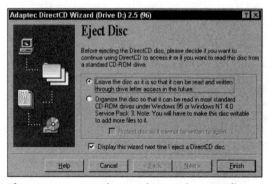

Figure 9.14 Preparing to eject a DirectCD disc

Note

You can disable this Eject Disc message in the future by clicking the check box at the bottom of the dialog box. DirectCD will take the action you choose now each time you eject the disc.

3. Once you've made your choice, click Finish to eject the disc. If you chose the Leave the disc as is option, you see the dialog box shown in Figure 9.15. If you chose the Organize the disc option, you see a dialog box with a progress bar that indicates how much time is left for the fix process.

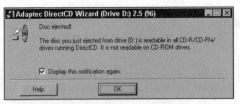

Figure 9.15 This disc has been ejected as is, so it can be reloaded immediately.

If you're planning on reading the disc on a computer that's *not* running Windows 95, you should finalize it as an ISO 9660 disc — remember the discussion of the ISO 9660 standard earlier in the book? Later in the chapter, in the section titled "Setting DirectCD Options," I describe how you can set this feature.

Adding Additional Files to an Existing Disc

In the last section, I showed you how to eject a DirectCD disc. If you left the disc writable, you can reload it by pressing the Eject button on the drive. The program will automatically take one of two actions, depending on whether you ejected it as is or organized it with the write option:

- If you chose the Leave the disc as it is option, DirectCD simply takes up where it left off, and no extra processing is required.

- If you chose the Organize the disc option and left the disc open, DirectCD will automatically update the disc's contents and you can write additional files to it. Once again, there is a short wait while the disc's Table of Contents is updated.

Erasing a DirectCD Disc

DirectCD takes full advantage of the rewritable CD-RW disc by enabling you to erase the contents of the disc, just as you would delete files from your hard drive. To erase a disc:

1. Select the files you want to erase within Windows Explorer.

2. Press the Delete key.

3. Windows displays a confirmation dialog box. Click Yes to confirm that you do want to erase the files.

As I mentioned earlier, you can do this same operation with a CD-R, but you won't reclaim any of the space from the deleted files. In effect, they're removed from the disc's directory (so they can't be retrieved) and they won't appear in Windows, but files deleted from a CD-R actually remain on the disc.

Setting DirectCD Options

Although DirectCD is just about as automatic as a CD recording program can be, there are a number of options you can set to fine-tune its operation, as well as changes that you can make to the read and write speeds the program will use.

Setting Wizard Options

To make a change in the operation of DirectCD:

1. Right-click the DirectCD icon on the taskbar.

2. Select Properties from the pop-up menu.

3. Click the DirectCD Wizard tab to display the screen shown in Figure 9.16.

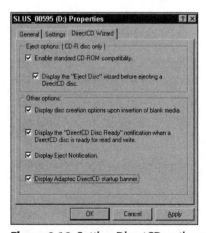

Figure 9.16 Setting DirectCD options

The fields you can change include:

- **Eject options.** I discuss these fields in the section "Setting ISO 9660 Compatibility" at the end of this chapter.

- **Display disc creation options.** If you disable this field, DirectCD will not prompt you for the information I discussed earlier when you load a blank disc. (I recommend that you leave this field enabled, because it gives you more control over the formatting and disc preparation process.)

- **Display the "DirectCD Disc Ready" notification.** If you disable this field, DirectCD will not display the notification screen when you've loaded a DirectCD disc.

- **Display Eject Notification.** Disabling this field turns off the notification screen you see when ejecting a disc.

- **Display DirectCD startup banner.** Disabling this field turns off the DirectCD banner image that's displayed during the Windows bootup process.

Setting Read and Write Speeds

Normally, you want to record a DirectCD disc at the fastest possible speed; therefore, this is the default setting. Some recorders, however, may experience problems with packet-writing at their maximum writing speed, particularly if

- You commonly experience media incompatibilities with a certain brand of CD-R disc, where you have to record at slower speeds. This may happen if your recorder returns errors when you try to write to a disc with a certain combination of reflective layer and dye color — for example, if your recorder seems to return errors more often when you use a disc with a gold reflective layer and a green dye layer. That same recorder may work much better with a brand of CD-R blanks that uses an aluminum reflective layer and blue dye.

- You often work with other applications on an older, slower PC while DirectCD is writing at maximum speed. If you're packet-writing in the background while you work on your word processing, for example, you may find that your application slows down to a crawl while you're writing data to a DirectCD disc at maximum speed. Slowing down the speed at which you write to a DirectCD disc reduces the performance penalty in other programs.

To change the read and write speeds used by DirectCD:

1. Right-click the DirectCD icon on the taskbar.

2. Select Properties from the pop-up menu.

3. Click the Settings tab to display the screen shown in Figure 9.17.

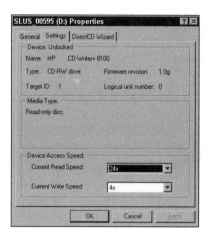

Figure 9.17 Setting the DirectCD read and write speeds

4. Click the Current Read Speed drop-down list box and click the desired speed.

5. Click the Current Write Speed drop-down list box and click the desired speed.

6. Click OK to save your changes.

Setting ISO 9660 Compatibility

As I mentioned earlier in the chapter, *unless* you've finalized the disc as an ISO 9660 closed session disc, a DirectCD disc can only be read on another computer running DirectCD. To create an ISO 9660 disc:

1. Format and record a DirectCD disc as usual.

2. When you're ready to finalize the disc, right-click the DirectCD icon on the taskbar.

3. Select Properties from the pop-up menu.

4. Click the DirectCD Wizard tab to display the screen shown in Figure 9.18.

5. Under Eject Options, select the Enable standard CD-ROM compatibility option and click OK. (If you'll be creating only ISO 9660 discs, you can disable the Display the "Eject Disc" Wizard option, and all of your discs will be ISO 9660 compatible; if you'll be creating DirectCD discs for a Windows PC as well, leave this option checked.)

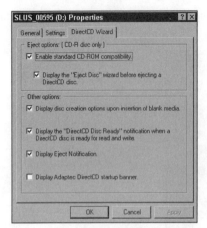

Figure 9.18 Setting ISO 9660 compatibility for a DirectCD disc

6. Right-click the CD icon on the taskbar again and select Eject from the pop-up menu.

7. When prompted on the Eject Disc screen, select the Organize the disc option.

8. Click Finish.

You can now read this disc under non-Windows operating systems such as DOS, Linux, and Mac OS.

In Review

This chapter delivers all the details about packet-writing with Adaptec's DirectCD. You learned how to format a DirectCD disc, how to read it and write to it, and how to check the free space remaining on the disc. You should be familiar with the options available in the program, as well as how to select an alternate read and write speed. Finally, you now know how to create a standard ISO 9660 disc, which can be read on other computers using just about any operating system.

CHAPTER
10

Introducing Adaptec's Toast Step-by-Step

IN THIS CHAPTER

- Using Adaptec Toast to record CDs

- Configuring Toast to meet your special recording needs

- Creating a temporary partition to make recording faster and easier

One of the most popular CD recording programs for the Macintosh is Adaptec's Toast, and it can match almost all of the features of Easy CD Creator. It also features the trademark ease-of-use that sets the best Mac OS applications apart from some of their Windows counterparts! Toast includes a Mac-specific version of the Spin Doctor utility you can use to create an audio CD from a vinyl album or cassette, and it offers the same features that make Easy CD Creator so powerful — including access to the Internet CD database, MP3 conversion, and bootable CD support.

If you have a Macintosh computer with a copy of Toast and a SCSI, IDE, or USB CD recorder, this chapter demonstrates the basics: How to record data and audio CDs, configuring Preference settings within Toast, and creating a temporary partition that you can use for recording.

Using Toast to Record a CD

Like most other Mac OS applications, Toast has fewer menu commands than a typical Windows application — you can "drag-and-drop" icons to perform most common functions, like selecting files or adding audio tracks.

Installing Toast on Your Macintosh

If you haven't already done so, install Toast by following these steps:

1. Load the Toast Installer CD in your CD-ROM drive. Your Macintosh automatically displays the contents of the disc in a new window.

2. Double-click the folder for the language you want to install to open it.

3. Double-click the Adaptec Toast Installer icon.

4. Click the Continue button twice to advance through the Installer's welcome screens.

5. If you agree to the software license, click Agree to continue.

6. Click Install to copy the files and complete the process.

Recording a Data CD-ROM

To record a simple data disc with files from your Macintosh's hard drive:

1. Run Toast from the location you saved it during installation. The program displays its main menu, which is shown in Figure 10.1.

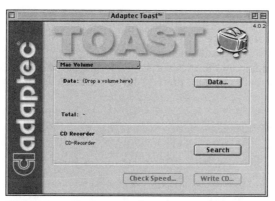

Figure 10.1 The Toast main menu

2. As shown in Figure 10.2, click the disc type drop-down list box and select Mac Volume (to record an entire Macintosh volume to a CD) or Mac Files & Folders (to record individual files and folders that you specify).

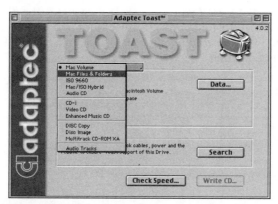

Figure 10.2 Selecting a disc type

Tip

If you like, you can drag and drop volumes or files into the Toast main window to add them.

3. Click Data. One of two different dialog boxes displays:

   • **Volume.** If you're recording a volume, the Select Volume dialog box shown in Figure 10.3 displays. Click the volume you want to record and click OK.

Tip

I recommend that you click the Don't copy free space check box to enable this option—otherwise, you'll spend time recording the empty space that remains on the volume! (Depending on the size of the volume that you've selected, recording empty space can actually result in "running out" of room on the blank CD.)

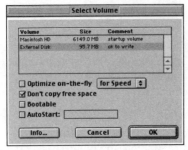

Figure 10.3 Selecting a volume for recording

- **Mac Files & Folders.** If you're recording a volume, the dialog box shown in Figure 10.4 displays. To select files and folders, drag and drop them from the volume into this dialog box, and click Done when you're finished.

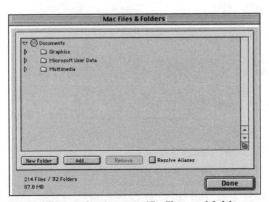

Figure 10.4 Selecting specific files and folders to record

4. Load a blank CD into your recorder.

5. Click Write CD.

6. Click Write Disc or Write Session. If the disc should be used again in the future, use Write Session—this leaves the disc open. To close and write-protect the CD you're recording, click Write Disc.

All done! As I said before, one of the advantages of Toast is the simplicity of its user interface.

Recording an Audio CD

Although I've said it throughout the book, this important rule bears repeating again: Remember, you need a standard CD-R blank disc if you'll be playing your new audio CD in your car or a standard audio CD player — CD-RW discs do not work correctly in audio CD players!

To record an audio CD from files on your hard drive and existing audio CDs, follow these steps:

1. Run Toast from the location you saved it during installation.

2. Click the disc type drop-down list box and select Audio CD.

3. Click Audio to display the Audio Tracks dialog box.

4. You can add tracks in either of two ways:

    • **Sound files.** If you're recording MP3 or Mac audio files, drag and drop them from your Mac hard drive into the dialog box. Toast adds them to the layout.

    • **Existing CD tracks.** If you're recording tracks from one or more existing audio CDs, load the audio CD and double-click the disc's desktop icon to display the track icons. Drag and drop the desired icons from the audio CD window into the dialog box. You can eject the disc and repeat this step with additional CDs.

Tip

You need a considerable amount of free hard drive space if you're going to fill an entire disc with tracks from existing audio CDs! Each minute of CD-quality music that you copy takes up 10 megabytes of hard drive space, so it's a good idea to have at least 1 or 1.5 gigabytes of free space before you fill an entire 74 minutes with music.

5. You can rearrange the tracks in any order you wish by dragging them to their new positions.

6. *If you've added files from existing audio CDs*, you must first extract the digital audio to your hard drive before you can record. (If your new audio CD only contains tracks from audio files already on your hard drive, you can skip this step.) Select the tracks that you've added from other CDs and click Extract To. Navigate through your system and choose the destination for the extracted digital audio. Click Save.

7. Once all the tracks are stored on your hard drive as audio files, click Done to return to the main Toast screen.

8. Click Write CD.

9. Click Write Disc or Write Session — for almost all audio CDs, the correct choice is Write Disc.

Warning

Although Write Session is an option when recording audio CDs, you should only use it if you're planning on adding data tracks later to create a Mixed-Mode disc! Most audio CD players are unable to read the disc you're recording if you don't choose Write Disc.

Note that Toast does not delete the audio files you created on your hard drive if you extracted tracks from an existing CD — you can do this manually, or keep the files on your drive if you plan on recording them again.

Configuring Toast for Optimal Performance

Naturally, a program as powerful as Toast includes a number of settings you can use to fine-tune the program's performance, which may help you cut down on recording errors if you're using an older PowerPC or 68000-series Macintosh. You can also choose default values for recording options that help streamline the recording process — the less mouse clicks I need to perform a task, the better. Finally, you can even change the appearance of the program's user interface to match your artistic side — as a Macintosh owner, I expect nothing less!

Setting Preferences in Toast

No, "light" or "dark" — sorry, couldn't help that one! Toast automates most of the configuration process, but the program does enable you to configure a number of preferences that globally affect the program's operation. Follow these steps to set your preferences:

1. Run Toast from where you saved it during installation.

2. Click the Edit menu and select the Preferences menu item to display the dialog box shown in Figure 10.5. You have the following options:

   - **Disk Cache.** This drop-down list box enables you to choose the location of the recording disk cache. As I mention earlier in the book, the faster the drive, the better. You can select the Startup Volume (the Mac OS startup volume), the Application Volume (where Toast was installed), or a volume by name. If you're using a Mac with a single hard drive, all of these selections are the same — it's usually a safe bet to choose Startup Volume.

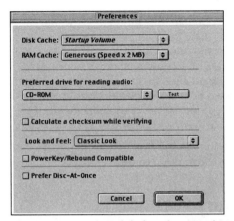

Figure 10.5 Setting global preferences in Toast

- **RAM Cache.** You can specify the size of the RAM cache that Toast creates to hold data before it's written to the disc. The more RAM your system has, the more you can specify here. Note that the standard amount of RAM is the total of the recording speed times 1 megabyte, whereas the generous amount is the total of the recording speed times 2 megabytes. If you can, choose the generous option (or select an even higher amount from the menu).

- **Preferred drive for reading audio.** You can choose any CD-ROM drive (including your recorder) as the drive you use to extract digital audio from existing audio CDs (typically, the faster the drive, the faster the extraction). However, some older CD-ROM drives can't extract audio — to check a drive, select it and click the Test button.

- **Calculate a checksum.** Enabling this option allows you to compare the checksum for a CD image created by another CD recording program with the disc that you've created with Toast. If the checksums match, then the CD you created with Toast matches the CD image exactly. (If you're not recording discs from images made by another recording program, leave this check box disabled.)

- **Look and feel.** Toast doesn't disappoint Mac owners with a taste for graphic design! You can click this drop-down list box to choose from one of four different window designs (which include color schemes): the Classic Look, which I've used here, Bondi, Noire, and Egor. The controls and menus do *not* change when you select a different look and feel.

- **PowerKey/Rebound Compatible.** If you're using the Mac OS applications PowerKey or Rebound, enable this check box to prevent these programs from automatically restarting. As you might expect, this can be a very unwelcome surprise in the middle of a recording session!

- **Prefer Disc-At-Once.** Enable this option if you would rather that Toast create discs using Disc-At-Once mode instead of Track-At-Once mode (as I explained earlier in the book, Disc-At-Once mode is preferred if you're creating a master disc for commercial duplication, and some audio CD players may generate an audible "click" between tracks recorded using Track-At-Once mode). Some CD recorders can't record using Disc-At-Once mode, so check your recorder's manual to see if you can enable this check box.

3. Once you've set the options in the Preferences dialog box, click OK to close the dialog box and save them to disk.

Creating a Temporary Partition for Convenient Recording

You may want to consider the creation of a temporary recording *partition* — a partition is a section of your hard drive that's identified as a different volume. It's been my experience that a separate partition is a great convenience when recording on the iMac using Toast; it enables you to create a custom volume for recording data from your hard drive directly to a new disc volume without the hassle of adding an external drive or trying to maintain a specific set of folders.

To create a temporary partition:

1. Run Toast from the location you saved it during installation.

2. Click the Utilities menu and select the Create Temporary Partition menu item.

3. Type a name for the volume.

4. Specify a size in megabytes for the partition. The default is 650 megabytes, but I personally recommend 750 megabytes (or 850 megabytes if you're using 80-minute blank CDs) to give yourself a little elbow room.

5. Choose the hard drive where the partition will be created (naturally, you need a drive that has at least that much free space remaining).

6. Click OK, and the new partition appears on your desktop with a special Toast icon.

7. Once you've recorded the disc, you can delete the partition (along with any data it contains) and recover the space by dragging the partition icon to the Trash.

In Review

Macintosh owners received basic training on Adaptec's Toast recording software in this chapter, including how to record a data CD, how to record an audio CD (from files on the hard drive or existing CDs), and how to set the program preferences. You also learned how to create a temporary hard drive partition to help simplify the recording of a discrete volume of data.

It ought to be possible to treat a RW disc somewhat like a floppy disc.

Maybe we ought not to expect a file to be fragmented
but we should be able to overwrite a file if it can be done without
fragmentation.

A limit of 1000 updates may mean not too much updating of
directory data, but surely we can get around this by a multi-level
hierarchic structure.

PART

III

Advanced Recording Topics

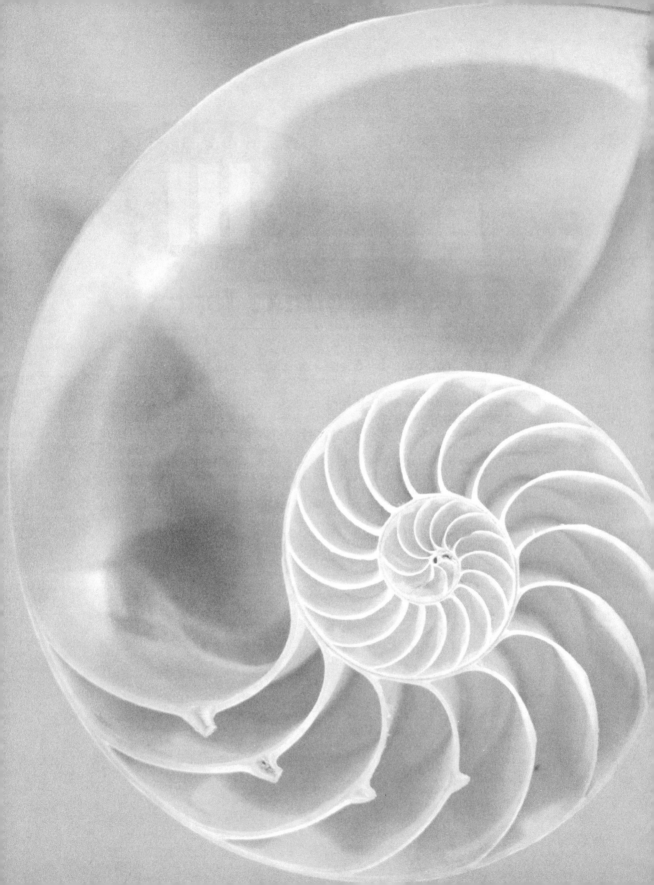

Adding HTML
Step-by-Step

IN THIS CHAPTER

- Making your disc accessible with menus

- Designing your HTML menu system

- Constructing your HTML menu

- Converting word processing documents to HTML

Now that you're busy recording all sorts of music, photos, and other stuff on recordable discs and passing them out to your friends, it's time to start thinking about ways to make all that data more user friendly and accessible. For example, you could add a READ.ME file to explain how to open the spreadsheet documents in a folder, or create a thumbnail index for a folder of images to help your friends find a specific picture. I like to add convenience and a professional touch to a recorded disc by creating a menu system, which can organize all the data on the disc and make it much easier to find. It's easy to do if you know a little HTML (that's short for *Hypertext Markup Language*), the programming language used to create Web pages.

Don't worry! You don't have to be a computer programmer to produce an HTML menu for your discs. In fact, if you use an HTML editor, you won't even have to open an HTML file or look at a single line of code. (And no, your discs don't necessarily have to have anything to do with the Internet, or communicate with the Internet at all.)

In this chapter, I discuss the HTML tags you need and provide code samples that you can use to create your own CD menus. By the time you're done, you'll know how to use HTML to add that finishing touch to your discs.

Why Create a Menu for My Discs?

Before we delve into the world of HTML, I'd like to clarify what type of applications benefit from an HTML front-end, and why they deserve the extra time and effort it takes. Here are some questions to consider:

■ **Are you recording work for distribution to others?** If you're creating a disc for distribution to other computer owners (especially if their experience with computers varies widely), then an HTML menu can add a professional "look-and-feel." HTML can also help automate the presentation of your material, so novice computer owners can access that material without loading additional software.

■ **Do your discs have an index or a large number of text files?** If you convert indexes or text files into HTML documents, your familiar Web browser provides built-in display and search capabilities (complete with text formatting and embedded hyperlinks to other documents on your discs).

■ **Do your discs primarily contain images or sounds?** HTML provides built-in tags for displaying images and digital video, and playing sounds automatically.

■ **Do you want to add Internet links to your discs?** If you'd like to provide links to your online Web page or your Internet e-mail address, an HTML menu can provide them with the click of a single button to computer owners with an Internet connection.

■ **Are you providing your Web site on disc?** Naturally, an HTML front-end is a perfect choice if you're creating a disc-based version of your online Web site. It can provide a menu for supporting material, as well as a "Table of Contents" to enable computer owners to access different pages directly.

Of course, if you're a programmer, you could write a menu system using another language — perhaps C or Visual Basic. However, HTML offers a number of unique advantages that make it ideal for use on your recorded CDs:

■ **Web browsers are familiar and easy to use.** Although Uncle Fred may not be familiar with an image display program — in fact, he may be downright afraid of it — he's probably already used a Web browser at least once before! The familiarity of a Web browser helps increase the "usability factor" of your material.

■ **Cross-platform acceptance.** Your HTML menu works on any computer with a Web browser — including Windows NT, Macintosh, Linux, UNIX, and other operating systems to come.

■ **HTML includes the functions you need.** With an HTML menu, you can display today's multimedia files, read and search through formatted text, link files together, download files, and connect automatically to the Internet to send e-mail and browse online sites. Not a bad selection of basic functions, especially for those of us recording CDs!

■ **HTML is easy to code.** HTML is nowhere near as difficult to learn as other, more powerful programming languages, and as I discuss in the next section, an HTML editor makes it easy to produce your menu with no programming work at all.

■ **HTML supports Java applets.** If you're familiar with Java programming or you have an application that can build Java applets, a disc with an HTML menu can run Java applets automatically (or from a menu command).

■ **Universal availability.** Like CD-ROM drives, it's a fair bet that most of the computers around today running Windows or Mac OS have a Web browser, even if they don't have a modem! Both of these operating systems include a Web browser as an integral part of the installation process. If you like, you can include the distribution version of Internet Explorer or Netscape Navigator on discs that are meant for Windows or Macintosh computers.

■ **It's free!** Let's face it, Web browsers are free, and there are dozens of freeware and shareware HTML editors available. For example, if you're running Windows, you may already have FrontPage Express on your computer.

As you can see, it's no coincidence that many software developers now distribute their programs using discs with HTML menus!

Note

I should also mention that dozens of commercial programs enable you to add functionality to your HTML projects, including animation and the loading of external programs. If you're willing to take the time and you can afford these programs, you can greatly extend the power of a simple HTML document.

Once you've created the HTML menu system for your disc, you can simply record those HTML files (along with any images, sounds, video, or Java applets required by the menu system) in the root directory of your disc. If you've designed an extensive menu system, you can keep the root directory of your recorded disc a little neater by saving those files in a separate folder. The menu system can be displayed by running a Web browser and opening the initial menu page.

Designing Your Disc Menu

Before you actually put fingers to keyboard to create your HTML menu system, it's important to take the time to design the pages you'll create on paper. What should they look like? Will you use full-color graphics, sound, and animation to create a multimedia menu, or should you stick with a strictly functional, utilitarian menu? What commands should you offer, and how many submenus should you include? To save yourself time and trouble during the actual creation of your HTML pages, decide these things now!

Note

If you've never designed a Web page and you'd like a complete tutorial on the subject, I'd recommend the book *HTML 4 for Dummies,* 2nd Edition, written by Ed Tittle and Natanya Pitts. It can fill in all the specifics that I can't cover in this chapter.

Three criteria help you determine what type of menu system you need for your disc:

- **The type of material that appears on the disc.** Will your files include multimedia material like images or sound files? Will it simply store data files, or are you recording text documents?

- **The retrieval method.** Will files be displayed seamlessly inside the browser (for example, image files or text that you've converted to HTML); will they be printed directly from the browser, or will they have to be "downloaded" to the hard drive and run from Windows Explorer? Is your disc meant for the quick retrieval of data, or would you like it to be scanned and explored at leisure?

- **Your target audience.** Finally, how do you plan for your target audience to use the disc? Are you recording material for potential customers, fellow employees, or yourself? Will most of the computer owners in your target audience have sound cards and faster processors?

I've built three basic types of disc menus for my projects, and you can apply the three criteria I just mentioned to determine which you should build for a specific disc. The three menu types are:

■ **Strictly data.** This is a spartan, no-nonsense menu with a single level, with no navigational controls. Interactivity and multimedia extras are held to a minimum. With this disc, you'll find only simple hypertext links that display or download a file. *This is a good choice for a simple storage disc for material that you won't retrieve often, or where files are accessed quickly and printed or copied to the hard drive. It's best suited for coworkers or your own use.*

■ **Balanced.** This type offers a mixture of simple backgrounds, including images for navigation buttons (perhaps an animated image or two as well). Menus should be nested up to three or four levels. *A balanced HTML menu is suitable for discs containing both multimedia and simple data files; files can be retrieved in any fashion, and it's a good choice for the average target audience for whom appearance is important, but not the primary concern.*

■ **Strictly multimedia.** This disc is made especially for the material you want to show off: high-resolution backgrounds, animation everywhere, and even background music and digital video! As you can imagine, most marketing and demonstration discs fall into this category. Your menus are practically unlimited in depth. Advanced HTML programmers might include Java applets on a multimedia disc. Note that a strictly multimedia disc requires a faster computer to perform well. *In most cases, this is the best choice for distributing material to potential customers whom you want to impress. The appearance and professional layout are all-important on a multimedia disc. Files are usually displayed within the browser; your target audience will require plenty of leisure time to explore a multimedia disc.*

Practical Menu Applications

Let's apply each of these disc menus to a particular application, so that you can see how each fits a specific set of requirements.

■ **An employee orientation disc.** Figure 11.1 illustrates a typical disc distributed to new employees for a large business. It contains company policy manuals in Adobe Acrobat format, the company-approved stylesheets and templates for Microsoft Office and Corel WordPerfect applications, the company logo in bitmap form and so on. This disc is designed for infrequent internal use only and the employee should be able to find specific material quickly, so there's no need to spice up the menu system for appearance. This is a perfect example of a strictly data disc menu — no frills, no extras.

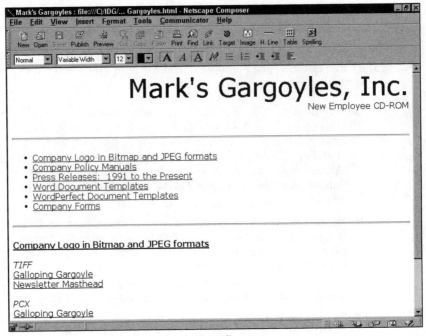

Figure 11.1 An example of a strictly data disc menu

■ **A beta-test disc.** In Figure 11.2, you see a typical balanced menu system: In this case, the disc contains software distributed by a software developer to selected beta testers. Because of the select distribution, appearance and presentation are somewhat more important than the previous example, and convenience is more important as well. For instance, the README file is displayed on-screen, and the beta-testers can watch a video message from the company's President. The disc may include a feedback form that can be printed for mailing or faxing, as well as an e-mail link to the company.

■ **An electronic catalog disc.** Figure 11.3 illustrates the strictly multimedia disc in action. In this case, it's an electronic catalog distributed by a company to its customers. You can bet that this disc includes plenty of animation, video, sound effects, music, and links to the company's Web site and sales staff e-mail accounts. Hopefully, customers will return to the disc many times, and they'll browse at their leisure.

Naturally, your disc menu may mix elements of each. These rough guidelines probably apply to the majority of your projects, but there are always exceptions to the rule. Once you've determined the design, you can use the HTML tags in the next section to create the menu pages.

Cross-Reference

In Chapter 14, "Practicing Advanced Recording," you'll go through the entire process of creating a balanced HTML disc menu.

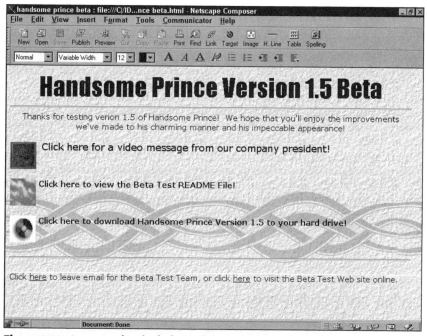

Figure 11.2 An example of a balanced disc menu

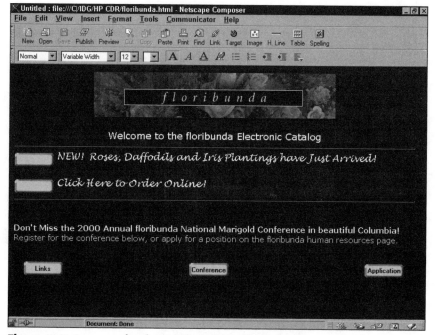

Figure 11.3 An example of a strictly multimedia disc menu

Using an HTML Editor

Strictly defined, an HTML editor is a program that enables you to create new HTML pages or edit existing pages, so it has to include at least a basic text editing function. However, the popularity of the Web has resulted in an explosion of very different programs that can fit into this broad category.

HTML editors range from the bare-bones text editing window (with not much more functionality than Windows Notepad) to a true "drag-and-drop" design system that creates Web pages that reproduce exactly what you add on-screen. The editor you choose depends entirely upon your taste and your level of experience. In fact, because I'm familiar with HTML, I often use Windows Notepad when I need to make a quick change to a page.

Figure 11.4 illustrates my HTML editor of choice, a fantastic "CareWare" program called Arachnophilia that includes professional features like real-time updating through internal browser code, a spell checker, table generation, macros, and templates. You can download your own copy for free at www. arachnoid.com/arachnophilia/index.html. Arachnophilia is the perfect choice for someone who's comfortable with HTML at the code level.

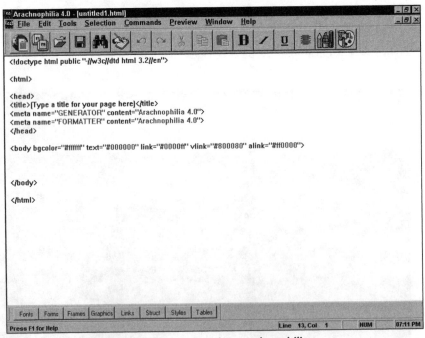

Figure 11.4 Editing a new HTML page using Arachnophilia

If you'd prefer a more visual "drag-and-drop" approach that uses wizards to help automate the coding process, consider Netscape Composer. It's free as well, at `www.netscape.com`; in fact, you may already have it if you've installed the full Netscape browser package recently. Figure 11.5 shows a page under development in Netscape Composer.

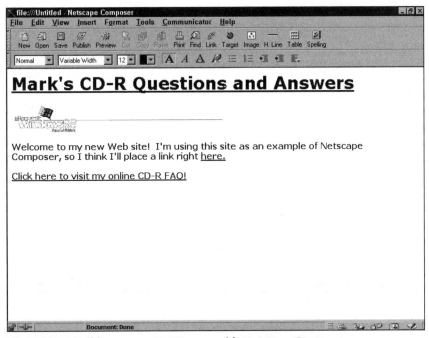

Figure 11.5 Building a new HTML page with Netscape Composer

Cross-Reference

Just about any HTML editor should be able to produce pages that you can use on your discs. If you're not using one yet and you're a novice to HTML coding, I would strongly recommend that you try out Netscape Composer, which I use in the HTML project in Chapter 14, "Practicing Advanced Recording."

Your HTML menu pages will be built from a series of standard HTML — each tag is a separate line in the file that affects the display or contents of the page. If you use a visual HTML editor, you'll probably never actually type one of these tags! For those who'd like to know more about how HTML works, however, I'd like to mention the specific tags I use most often while building a menu. The following examples help illustrate how you can format the appearance of your HTML text.

Adding Text Using the BODY Tag

The <BODY> tag encloses the text and visual contents of every HTML page. For example:

```
<html>

<head>
<title>This Title Appears in the Menu Bar</title>
</head>

<body>

This text appears within the BODY tag. I can assign it font and
color characteristics, or add tags to display images or link
other HTML pages. Note the ending BODY tag (preceded by a forward
slash) that effectively ends the contents of the page.

</body>

</html>
```

This HTML file will produce the page shown in Figure 11.6—nothing special, but the display of text was the original idea behind the HTML language, and it will make up the bulk of your menu system if you're designing a strictly data or balanced HTML menu system.

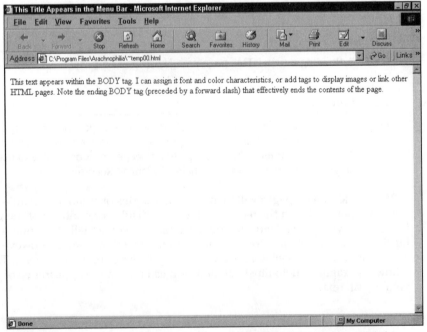

Figure 11.6 The HTML BODY tag enables you to display regular text like this.

Formatting Headers

Using the header tag, a total of six header levels can appear in the body of your page. The HTML code looks like this:

```
<html>

<head>
<title>This Title Appears in the Menu Bar</title>
</head>

<body>

<H1>This is a Level 1 Header!</H1>
This is standard text.
<H2>This is a Level 2 header.</H2>

This text appears within the BODY tag. I can assign it font and
color characteristics, or add tags to display images or link other
HTML pages. Note the ending BODY tag (preceded by a forward slash)
that effectively ends the contents of the page.

</body>

</html>
```

Figure 11.7 illustrates what the header tags look like when they are displayed by your browser.

Drawing a Horizontal Rule

Figure 11.8 shows a horizontal rule created with the <HR> tag. A horizontal rule can divide areas of text in your menu, separate images from text, or be used to underline the commands in your menu:

```
<html>

<head>
<title>This Title Appears in the Menu Bar</title>
</head>

<body>

<H1>This is a Level 1 Header!</H1>
This is standard text.
<HR>
<H2>This is a Level 2 header separated by a horizontal rule.</H2>

This text appears within the BODY tag. I can assign it font and
color characteristics, or add tags to display images or link other
HTML pages. Note the ending BODY tag (preceded by a forward slash)
that effectively ends the contents of the page.
```

```
</body>

</html>
```

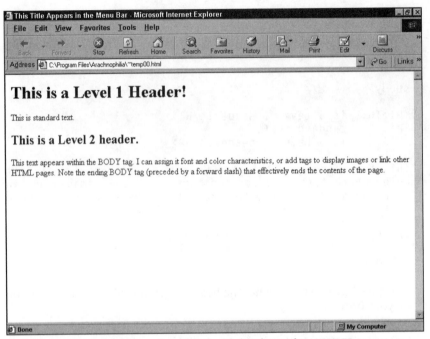

Figure 11.7 Examples of text formatted with level 1 and 2 HEADER tags

Inserting Graphics

With the IMG tag, you can place images directly into the page as a design element (these graphics are called *inline* images). Figure 11.9 shows an inline image used in a menu generated by this code:

```
<html>

<head>
<title>This Title Appears in the Menu Bar</title>
</head>

<body>

<H1>This is a Level 1 Header!</H1>
This is standard text.
<HR>

<H2>This is a Level 2 header separated by a horizontal rule.</H2>
```

This text appears within the BODY tag. I can assign it font and
color characteristics, or add tags to display images or link
other HTML pages. Note the ending BODY tag (preceded by a forward
slash) that effectively ends the contents of the page.

```
<IMG SRC="spotlight.gif" ALIGN=MIDDLE>
```

```
</body>
```

```
</html>
```

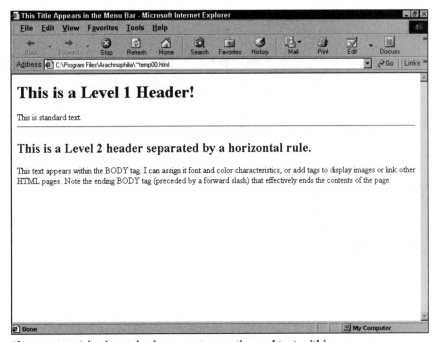

Figure 11.8 A horizontal rule separates sections of text within a page.

You can use three different alignment modes for this tag: BOTTOM, MIDDLE,
and TOP. Each mode indicates where the graphic should line up with the text
that follows it.

Adding Music

Remember the MIDI music standard that I mentioned earlier in the book? To add
a background MIDI song to your menu, try this trick:

```
<html>
```

```
<head>
```

```
<title>This Title Appears in the Menu Bar</title>
</head>

<body>

<H1>This is a Level 1 Header!</H1>
This is standard text.
<HR>
<BGSOUND SRC="background.mid" LOOP=INFINITY>

</body>

</html>
```

IE but not Firefox.

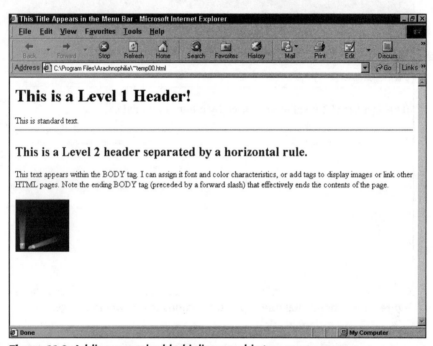

Figure 11.9 Adding an embedded inline graphic to a menu page

When you set LOOP equal to INFINITY, the music continues indefinitely—to have it play a finite number of times instead, simply substitute the number as the value for the LOOP attribute. Naturally, the computer needs a sound card and speakers.

Retrieving Files

If you'd like to include a link that retrieves any type of file from your disc (including images, audio, video, and programs), use the <A HREF=> tag, which uses the form:

```
<A HREF="filename">Descriptive text or filename here</A>
```

Note

To use this form, the file would have to be in the same directory as the HTML file—this is called a *relative* link, because the path is assumed relative to the location of the HTML document itself.

If the file type is recognized within the browser, it is automatically opened—otherwise, your browser should enable the file to be downloaded directly to the hard drive.

Accessing Web Sites

How about offering an automatic link to your Web site? You'd use this form of the A tag:

```
<A HREF="http://website/address.com">Descriptive text here</A>
```

If the computer is properly configured and can reach the Internet, the browser automatically connects and displays the page.

Linking to E-Mail

Finally, you can use this form of the A tag to link to an e-mail address. This will allow people to click on the link and send you an e-mail message. To add an e-mail link to your CD menu, use the following code:

```
<A HREF="http:/website/youraddress@domain.com">Descriptive text
here</A>
```

In my example, the code for the CD menu with the e-mail link added looks like this:

```
<html>

<head>
<title>This Title Appears in the Menu Bar</title>
</head>

<body>
```

```
<H1>This is a Level 1 Header!</H1>
This is standard text.
<HR>

<H2>This is a Level 2 header separated by a horizontal rule.</H2>

This text appears within the BODY tag. I can assign it font and
color characteristics, or add tags to display images or link
other HTML pages. Note the ending BODY tag (preceded by a forward
slash) that effectively ends the contents of the page.

<A HREF="mailto:mlcbooks@home.com">Send me an email message!</A>

</body>

</html>
```

When viewed by your browser, the e-mail link will appear like it does in Figure 11.10 below.

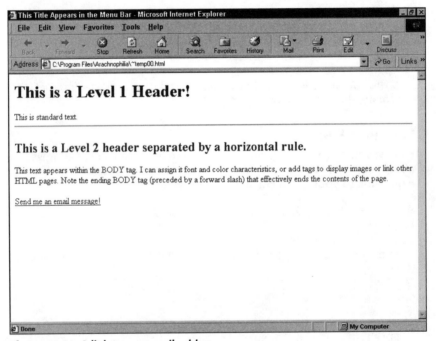

Figure 11.10 A link to an e-mail address

When you click this link, your computer should open your e-mail program and present you with a message editing window—the To: field will already be filled in with the correct name.

Converting Text to HTML

Before I close this chapter, I'd like to describe how you can convert a word processing file into a formatted HTML file. This comes in handy in two situations:

■ If you create an extensive menu system with text you've prepared on a word processor.

■ If you have a large number of existing word processing documents that you'd like to display on a disc as HTML files within a browser.

Because most word processors save documents in a proprietary binary format, you can't simply open your document in Windows Notepad and add a tag or two—most people use a word processor such as Microsoft Word or Corel WordPerfect and save files in the default format, so that's not usually an option. Besides, adding tags by hand to a twenty-page document rapidly becomes very tough going, especially if the document has a large number of heads, subheads, and bold or italicized type.

So what's the solution? Export as HTML! Most current major word processing and desktop publishing programs include an export (or *Save As*) option that can save a copy of a document in HTML format. Depending on how good the conversion is, you <u>may</u> end up with an on-screen presentation in your browser that's quite close to the original format of the word processing document! For example, Figure 11.11 illustrates the text from a word processing document converted to HTML format within Word 2000; I simply saved the original document under a new name with the "Web page" file type.

Note

Are you using an older word processing program that can't convert and save documents as HTML files? All may not be lost: If your program can save documents as RTF (*Rich Text Format*) files, you're in luck. With a little searching on the Web, you'll find a number of shareware and commercial tools available that can convert RTF files to HTML.

Most conversion to HTML is crap!

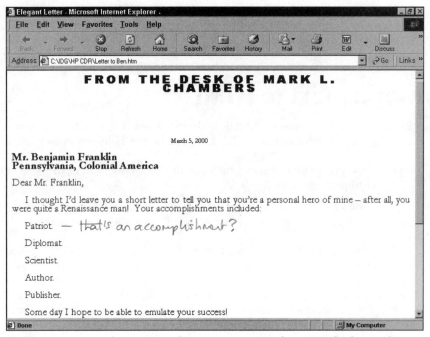

Figure 11.11 A word processing document converted to HTML looks nearly as good as the original.

In Review

In this chapter, you learned why you should add an HTML menu system to your recorded CDs. You were introduced to two different types of HTML editing applications, and you learned how to design your menu system to appeal to your target audience. You also took a quick tour of HTML commands that you're most likely to use to create your menu system, and you saw how to convert word processing files to HTML by exporting them.

Recording Multisession CDs Step-by-Step

As I mention earlier in the book, programs like DirectCD make it easy to copy additional files to a recorded CD and copy files from a recorded CD to a hard drive or other storage medium. You can even "delete" files from a CD-R, although the files aren't actually erased from the disc. However, not all CD recorders support packet-writing mode, where files can be copied to a blank CD as you would copy files to a floppy disk—so there are drives (especially older CD recorders) that can't use DirectCD to record files. How can you record information incrementally to a CD-ROM with one of these drives?

Luckily, there is an answer: You can write a *multisession* CD. On a multisession disc, you can record separate sessions (think of them as separate volumes on the same disc), or you can "update" the same session with new information in the same fashion as a DirectCD disc. Multisession discs can be used to back up files in separate sessions, too, which makes them a good choice for archiving data.

In this chapter, I describe both types of multisession recording, and I show you how to create a disc of each type. I also demonstrate the Session Selector program that you need in order to switch between sessions on the disc.

Distinguishing between Incremental and Multivolume Recording

Recording a traditional single-session data CD-ROM requires a single recording session, and the disc is usually fixed and closed so that it can't be recorded again. With a multisession disc, however, you can record it once, use it, and then record on it again; for example, you could record the images you take at your family reunion each year with a digital camera, "appending" them each year until you fill the entire disc. Each session you record is separated from the previous section by a "dividing line" of empty space (which can range anywhere from 14 to 30 megabytes, depending upon its position on the disc surface). Because of this lost space, you never get the storage capacity from a multisession disc that you get from a single session disc. It's a good idea to avoid recording a session that contains only a small amount of data, because you're guaranteed to lose at least 14 megabytes when you add another session!

You can record two different types of multisession CD-ROMs using Easy CD Creator:

■ **Incremental.** An incremental multisession disc makes it easy to "update" previous data that you've recorded. All the information that you've recorded within the previous session is available; as the name suggests, you can add files to that existing information. Where does that information come from? Easy CD Creator includes an Import Session function that enables you to read the contents of the previous session into your data CD layout, as shown in Figure 12.1. You can even "delete" files from an incremental multisession disc. (I'd better qualify that—files deleted from this type of disc are actually not erased and you don't regain any of the space they used; instead, the location of the file isn't updated in the disc's Table of Contents, so it effectively disappears and can't be recovered.) Incremental discs are fast to create, too, because the information in the previous session is not actually re-recorded. Instead, the session's directory information is retained and updated with the new data. If you're running Windows 95, a program like Session Selector isn't required to read an incremental multisession disc. However, your drive can <u>only</u> read the <u>latest</u> session you've recorded!

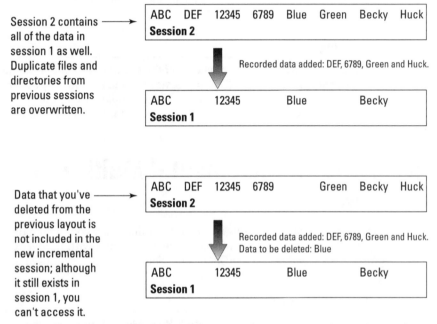

Session 2 contains all of the data in session 1 as well. Duplicate files and directories from previous sessions are overwritten.

Data that you've deleted from the previous layout is not included in the new incremental session; although it still exists in session 1, you can't access it.

Figure 12.1 Updating data from a previous session is easy with an incremental multisession disc.

■ **Multivolume.** As you might have guessed from the name, a multivolume multisession disc stores data in discrete sessions; each volume can be accessed with a program like Session Selector, which enables you to switch between volumes whenever you like without rebooting your computer. However, there's a downside: You can only read data from one volume at a time, and you can't modify the data stored on a session (so files can't be erased). Figure 12.2 illustrates how data is written to a multivolume disc.

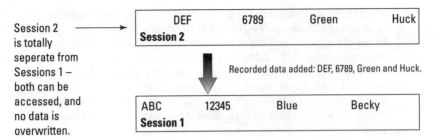

Session 2 is totally seperate from Sessions 1 – both can be accessed, and no data is overwritten.

Figure 12.2 Each session is a separate volume on a multivolume multisession disc.

Warning

Not every CD-ROM drive can read all of the sessions on a multivolume disc! Older first-generation CD-ROM drives may be able to read only the first or the last session on the disc, so if you're creating a multisession disc for distribution, consider using incremental multisession mode for the widest compatibility.

Recording an Incremental Multisession CD-ROM

Before you record an incremental multisession disc, you need a disc that you've recorded earlier. This disc *must* have been recorded with the Write Method set to *Close Session and Leave CD Open*. This field appears in the Advanced portion of the CD Creation Setup dialog box.

Cross-Reference

To learn how to set Easy CD Creator's Write Method, check out the section "Recording a Data CD-ROM" in Chapter 8, "Introducing Easy CD Creator Step-by-Step."

To record an incremental multisession disc:

1. Load the disc with the existing session into your drive. Easy CD Creator automatically displays the Create CD Wizard welcome screen.

2. Click the Data button to display the different types of data disc you can record.

3. Click Data CD to load the Data CD Layout screen.

4. Before you add any files, click the File menu and select CD Layout Properties to display the dialog box shown in Figure 12.3. Make sure that the Automatically import previous session check box is enabled, and click OK.

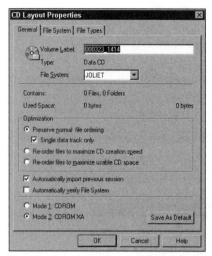

Figure 12.3 Configuring the CD layout properties for an incremental multisession disc

5. Build the layout for the new session just as you would with a standard single-session data CD. Notice that when you add the first new file or folder, Easy CD Creator automatically imports the files and folders recorded during the previous session.

6. Click the Create CD button on the toolbar to display the CD Creation Setup dialog box. Click OK to continue.

7. You can follow the progress of your recording from the Process dialog box.

Recording a Multivolume Multisession CD-ROM

You need the same type of existing destination disc required in the previous section (with the Write Method set to *Close Session and Leave CD Open)* to record a multivolume multisession disc. Follow these steps:

1. Load the disc with the existing session into your drive. Easy CD Creator automatically displays the Create CD Wizard welcome screen.

2. Click the Data button to display the different types of data disc you can record.

3. Click Data CD to load the Data CD Layout screen.

4. Before you add any files, click the File menu, select CD Layout Properties, and make sure that the Automatically import previous session check box has been disabled. Click OK to return to the layout.

5. Build the layout for the new session just as you would with a standard single-session data CD.

6. Click the Create CD button on the toolbar to display the CD Creation Setup dialog box. Click OK to continue.

7. Easy CD Creator displays the dialog box shown in Figure 12.4, prompting you to confirm that you want to add a new volume to the disc. Click Yes to begin the recording.

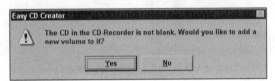

Figure 12.4 Confirming the creation of a multivolume multisession disc

8. You can follow the progress of your recording from the Process dialog box.

Using Session Selector

If you've created a multivolume multisession disc, Adaptec provides you with a method of selecting and reading a different volume — it's a program called Session Selector. To choose a new session from a multivolume disc:

1. Run Session Selector from the Windows 98 Start menu by clicking Start and choose Programs ➪ Adaptec Easy CD Creator 4 ➪ Features ➪ Session Selector. The program displays the main window shown in Figure 12.5.

2. If you have more than one CD-ROM drive on your system, click the correct drive in the left pane of the window. Session Selector displays the sessions on the selected disc in the right portion of the window.

3. The current session being read is reported with a drive letter. To select another session, click the session to highlight it, click the Tools menu, and choose Activate Session. After a short delay, the new session is active.

4. Click File and select the Close menu item to return to Windows.

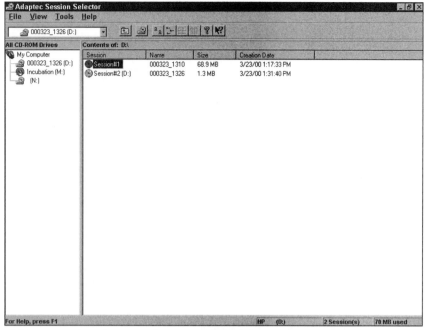

Figure 12.5 Choosing a session on a multivolume multisession disc

5. You can also select another session and automatically open it within Windows Explorer. To do this, click the session to highlight it, click the Tools menu, and choose Explore.

In Review

In this chapter, you learned how to create both types of multisession data CD-ROMs, which enables you to copy additional files to a recorded CD. In addition, you now know how to use Adaptec's Session Selector to switch volumes on a multivolume multisession disc.

Q Where can info about the tracks on an audio CD be kept?
Is there a standard for this?
If so, <u>why</u> don't you tell us about it? If not, why not?

p196 p252

Recording Projects

Doing Basic Recording

Earlier in the book, I showed you how to accomplish the most common tasks in CD recording: creating simple data discs and creating audio discs. Those two "vanilla" procedures will work fine for the great majority of your projects, and you will find they make up the bulk of the work done by your CD recorder.

In this chapter, you apply what you've learned in the book to create three specific projects using three different software applications: Easy CD Creator, DirectCD, and Spin Doctor. Each of these applications addresses a unique need, and you will discover why each program is best-suited for a particular application.

Welcoming New Employees on CD

In our first scenario, let's suppose that you need to record a CD-R disc for a new employee who's just joined your company's Marketing department. You want to save the information first as a disc image to your hard drive, so that you can make additional copies as more people are hired. The image will include the company logo in several different formats, templates for Microsoft Office and WordPerfect, several years of company press releases, and high-resolution digital images of each of your products. Let's also suppose that the information will be arranged into four folders by the type of data. For example, you'll have an Images folder for the product shots, a Press Releases folder, a Logo folder, and a Templates folder for the company's example templates.

Why use Easy CD Creator in this case? Two reasons:

- The disc is written at one time, and no additional data will be added later. (Therefore, there's no need to use DirectCD.)

- Easy CD Creator can save and record disc images. (DirectCD can't use disc images.)

MATERIALS

An installed copy of Easy CD Creator

The files to be recorded

A blank CD-R or CD-RW disc

Creating an Employee Orientation Disc with Easy CD Creator

To create a disc image for a disc that will be given to new employees:

1. Load a blank CD-R or CD-RW disc into your drive—Easy CD Creator detects this and automatically display the Create CD Wizard welcome screen.

2. Because this will be a data CD, click the Data button.

3. We want to use Easy CD Creator, so click Data CD. After Easy CD Creator loads, you'll see the Data CD layout screen shown in Figure 13.1.

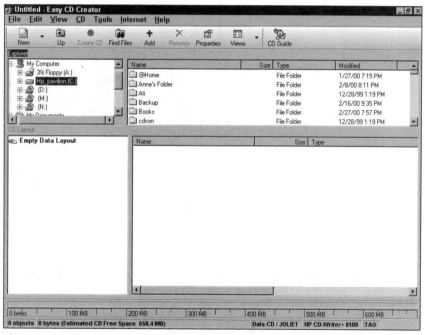

Figure 13.1 Our empty Data CD layout, ready to customize

4. Next, you should create the four empty folders that will hold the data. Click the title Empty Data Layout in the left pane of the CD layout window, then choose New Folder from the Edit menu. Type the name for the new folder and press Enter to save the change. You'll have to repeat this step four times; once you're done, your layout will look like Figure 13.2.

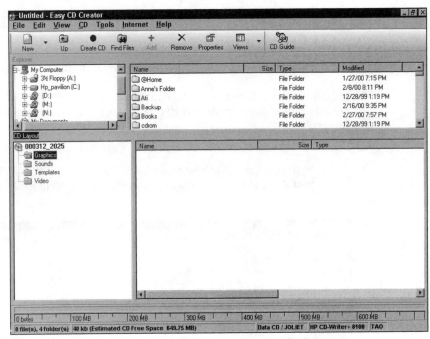

Figure 13.2 Four empty folders have been added to the layout.

5. You must open the target folder to copy files to it, so click the first new folder you've created (in our example, the Graphics folder).

6. Use the Explorer display within the top half of the window to locate the files you'll need to fill the Images folder. As you can see, I've got an entire directory of images, so I click the Edit menu and choose Select All to save time.

7. Click the Add button in the Toolbar to copy the files. Your layout should now look like Figure 13.3.

8. In Figure 13.4, you can see that I repeated steps 5 through 7 until all the files have been added to each of the four folders.

Tip

Here's an easy way to copy an entire folder and all of its contents to the CD layout: use the Explorer display to navigate to the folder, click it, and drag the entire folder over the top of the disc icon in the CD layout.

9. Now that our layout is finished, it's time to save it as an image. From the File menu, choose the Create CD Image menu item. Easy CD Creator displays the Select Image File dialog box.

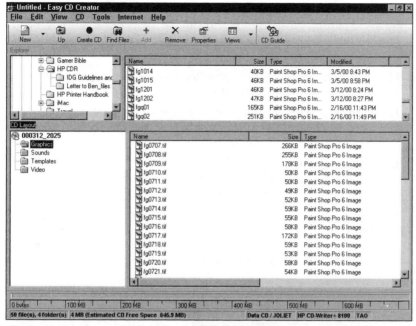

Figure 13.3 A directory full of files in our new data CD layout

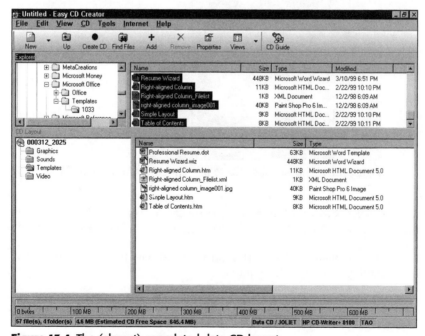

Figure 13.4 The (almost) completed data CD layout

10. Store this disc image in the root directory of your C: drive. Click the Save In drop-down list box and choose the C: drive, and enter a filename for the image in the File name field (I use newemp). Remember, Easy CD Creator adds the extension .CIF for you.

11. Click Save, and allow the recording process to complete. Press OK to return to the Data CD layout window.

12. Okay, you've saved your disc image for later use. Now, without closing Easy CD Creator, let's record our first copy! Click the File menu and choose Create CD from Image.

13. Easy CD Creator displays the Select Image File dialog box; once again, navigate to the root (or top) of your C: drive and double-click the newemp file to open it.

14. Easy CD Creator displays the same CD Creation Setup dialog box you would see if you were recording from a layout. Because we want to finalize this disc so that it can't be modified, click Advanced to display the dialog box shown in Figure 13.5 and choose Track-at-Once and Close CD.

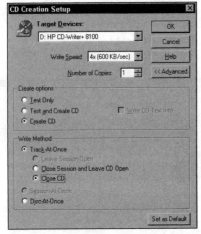

Figure 13.5 Choose Close CD to prevent others from writing to the disc.

15. Click OK to start the recording process. You can monitor the progress of your recording, or take a break to grab a cup of coffee or a glass of water.

That's it! Thanks to Easy CD Creator, you should have a disc ready for your new employee in 15 to 20 minutes.

Saving Those Oldies But Goodies on CD

Next, turn your attention to audio CD recording. This recording will be somewhat different from the process I describe in Chapter 8, because we'll be creating an audio CD from an older vinyl record album using the Adaptec program Spin Doctor. I think any audiophile would agree that losing a precious recording to scratches and worn-out equipment would be a tragedy — but by "re-recording" that audio to a CD, you'll be able to enjoy it for many years to come.

Why use Spin Doctor instead of Easy CD Creator? The answer is in the input source: Easy CD Creator can only record audio from files on your hard drive or from tracks on an existing audio CD. Spin Doctor can also use the input from your stereo system, so you can use audio from any of your stereo components.

Before we start, however, you'll have to set up your computer's sound card to accept input from your stereo system and turntable. Because sound card hardware varies by manufacturer, check your card's manual for specific instructions on the cables you need and what connector you should use.

> **MATERIALS**
>
> An installed copy of Spin Doctor
>
> A cable connection between your sound card and your stereo system
>
> The album you want to record
>
> A blank CD-R disc

Archiving Vinyl Records with Spin Doctor

Once your card is properly connected to your stereo, follow these steps to record your old vinyl records using Spin Doctor:

1. Load a blank CD-R disc into your drive. Remember, *CD-RW discs should not be used when recording Red Book audio CDs!* Easy CD Creator detects the disc and automatically displays the Create CD Wizard welcome screen.

2. Click the Audio button.

3. Click Spin Doctor. Once the program loads, you see the screen shown in Figure 13.6.

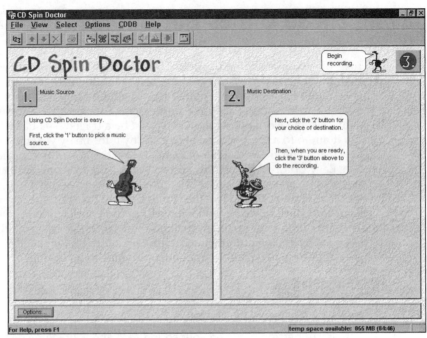

Figure 13.6 The Spin Doctor main screen

4. Our first step is to select the source for our audio. Click the 1 button to display the Select Music Source dialog box shown in Figure 13.7.

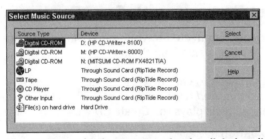

Figure 13.7 Selecting a source for the digital audio you'll record

5. Although we can choose digital extraction from an existing audio CD and digital audio files from the hard drive, the recording source for this disc is an existing LP, so click LP and click Select. Note that the audio from both LPs and cassettes is routed through your sound card.

6. Enter the name for the audio you're about to copy (or use the default title, Sampled Audio, as shown in Figure 13.8), and click 2.

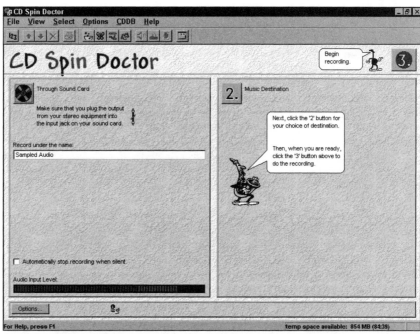

Figure 13.8 Entering a name for the audio from our LP

7. From the Select Music Destination dialog box shown in Figure 13.9, you can choose to record the audio directly to your CD recorder, save the audio as WAV files on your hard drive, or save it as MP3 files. Because we're recording a CD, choose the CD Recorder entry and click Select.

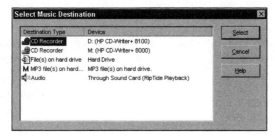

Figure 13.9 Choosing a destination for our digital audio

Tip

If you'd like to edit the audio that you've copied from an album or cassette before you actually record it to CD—for example, to remove additional silence from the beginning and end of one or more tracks—you can always select MP3 as the music destination and record the audio as MP3 files on your hard drive instead. Once you've edited the files and pronounced them ready to record, you can use Easy CD Creator to record them as I described in Chapter 8, "Introducing Easy CD Creator Step-by-Step."

8. At this point, we're ready to begin recording, but what if this is an older LP with a number of scratches and pops? And what if we want separate tracks for each song on the album (rather than a single long track that contains all of the songs)? You can enable these special functions from the Options menu before you record. Click Options to display the screen illustrated in Figure 13.10.

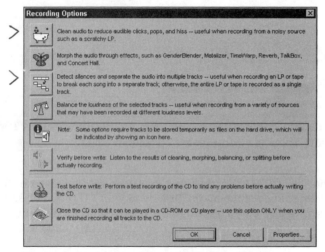

Figure 13.10 Setting options within Spin Doctor

9. To help remove the pop and hiss from an older LP (imperfections that affect just about every album I still own), click the Clean Audio button.

10. To divide each song on the album into a separate audio track, click the "Detect silences and separate the audio into multiple tracks" button. Finally, click the Close the CD button at the bottom—this finalizes the CD so that it can be read in your audio CD player. Click OK to return to the main Spin Doctor screen.

11. Click the Record to CD button at the top-right corner of the Spin Doctor screen.

12. Spin Doctor displays the prompt dialog box shown in Figure 13.11 to help you synchronize the music from your turntable. Start the turntable and immediately click Record. Spin Doctor displays an animated progress dialog box.

Figure 13.11 Ready to record from LP!

13. Once the album has finished playing, click Stop to finish the recording and close the disc.

■   ■   ■   ■   ■   ■   ■   ■   ■   ■   ■   ■   ■   ■

Growing Your Family Tree on a CD

Our last project in this chapter is a great example of a DirectCD application: Saving genealogical records from a database to a CD for archival storage. These records won't be changed in the future, so you can consider this project as a "backup" procedure.(It's hard to think of a more catastrophic event for a genealogy buff than the loss of all of those records that you've painstakingly researched and gathered!)

As I mentioned earlier in the book, recordable CDs are perfect for archival backup; unlike with tapes, data doesn't have to be restored first before it can be used, and a blank CD-R disc is far less expensive and stores much more than a Zip disk. Therefore, you can use this procedure to back up your other important information as well, such as financial records or a database of your professional contacts.

DirectCD is the best choice for a project like this one for three reasons:

■ Unlike Easy CD Creator, DirectCD doesn't require you to design a CD layout before recording, so you save time if you're just backing up files for simple archival storage.

■ Data can be appended to a DirectCD disc at a later time—this is more efficient than recording an entire disc for five or six megabytes of data! (Remember, you can add extra data even if you're using a CD-R disc instead of a CD-RW disc. Therefore, I recommend that you use the cheaper CD-R discs with DirectCD whenever possible.)

■ A DirectCD is not a multisession disc, so you won't need to switch sessions to read data recorded at different times.

> **MATERIALS**
>
> An installed copy of DirectCD
>
> The files to be recorded
>
> A blank CD-R disc

Recording Genealogy Records with DirectCD

First, our genealogy data should be arranged in the proper fashion. For this project, we need to back up the complete database folder, which contains over a hundred files. Although DirectCD enables you to "overwrite" the directories on a CD-R, it's a good idea to store successive database backups as separate folders. This way, you can return to a "snapshot" of your data each time you record a new copy.

Note

If you don't want to create a genealogy database from scratch, there are several good genealogy-related software applications that can help you organize your family tree. Two such software programs are **Family Tree Maker** (www.familytreemaker.com) and **Legacy Family Tree** (http://www.legacyfamilytree.com/).

For example, let's suppose that you've recorded a backup of the data in June 2000 and one in August 2000, so you can return to the June backup in case you find that your database was corrupted at the time of the August backup. It's easy to create backups organized by date: simply save the folder on your DirectCD disc with the date as the folder name. In our previous example, you'd have two folders named June 2000 and August 2000.

Once you've organized your data as you like, follow these steps to back up the data:

1. Load a blank CD-R or CD-RW disc into your drive to display the Create CD Wizard welcome screen.

2. Click the Data button.

3. Click DirectCD and click Next to continue on the Welcome screen.

4. If you have multiple CD recorders on your system, DirectCD displays the Drive Information screen shown in Figure 13.12. Click the desired recorder and click Next to continue.

5. Click Next to confirm the formatting process and continue.

Figure 13.12 Choosing a destination CD recorder

6. Type a descriptive Volume name of up to 11 characters for this disc on the Name Your Disc screen. Once you've entered a name, click Finish to start the formatting, and watch the progress of the formatting process.

7. The Disc Ready dialog box appears when your new disc is ready to use. Click OK.

8. Next, open Windows Explorer and navigate to the location of the database folder, as shown in Figure 13.13.

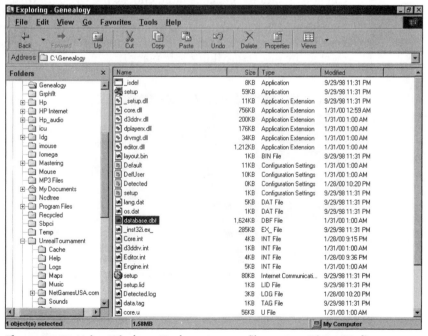

Figure 13.13 Using Windows Explorer to copy files onto a DirectCD disc

9. Click the folder to select it, then drag it on top of the DirectCD drive and release the mouse button. (If we were copying multiple folders or files, you could hold down the Ctrl key while clicking to select each of them as a group.) Windows displays the Copy progress dialog box.

10. When the database folder and all of the files it contains have been copied, you should change the folder name to the month and date on the DirectCD disc — click the DirectCD drive in the left pane of the Explorer window to display the folder, and then click the folder name once. Type in the new folder name and press Enter to save it.

11. As a precaution, it's a good idea to use your genealogy program to open the database you've created on your DirectCD disc — it only takes a second, and if you can load the database without error, you've verified that your data has been properly backed up.

Tip

Unsure of how much room remains on your DirectCD disc for future backups? Right-click the DirectCD drive icon in Windows Explorer and choose Properties from the pop-up menu to display the current disc usage and the amount of free space remaining.

12. Now that the recording is complete, press the Eject button on the drive to display the Eject Disc screen shown in Figure 13.14. Because this disc can hold additional backups later, choose the Organize the Disc option and <u>disable</u> the "Protect the disc so that it cannot be written to again" check box. (This option enables you to read the disc using most PCs running Windows 95 or later without write-protecting it.) Once you've ejected the disc, store it in a safe place.

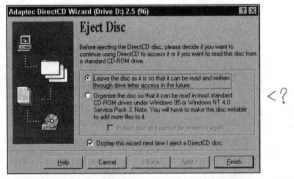

Figure 13.14 Selecting Eject options for a new DirectCD disc

13. When you're ready to add the next backup to your DirectCD disc, simply reload it into the CD recorder—DirectCD automatically detects that you've loaded a DirectCD disc, and displays the Make Disc Writable dialog box you see in Figure 13.15. Click Next to continue.

Figure 13.15 Making a DirectCD disc writable again

14. DirectCD displays the Name Your Disc dialog box again to give you the option of changing the Volume Name—you don't have to change it, of course. Click Finish to start the procedure.

15. Once the disc has been made writable again, DirectCD displays the confirmation dialog box that you see in Figure 13.16. Click OK to begin using your DirectCD disc again.

Figure 13.16 Ready to write again!

In Review

In this chapter, you completed three projects step-by-step. Each of these projects is a good demonstration of the variety of recorded discs you can produce. In the course of doing these projects, you used three different programs, proving once again that it's always a good idea to use the right tool for the job. As you discovered, each program is best suited for a particular application, and you can use these general guidelines to determine what program is the right one to use for your next recording project.

CHAPTER

14

Advanced Recording Projects

Ready to try your hand at recording something else besides a standard audio or data CD, or adding a professional "finishing touch" to a recording? If so, keep reading: The projects in this chapter cover the advanced features of Easy CD Creator, along with Adaptec's Jewel Case Creator and VCD Creator, Ritz Camera's Photo Manager, and Netscape's Composer.

Just a few years ago, many CD recorders didn't even *support* the specialized disc recording modes and formats I describe in this chapter — they were considered "exotic" — and the multimedia authoring software required to finish these projects might have cost you several hundred dollars. Today, however, thanks to the popularity of CD recording and the availability of programs like Easy CD Creator and Ritz Photo Manager, your home computer's CD-RW drive can create a stunning multimedia "photo album" on a disc or record Video CDs with your family home movies that will last through the next century.

Finally, I also show you how to enhance the appearance of your disc with a custom label and jewel box insert, and I build an example CD menu using HTML.

Making Your Own Video CD

You can use VCD Creator to record digital video as a *Video CD,* which can be played on Video CD players, CD-I players, and any DVD player that supports the standard Video CD format. As an example, let's use the most common scenario for a home PC owner: You have a number of home video clips that you've recorded and saved on your hard drive in MPEG format, and you'd like to create a Video CD with these clips that runs the clips one after another in a seamless show.

Note

VCD Creator is available as part of the Deluxe version of Easy CD Creator. Depending on the version of the Adaptec software that shipped with your drive, you may have to upgrade your copy before you can create a VideoCD.

MATERIALS

Computer with a CD-R or CD-RW drive

Installed copy of Easy CD Creator

Blank CD-R disc

MPEG video files

Recording a Video CD

To create this type of Video CD:

1. Load a blank CD-R disc into your drive. Easy CD Creator will detect this and automatically display the Create CD Wizard welcome screen.

Note

To assure the widest compatibility, use only CD-R discs to create Video CDs.

2. Click the Photo & Video button.

3. Click Video CD. After Easy CD Creator loads, you'll see the VCD Creator Wizard screen shown in Figure 14.1. Click Next to continue.

Figure 14.1 The Welcome screen for the VCD Creator Wizard

4. For this project, we use the Simple Video Sequence type (which also offers a higher level of compatibility with DVD players). Choose Simple Video Sequence and click Next.

5. Click Add to select the MPEG video clips from your hard drive. VCD Creator displays the standard Add Play Items dialog box shown in Figure 14.2. Navigate to the location of the MPEG files and double-click the first file to open it.

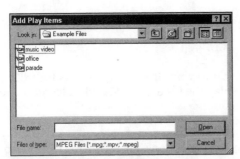

Figure 14.2 Use the Add Play Items dialog box to select a video clip to add to a Video CD layout.

6. The clip is loaded and displayed in the Add New Play Item dialog box. You can preview the clip frame-by-frame by dragging the slider bar below the Video Clip Preview window. Click OK to accept the clip. Notice that a thumbnail of the clip appears in the Video CD layout screen, as shown in Figure 14.3.

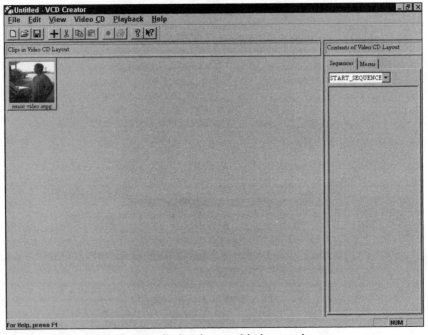

Figure 14.3 An MPEG movie clip has been added to our layout.

7. Repeat steps 5 and 6 to load each of the clips into the VCD Creator layout screen.

8. Once you've added all of the clips, click Next to continue, and click Next again on the Creating Play Sequence screen.

9. On the screen shown in Figure 14.4, you determine the play order of the clips you've loaded. Click the thumbnail in the left column for the clip that should appear first and click Add>>. Continue this process until you've added all the clips in the order they should appear. If you need to remove a clip from the sequence you're building, click the thumbnail in the START_SEQUENCE column to select it and click <<Remove.

Figure 14.4 Building the sequence for our Video CD

10. Once you've added and arranged all of the clips in the order that you want them in the START_SEQUENCE column, click Next to continue.

11. If you'd like to view the video sequence you've created, click Playback. VCD Creator displays the control panel shown in Figure 14.5, which is much like a set of VCR controls — you can use these to play, pause, or skip to the next or previous clip. Once you've finished the playback, click Close on the MPEG Playback panel, and click Next to continue.

Tip

Suddenly discover that the sequence you build needs to be changed? No problem! Click Back to return to the Play Sequence screen, and change your sequence as necessary.

Figure 14.5 The MPEG Playback controls

12. That's it! You're ready to record your Video CD. VCD Creator displays the screen shown in Figure 14.6 — click Create the CD now and click Finish to start the process.

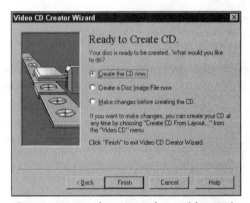

Figure 14.6 Ready to record our Video CD!

Before the recording actually starts, VCD Creator automatically "builds" the sequence and generates the Video CD data file — this can take a few minutes on a slower PC, especially if you've selected a large number of clips. Once the build step is complete, however, you see the same familiar CD Creation Setup dialog box, and the rest of the process is the same as recording a standard data CD.

Developing a Photo Album Slideshow

One application for compact discs that many computer owners are already familiar with is the storage of digital photographs. In fact, many photo development labs already offer you the option of recording your photos onto a CD. However, if you have a scanner or a digital camera and you've built your own library of digital photographs, you can save yourself the money and create your own custom photo album disc to show off those pictures on any computer running Windows 98 or Mac OS!

For this project, we use Ritz Camera Photo Manager, a photo organizing and editing program that ships with Hewlett-Packard CD-Writer Plus series CD-RW drives. Photo Manager includes a neat feature called a *slideshow*, in which your images are shown one after another on the computer's monitor. Using this feature, you can create an automated "photo album slideshow." As an example, I use a number of images I took in St. Louis, Missouri, during a Cardinals baseball game. I call my slideshow "A Day At the Ball Game." I'm sure you've already built up a collection of your own digital images, so use them instead as you follow the steps in this project.

Note

Although we're using images I've shot myself with a digital camera, I won't explain how those pictures were transferred from the camera to my computer's hard drive—there are many methods of downloading images from a camera, and each camera uses a slightly different process. For all the details on getting those images you took from your camera to your computer, consult your camera's manual. (If you'd like to learn more about digital photography, I recommend *Fun with Digital Imaging: The Official Hewlett-Packard Guide,* written by Lisa Price and Jonathan Price and published by IDG Books Worldwide.)

MATERIALS

Computer with a CD-R or CD-RW drive

Installed copy of Easy CD Creator

Installed copy of Ritz Camera Photo Manager

Blank CD-R or CD-RW disc

Images in JPEG or bitmap format

Recording Your Slideshow

Follow these instructions to create a photo album slideshow CD that you can send to your friends and relatives:

1. To run the Photo Manager program from the Windows 98 Start menu, click Start and choose Programs ⇨ Ritz Photo Manager ⇨ Photo Manager. The Photo Manager main screen appears, as shown in Figure 14.7

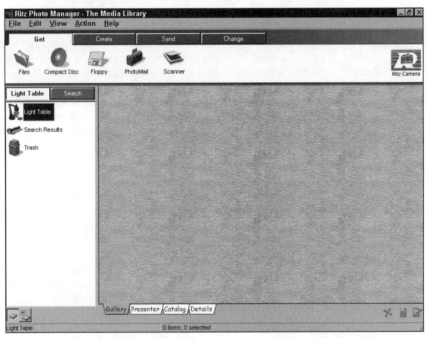

Figure 14.7 The Photo Manager main screen

2. First, you need to create a *photo album,* which is Photo Manager's apt term for a collection of pictures. Click the Create tab at the top of the screen and click the Album toolbar button to display the Create Album dialog box shown in Figure 14.8.

3. Enter the name for your album (I call my album, "A Day At the Ball Game") and click OK. The album icon appears at the left side of the screen; click it once to select it as the destination for the images.

4. Click the Get tab and click the Files toolbar button to display the Import Photographs dialog box. Click Next to continue.

Figure 14.8 Creating a new photo album

5. On the screen shown in Figure 14.9, click the Look in: drop-down list box and navigate to the folder containing your pictures. You can click individual images to select them, or hold down the Ctrl key to choose multiple images. To place all the pictures in the same folder, click Select All and then click Next to continue.

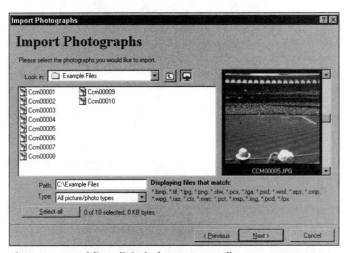

Figure 14.9 Adding digital photos to an album

6. On the Specify Photograph Attributes screen, you can enter the photographer's name, search keywords, include the date the images were taken, and add other comments. However, because these won't be displayed in the slideshow, leave these optional fields blank and just click Next.

7. Finally, specify the current album as the destination for the images and click Finish to add the pictures.

8. Your Photo Manager screen now contains thumbnails of all the images you've added to this album, so it should look something like Figure 14.10. Now that you've built an album, you're ready to create the slideshow.

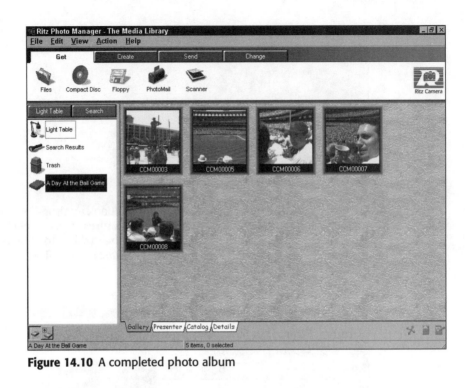

Figure 14.10 A completed photo album

9. Click the Create tab and click the Slideshow toolbar button to display the Slideshow Publisher Wizard. Click Next to continue.

10. Because our new album was still selected, it's automatically the source for our slideshow images. On the Select Photographs screen shown in Figure 14.11, simply click Select All and click Next to continue.

11. Click Folder and select a directory where the presentation should be stored (this step enables you to add text files, sound files, or other documents to your slideshow CD before you record it) and click Next.

12. Photo Manager will prompt you for permission to create the new folder to hold your presentation. Click Yes to continue.

13. Now select the type of operating system that the disc will play under. You can choose either Windows or Macintosh, as shown in Figure 14.12. Click Next to continue.

14. Photo Manager displays the final statistics on how many images the slideshow will contain and how much space they will take. Click Finish to create the slideshow.

15. Photo Manager will ask whether or not you want to view your slideshow. Because we're going to record it, click No. Click the File menu and choose the Exit menu item to close the program.

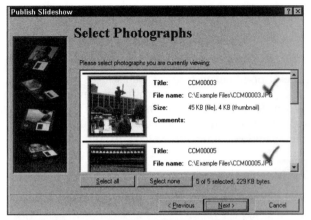

Figure 14.11 Selecting photos for our slideshow

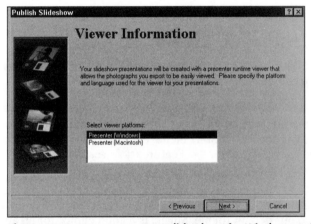

Figure 14.12 You can create a slide show for Windows or for Macintosh.

That takes care of creating the slideshow! Now you can run Easy CD Creator and record the files, just as with a simple data CD. Create a data CD layout that contains the files from the directory created by Photo Manager. Notice that I've placed all the files in the root directory of the disc, but you can put them in a separate directory if you like. As I mentioned earlier, I can also include any additional files that I want on the disc. It's a good idea to add a short README file explaining that the recipient can click the presentr.exe file to watch the slideshow. (If you like, it's also a good time to add sound files or video clips as well, to create a truly multimedia "album on a disc!")

Creating Professional-Looking CDs

Once you've finished a recording a CD, you *could* simply write a title on the disc with a felt-tipped permanent marker, stick it in an empty jewel case, and call it complete. If your computer has a printer, however, why not take a final step to add a professional touch to your new disc? In this section, you learn how to print a custom jewel case insert and a custom CD label for your recorded CDs. It doesn't take long, and you'll be impressed with the results!

MATERIALS

Computer with a laser or inkjet printer

Installed copy of Easy CD Creator

Recorded audio or data CD

Making Custom CD Liners and Labels

In this project, let's suppose that you've just created an audio CD of your favorite music. As an example, I use one of my favorite jazz compilation discs. Follow these steps:

1. To run the Adaptec Jewel Case Creator program from the Windows 95/98 or Windows 2000 Start menu, click Start and choose Programs ⇨ Adaptec Easy CD Creator 4 ⇨ Features ⇨ Jewel Case Creator. The Jewel Case Creator main screen appears, as shown in Figure 14.13.

2. Jewel Case Creator includes a number of preconfigured themes. Each theme includes a coordinated jewel case insert and CD label design. Although our default theme, Music, is a good choice for an audio CD, let's pick another to reflect the days of jazz radio; click Format and choose the Change Theme menu item to display the Change Theme dialog box shown in Figure 14.14.

3. Click Radio to select the Radio theme, and Jewel Case Creator updates the Preview window on the right. Click OK to accept the new theme and update the main screen.

Note

Some of the themes provided with Jewel Case Creator are designed only for use with audio CDs (such as Music and Radio), whereas others are designed only for data CD-ROMs (such as Composition and Datafiles). The data-only themes are marked in the Change Theme dialog box, but Jewel Case Creator will also alert you if you try to use a theme with the wrong type of disc.

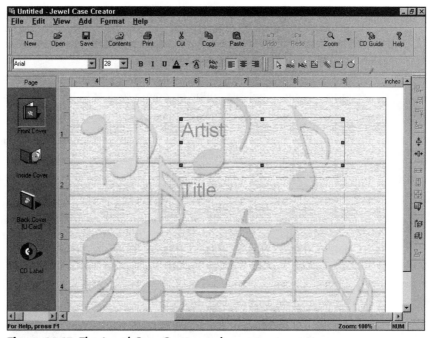

Figure 14.13 The Jewel Case Creator main screen

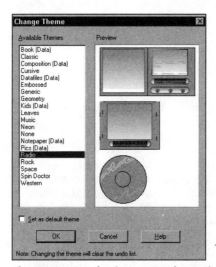

Figure 14.14 Selecting a new theme for an audio CD jewel case

4. Now that you've selected a theme, load your audio CD into the CD recorder or any CD-ROM drive on your system.

5. Click the Add menu and select the CD Contents item. Jewel Case Creator will automatically update the disc title, artist name, and track list with the information you entered when you recorded the disc.

Tip

You can also click Contents on the program's toolbar to update the main screen with the title, artist, and track names.

6. If you didn't enter the artist, disc title, or track names for your audio CD when you recorded it, you have two options:

- **Accessing the Internet.** If you copy an existing audio CD and you enable audio CD information downloading, the program will automatically attempt to connect to the Internet and download the title, artist, and track names from the CD database. Audio CD information downloading is enabled by default; if it's been turned off and you need to enable it, select Preferences from the Edit menu and click the Internet tab to display the screen shown in Figure 14.15.

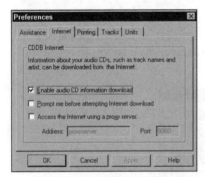

Figure 14.15 Enabling access to the Internet CD database

- **Typing the information.** You can always enter the disc title, artist, and track names manually. You use this method if you recorded your audio CD with tracks taken from more than one source disc, or if the audio CD you've recorded is not recognized within the Internet CD database. Manual entry also works when you don't have an Internet connection. Click the Add menu and select Track to display the Insert New Track dialog box shown in Figure 14.16. Type in the track number, the title, and the duration, and click Add Track—repeat this procedure for each track on the disc, and click Done when you're finished. To enter the disc name and artist, double-click the word Artist or Title within the main screen; the program displays an edit box, and you can type the new text. Hit Enter to save your changes, and they'll appear in the main screen.

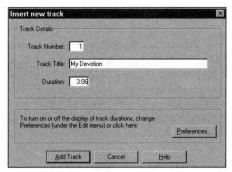

Figure 14.16 Adding track information to an audio CD jewel box insert

7. Once all the information has been added, you can print your new front cover! Click Print on the toolbar and click OK to start printing.

8. As you may have already noticed, Jewel Case Creator can also print an inside cover, a back cover, and a disc label—luckily, you only have to enter the information once, and it's automatically updated for these other templates. Let's create a CD label as well—click the CD Label button in the column on the left side of the screen to display the CD label template shown in Figure 14.17.

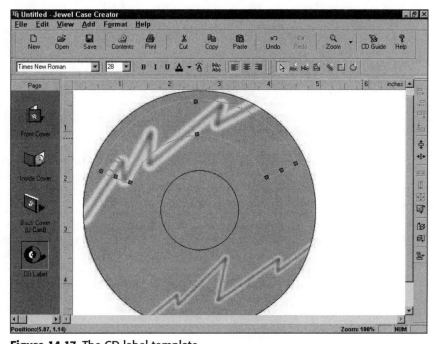

Figure 14.17 The CD label template

9. Load your printer with precut CD labels—typically, most labels are loaded upside-down, but check the instructions that came with your CD labels. Click Print on the toolbar to display the Print dialog box, and click Page Setup to display the dialog box in Figure 14.18.

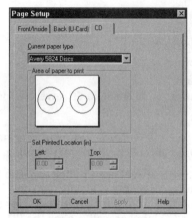

Figure 14.18 Selecting the proper brand of CD labels

10. Click the Current Paper Type drop-down list box and click the brand and type of disc labels you're using, then click OK.

11. Click the proper label position that you want to print—for example, if you've already used the first label on a two-label sheet, click the second label position. If you forget this step, you may end up attempting to print on a label that's no longer on the sheet!

12. Click OK to start printing.

13. Once the label has printed, apply it according to the label manufacturer's instructions.

Some labels can be aligned and applied by hand, whereas others require a special application device like the NEATO CD labeler shown in Figure 14.19.

Warning

I recommend that you *do not* try to manually align and apply a CD label that has been designed for use with a labeling device! Once you've applied most CD labels, they can't be removed without destroying the disc—and if a label is improperly aligned, it can unbalance a disc and render it unreadable!

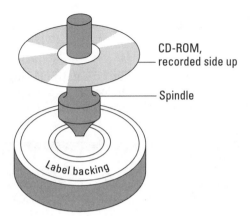

CD-ROM,
recorded side up

Spindle

Label backing

Figure 14.19 The NEATO CD labeling device

■   ■   ■   ■   ■   ■   ■   ■   ■   ■   ■   ■   ■   ■   ■   ■

Designing a CD Menu

In Chapter 11, I introduce you to the idea of adding HTML to your recorded discs. As I mentioned there, you can use an HTML editor to help automate the creation of your menu. In this section, I use Netscape Composer, which is a good choice for a single-level menu example. (If you're familiar with coding more complex HTML, then you can expand the simple menu I build here within your own editor.)

This menu will be added to a disc I'm recording that contains material from one of my Web sites. Our example menu will include download links for text files and an image, a link to my e-mail address, and a link to the Web site itself. This is what I call a "balanced menu."

Cross-Reference

In Chapter 11, "Adding HTML Step-by-Step," I discuss balanced CD menus in more detail.

MATERIALS

Computer with an Internet connection

Installed copy of Netscape Communicator with Composer

Programming Your CD Menu

To create a balanced menu for your CD:

1. Run Netscape Composer from the Windows 98 Start menu by clicking Start and choosing Programs ⇨ Netscape Communicator ⇨ Netscape Composer. The program displays the main window shown in Figure 14.20.

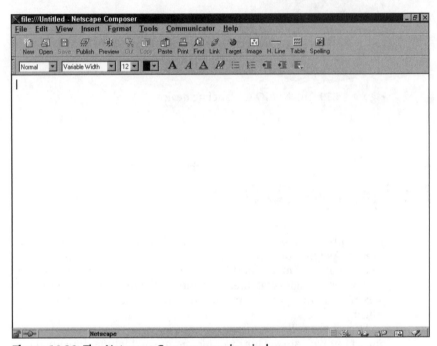

Figure 14.20 The Netscape Composer main window

2. Click the File menu, select New, and choose Page from Wizard.

Note

To use the graphics available from Netscape, you have to be connected to the Internet!

3. Click Start.

4. Click the Give your page a title link in the left window. Enter the title **My Example Menu** and click Apply to display the change in the Preview window.

5. Next, scroll through the left window to the Looks section and click the A preset color combination link. The color combinations shown in Figure 14.21 appear — click one to apply it. (I choose the second combination.)

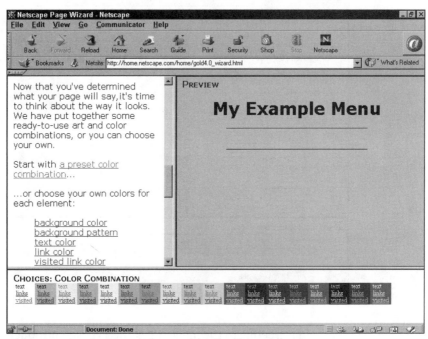

Figure 14.21 Selecting a color combination for our menu

6. Now let's add links to download an image and a text file to the computer's hard drive. Click the Add some hot links to other Web pages link, and enter the text **Download my photo catalog!** in the Name field. In the URL field, type **/photos/catalog.zip** and click Apply. (When the disc is recorded, you should create a folder in your CD layout called photos, where the catalog.zip file should be saved.)

7. Add another link in the same fashion, but enter the text **Download my file catalog!** in the Name field. In the URL field, type **/files/catalog.doc** and click Apply. (Once again, you must create a folder called files within your CD layout that contains catalog.doc for this to work.)

8. Don't forget a link to the Web site! Add a third link with the text **Visit my Web site!** and the URL **http://batcave.somewhere.net** to create a Web link. Your Preview window should now look something like Figure 14.22.

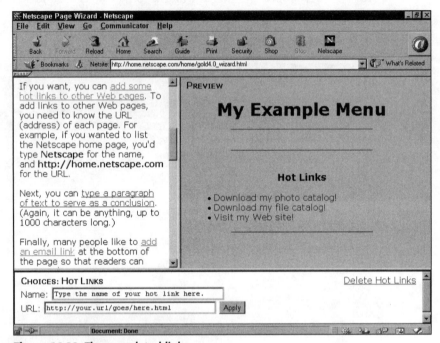

Figure 14.22 The completed links

9. Let's add a greeting to the menu. Click the Type an introduction link and enter a short introduction to your disc, then click Apply to add it to the Preview window.

10. Finally, let's add an e-mail link. Click Add an email link, type in your e-mail address, and click Apply. Your Preview window should now look something like the example I've created in Figure 14.23.

11. Now scroll to the bottom of the left window and click Build to prepare the HTML code. The finished menu is displayed in Communicator, as shown in Figure 14.24.

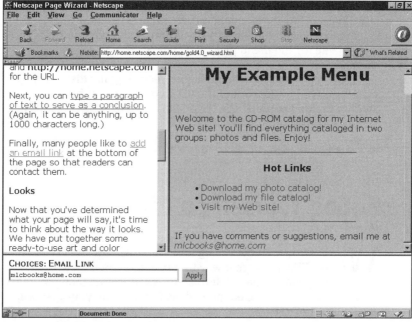

Figure 14.23 Our completed menu, ready to build

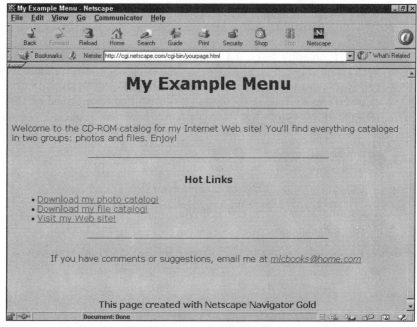

Figure 14.24 The completed menu as it appears in Communicator

12. Click the File menu and select Save As to save the menu page to your hard drive. (I recommend that you create a new folder, so that you can easily locate the file and any graphics that you may add later.) Enter a name for the menu page and click Save.

You've just created a menu! Before recording my disc, I copy the HTML file that I've saved to the root of the CD layout — remember, for the download links that we created to work, the HTML file must not be saved within a folder.

■   ■   ■   ■   ■   ■   ■   ■   ■   ■   ■   ■   ■   ■

Promoting Yourself on CD

Whether you are advertising for your small business or running for public office, CDs are a great way to mix audio and data to create an attractive yet compelling promotional ad. If this idea excites you, then you're ready to try your hand at recording a mixed-mode disc. In this case, your disc will contain two different types of data:

■ The digital pages of a print advertising campaign saved as Word documents, and all of the clip art and fonts needed to reproduce those pages.

■ The audio tracks you've created for the radio promotional spots that will supplement the print campaign.

This is an application that's perfect as a demonstration of a mixed-mode CD; both types of data can be retrieved on a computer from a single disc. (Remember, you can't play a mixed-mode CD in an audio CD player, so audio tracks you record must be played back on a computer — or, in this case, saved as MP3 files on the radio station's computer. To create a disc that can be played on your stereo's CD player, create a CD Extra disc by following the instructions in the next section.)

MATERIALS

Computer with a CD-R or CD-RW drive

Installed copy of Easy CD Creator

Blank CD-R disc

Digital audio tracks in MP3 format, images, and word processing documents

Recording a Mixed-Mode CD

To create this type of mixed-mode CD:

1. Run Easy CD Creator program from the Windows 98 Start menu by clicking Start and choosing Programs ⇨ Adaptec Easy CD Creator 4 ⇨ Features ⇨ Easy CD Creator.

2. Click the File menu, select New CD Layout, and choose Mixed-Mode CD. Notice that the screen shown in Figure 14.25 is slightly different from a typical data CD layout.

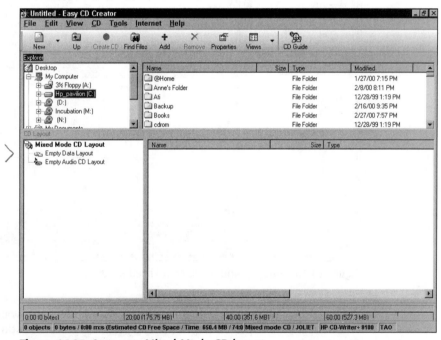

Figure 14.25 An empty Mixed-Mode CD layout

3. Within the Explorer display at the top right of the Layout window, navigate through your hard drive until you find the files and folders to record. Click the icon for the file or folder you want to add to your data CD to highlight it. To highlight multiple files and folders, hold down the Ctrl key while you click each icon.

4. Click Add to add the files and folders to the data portion of the layout.

5. Repeat steps 3 and 4 until you've added all the files you want to the layout.

6. Now click the Empty Audio CD Layout in the CD Layout window to add your audio tracks—note that the Easy CD Creator screen changes to an Audio CD layout, as shown in Figure 14.26.

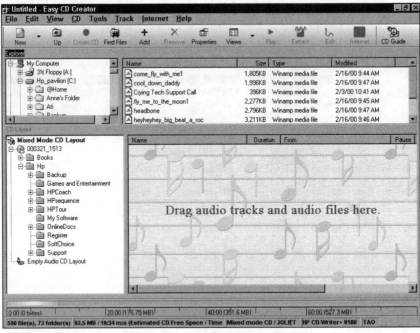

Figure 14.26 Ready to add tracks to a Mixed-Mode CD

7. Navigate through your system and locate the audio files you want to record using the Explorer display, or copy tracks from an existing audio CD by loading it and selecting that drive to display the tracks as "files."

8. Click the audio files to highlight them. To select multiple files, hold down the Ctrl key while you click.

9. Click Add in the toolbar to copy the files.

10. Repeat steps 7, 8, and 9 until you've added all the tracks you want to the audio layout. Your Mixed-Mode layout should look something like Figure 14.27.

11. Click the Create CD button in the toolbar, and complete the recording process as you normally would with a standard data CD.

Tip

Remember, if you're sending your disc to another computer, don't forget to close the CD after the recording has completed. If necessary, click Advanced in the CD Creation Setup dialog box to set this option. I'd also recommend Track-at-Once recording for a Mixed-Mode CD.

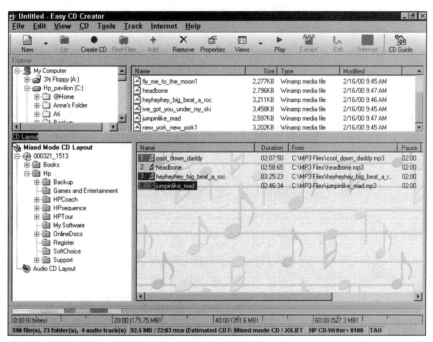

Figure 14.27 A completed Mixed-Mode CD layout

Recording Music and Video on CD

Earlier in the book, I mention CD Extra discs—a special format that places the audio tracks first on a multisession CD, followed by a separate session containing computer data. Unlike Mixed-Mode CDs, CD Extra discs are perfect for carrying a combination of Red Book audio and data. They can be played on both a standard audio CD player and a computer's CD-ROM drive.

In this section, we create a CD Extra disc for your up-and-coming rock band, with a number of MP3 files as the audio component, followed by a data track containing the band's latest video!

MATERIALS

Computer with a CD-R or CD-RW drive

Installed copy of Easy CD Creator

Blank CD-R disc

Digital audio and digital video files

Creating your CD Extra Disc

To record music and video on a CD Extra disc:

1. Run Easy CD Creator program from the Windows 98 Start menu by clicking Start and choosing Programs ➪ Adaptec Easy CD Creator 4 ➪ Features ➪ Easy CD Creator.

2. Click the File menu, select New CD Layout, and choose CD Extra to display the layout shown in Figure 14.28.

3. Click the Empty Audio CD Layout in the CD Layout window to add your audio tracks.

4. Navigate through your system and locate the audio files you want to record using the Explorer display. You can also copy tracks from an existing audio CD by loading it and selecting that drive to display the tracks.

5. Click the audio files to highlight them. To select multiple files, hold down the Ctrl key while you click.

6. Click Add in the toolbar to copy the files.

7. Repeat steps 4, 5, and 6 until you've added all the tracks you want to the audio layout.

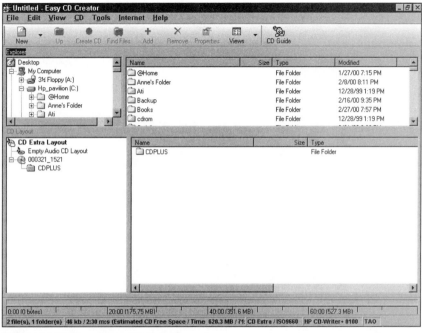

Figure 14.28 An empty CD Extra layout

8. Click the disc icon in the CD Layout window to add files and folders to the disc. Note that the volume label for the data session is automatically assigned, but you can change this if you like by clicking the label. The files and folders you add do not need to be added into the CDPLUS folder — this folder is automatically added by Easy CD Creator to hold information you enter for the audio tracks.

Warning

Don't delete the CDPLUS directory or any of the files it contains!

9. Within the Explorer display at the top right of the Layout window, navigate through your hard drive until you find the files and folders to record. Click the icon for the file or folder you want to add to your data CD to highlight it; hold down the Ctrl key while you click each icon to highlight multiple files and folders.

10. Click Add to add the files and folders to the data portion of the layout.

11. Repeat steps 9 and 10 until you've added all the files you want to the layout. Your finished layout should look something like Figure 14.29.

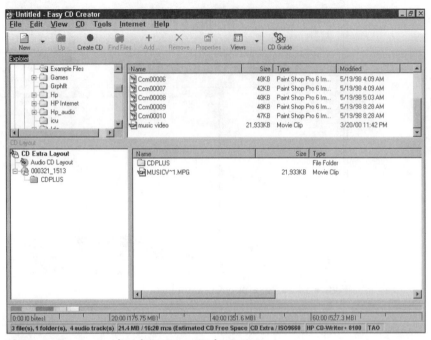

Figure 14.29 A completed CD Extra CD layout

12. If you like, you can enter additional information that can be displayed by audio CD players that support the full CD Extra format. To do this, click File and choose CD Layout Properties, then click the CD Extra tab to display the dialog box shown in Figure 14.30. All fields in this dialog box are optional. Click the Created: and Published: drop-down list boxes to choose the desired date from a calendar pop-up display, and type text directly into the other fields. Once you're done, click OK to save the information to your layout.

13. Click the Create CD button in the toolbar, and complete the recording process as you normally would with a standard data CD.

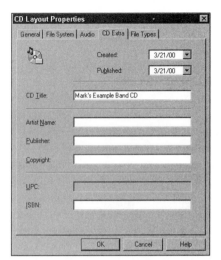

Figure 14.30 Entering CD Extra information before recording the CD

In Review

In this chapter of advanced projects, you used Easy CD Creator, Ritz Camera Photo Manager, VCD Creator, Netscape Composer, and Jewel Case Creator to record a Video CD, a photo album slideshow disc, a mixed-mode promotional CD, and a CD Extra disc that contains both music and video. In addition to that, you also created a professional-looking custom disc label and jewel case insert for a n audio disc, and you made your data CD more accessible by creating a multimedia HTML menu.

APPENDIX

A

Troubleshooting Recording Problems

IN THIS APPENDIX

- Buffer underrun problems
- Common recording problems
- Problems while reading recorded CDs

I n this appendix, I provide possible solutions for the problems you may encounter while recording discs.

Note

Although this book focuses on Adaptec's Easy CD Creator and DirectCD programs, the errors and solutions I describe here should apply to any CD recording software.

Buffer Underrun Problems

One of the most common problems you'll encounter while recording discs is the dreaded buffer underrun error. Although an underrun can be caused by a number of factors, the end result is the same: your computer can't transfer data to the CD recorder at the necessary rate to ensure a successful recording. Try these solutions:

- **Record at a slower speed.** Although your system may not be able to support the highest speeds available with your recorder, you can always record at a slower speed—for example, if you can't record at 8x, try recording at 4x instead.

- **Record from a disc image.** Rather than recording a number of smaller files "on-the-fly," try creating a disc image and then record from the image—this is much more efficient and requires less overhead.

- **Don't multitask while recording.** Dedicate the entire resources of your computer to recording by shutting down all unnecessary applications (including those running on the Windows taskbar).

- **Defragment before recording.** A defragmented drive transfers data significantly faster.

- **Use the fastest drive on your system.** Whenever possible, choose the fastest drive on your system as the location for source data and temporary files created by your recording software.

- **Use simulation/test mode.** If you're unsure about the possibility of a buffer underrun error after trying the previously mentioned tips, there's no reason why you still can't attempt a recording—the trick is to use your recording software's simulation or test mode first, before the actual recording begins. If the data can be successfully recorded in test mode, you can be certain there will be little likelihood of errors during the recording process.

Common Recording Problems

If you've been recording discs for some time, you're likely to encounter one or two of these common errors:

My computer locks up when I try to record, and I don't know why.

- **Create a log file.** Because your computer locks up and you don't see an error message, use the log file option if your recording software supports it — the log file may contain error messages that help in troubleshooting the problem.

- **Reinstall CD recorder drivers.** If your recorder doesn't work at all, your drive's software drivers have probably been corrupted or deleted. Reinstall the software drivers that you received with your drive, or download the updated drivers from the manufacturer's Web site and install them.

- **Check your SCSI termination and device IDs.** If either is configured improperly, a SCSI CD recorder will probably not work at all, and trying to use the device will likely lock up your system.

My recording software tells me that the blank disc I'm loading isn't empty, doesn't have enough room, or is incompatible.

- **Reformat.** If you're writing a CD-RW disc, this error message often indicates either that the disc has not been formatted or that a previous formatting operation was interrupted before it could complete. Reformat your CD-RW to refresh it.

- **Wrong disc type.** Naturally, you won't be able to use a blank CD-RW disc in an older recorder that records only CD-R — however, this message can also be caused by attempting to write 80-minute "extended" discs in an older recorder (a process called overburning).

- **Reinstall CD recorder drivers.** This error message is can also be caused by corrupted or deleted software drivers — in effect, your CD recorder actually thinks there is data on that disc. Reinstall the software drivers that you received with your drive, or download the updated drivers from the manufacturer's Web site and install them.

- **Previous session.** You may be running out of room on the disc because of a previous session that you've recorded — within Easy CD Creator, you can click the CD menu and select the CD Information menu item to display the disc summary and see if that disc is *really* blank.

- **Bad media.** Although it doesn't happen often, it's certainly possible that the blank disc you're trying to use is bad. Try recording with another disc from another manufacturer.

The CD recorder keeps telling me it's not ready — it won't eject the disc — it just sits there!

- **Mounting delay.** Some CD recorders take longer than others to recognize a blank CD (or if you're trying to read an existing audio CD, to extract tracks). It's important to wait until the drive is ready before continuing — check your recorder's documentation for specifics on front panel indicators that you can use to determine when the drive is ready.

- **Lead-in/lead-out recording.** There may not actually be a problem with your recorder — instead, it may still be recording the lead-in or lead-out portions of the disc. Unfortunately, many recording programs don't indicate these delays (which occur at the beginning and end of most recording sessions), and it's easy to think that your computer is locked up. Give your recorder at least a couple of minutes to finish this processing.

- **Check your SCSI termination and device IDs.** This is another classic symptom of an incorrect SCSI installation. Run the diagnostic software supplied by your SCSI adapter card or drive's manufacturer to verify that you've correctly installed the drive.

- **Reinstall CD recorder drivers.** Your drive's software drivers may have been corrupted or deleted. Reinstall the software drivers that you received with your drive, or download the updated drivers from the manufacturer's Web site and install them.

I get a fixation error when I try to write a new session to this disc. What's the problem?

- **Interrupted recording.** You may receive this message if the recording session is interrupted by a power failure or your computer locks up. Unfortunately, the disc may be unreadable — however, you can try using Session Selector to read data from the disc. (If it's a multisession disc, you should be able to read data from previous sessions this way.)

- **Attempt a recovery of the data.** If you're using Easy CD Creator, you may be able to recover some or all of the data even if the fixation process didn't complete properly. Click the CD menu and select the CD Information menu item to display the disc summary — if your recorder is able to recognize the data on the disc, use the Recover feature to attempt fixation again.

I can't record my MPEG, AVI, MOV, or ASF files to a Video CD.

- **Compression/codec problems.** Your recording software may not support the compression and codec used to record a particular video clip. If possible, use a video editing program to convert them to the standards supported by your recording software.

- **Unsupported formats.** Although most Video CD recording programs recognize AVI and MPEG, your video clips may be in a format that your recording software can't handle. Again, use a video editing program to convert them if possible.

The Windows (or Mac OS) long filenames on my hard drive are truncated on the disc I recorded.

■ **Long filenames not enabled.** If you're recording a disc for a Windows system, use Microsoft Joliet file format, which enables long filenames, instead of ISO 9660 file format. If you're writing a Mac disc, check the documentation for your recording software to determine where you can enable support within the program for long filenames.

My recording software says it won't allow me to create a nested folder.

■ **Use Microsoft Joliet.** You're attempting to create a disc using the ISO 9660 file format, which won't allow more than eight levels of nested folders (subdirectories). Use Microsoft Joliet if possible, or disable DOS/ISO 9660 conventions. You also have a limitation of 255 characters on your pathname under ISO 9660.

Problems While Reading Recorded CDs

Consider these solutions for the general problems that crop up with CD recording:

I can read the discs I record everywhere except for one particular CD-ROM drive. What's wrong?

■ **Drive is not a MultiRead model.** Most older CD-ROM drives can't read a CD-RW disc you've recorded because the frequency of the laser is too weak. Record the data on a standard CD-R instead.

■ **Alignment problems.** It's possible that the drive is incorrectly calibrated — if this is the case, it will probably have problems reading any recorded CDs (and possibly might even return errors with a commercial disc)! Bring the drive to your local computer repair shop and ask the technician to check it.

■ **Media incompatibilities.** Some CD-ROM drives and CD recorders simply don't work well with certain combinations of dye color and reflective layers — for example, a drive may be able to read a recorded CD that uses a blue dye layer and silver reflective layer, but it may not reliably read a recorded CD with a green dye layer and a gold reflective layer. Try reading a disc recorded with another combination of dye color and reflective layer.

My CD-ROM drive doesn't recognize the disc I just recorded. Did I make a mistake?

■ **Dirty disc.** Dust, grease, and oil on the surface of a CD can prevent your drive from reading data. Follow the cleaning procedure I describe earlier in the book.

- **Session remains open.** If you recorded a session and left it open, a standard CD-ROM drive will not be able to read it — you have to either close the session using Easy CD Creator or read the disc in your CD recorder.

- **Auto insert notification disabled.** If a program is supposed to automatically run when you load the disc, try using Windows Explorer to run the program from the disc — if you can, then Auto insert notification has been disabled within the Properties panel for the drive you're using.

- **Unrecognized format.** Depending on the recording format you used, a disc created on the Macintosh may not be recognized by a PC. Consider recording cross-platform discs in true ISO 9660 format.

- **Faulty recording.** Although rare, it is possible for a recording program to indicate that a disc has been recorded successfully, when in fact something went wrong during the process. Check and see if you can read your new disc from the recorder or another CD-ROM drive.

I hear a click between every track of the audio CDs I've recorded.

- **Use Disc-at-Once.** This problem usually appears only on some audio CD players — in fact, you may be able to listen to the disc on another player without any problem at all. You should be able to eliminate these clicks by recording your audio CDs using Disc-at-Once mode (if your recorder supports it), which enables the laser to record the entire disc without shutting off between tracks — this area between the tracks is causing the clicks.

The MP3 tracks I recorded to my audio CD play in mono instead of stereo, and some of them are "chopped off."

- **Sub-standard MP3 files.** Not every MP3 file you receive is recorded with CD quality, and it's likely that the original audio was recorded in mono. Also, it's a good idea to preview an entire MP3 track *before* you record it, because these files are often badly edited!

I'm having problems trying to read a disc I recorded for a Linux/UNIX system.

- **Use ISO 9660.** Most variants of these operating systems don't recognize Joliet or Mac HPFS file formats, so use ISO 9660 file format when recording for Linux/UNIX.

- **Case-sensitivity.** Linux and UNIX are case-sensitive, which may cause problems when running programs directly from the disc.

I can play the audio tracks, but I can't read the data track on a CD Extra disc on my computer.

- **Unsupported format.** Your computer's CD-ROM drive doesn't support the CD Extra format.

- **Disc incorrectly closed.** The data track may have been incorrectly saved. If you're using Easy CD Creator, load the disc into your CD recorder, click the CD menu, and select the CD Information menu item to display the disc summary. If your recorder is able to recognize the data on the disc, use the Recover feature to attempt fixation again.

I can't read Kodak PhotoCDs on my computer.

- **Proprietary format.** Discs created for use on a Kodak PhotoCD player cannot be used on a computer, and your recorder can't create Kodak PhotoCDs — they use a proprietary format.

My CD and DVD drives refuse to recognise CD's, though I know they work alright at other times.

APPENDIX

B

Hewlett-Packard Technical Support's Frequently Asked Questions

Thix appendix contains material concerning CD recording collected by the Hewlett-Packard technical support staff at Customer Care Centers around the world.

Note

If you don't own an HP CD recorder, you'll still find this appendix a valuable resource. Although the solutions presented in this appendix address specific drives manufactured by Hewlett-Packard, much of this material applies to any CD-RW drive used on a PC under Windows 95, 98, or 2000, or under Windows NT.

Frequently Asked Questions

Take a look at the following questions and problems to see if your particular situation is covered. Or if you prefer, check out the Hewlett-Packard CD Writer home page at http://www.hpcdwriter.com/.

How much can I fit on a 74-minute CD?

For audio, the answer is simple enough: you can place 74 minutes of audio on a 74-minute CD. Some people believe that this can vary if you are using the option to write in DAO (Disc at Once), which takes out the two-second gaps between tracks. This process will not actually increase the disc capacity, but it will maximize the 74 minutes that are available. Audio is a fairly simple calculation; data burns, by contrast, introduce some complicated variables.

Easy CD-Creator

Using this software, you should be able to place 650 megabytes of data on the disc.

DirectCD

Using this software, you will find that capacity depends on whether you are using a CD-R or CD-RW disc. CD-R, when formatted with DirectCD, usually will have between 550 and 600 megabytes left after format. A CD-RW disc will generally have between 500 and 550 megabytes left after format.

Why do my recorded audio CDs hiss and pop?

This is caused primarily by the source drive used to extract the audio tracks for burning. Many older CD-ROM drives were not designed to perform the audio extraction technique required by the HP CD-Writer drive at a fast enough speed. Errors normally not audible in the source content often surface during this process. To test and verify the issue, use the HP CD-Writer drive as the source and the destination drive for an audio CD burn. Select the HP CD-Writer drive as both the source and the destination drive in CD-Copier Deluxe. On the resulting disc, the audio quality should be corrected. If this resolves the issue, you may continue to use the HP CD-Writer drive as your source drive, or you may wish to investigate a new CD-ROM for you computer, capable of faster audio extraction.

Why can't I read my recorded CDs on another computer?

There are a few different issues that can affect what we call "disc interchange," or reading a burned CD on another computer system or CD device.

CD-R versus CD-RW Media

CD-R discs are recommended for any CDs you wish to take to another computer system. CD-RW can be used, but some older CD-ROM readers will have problems accessing the information on these discs. If the CD-ROM reader has a MultiRead icon like the one you see on the CD-Writer, then that drive will be able to read RW media.

Using Adaptec's DirectCD

If you are using a CD-R disc, formatted with DirectCD, an options window appears when you eject these discs. The window will give you a choice to leave the disc "open" for further writing or to "close" the disc to be read on other computers. Choosing the second option will place a Table of Contents on the CD that most CD-ROMs need in order to access the information. If you are using CD-RW discs, you will not see the eject options, because these CDs cannot be "closed." Because of the specialized format that DirectCD uses, even after the disc is "closed" to be read on other computers, many systems will not be able to read these discs. The reason for this is two-fold:

1. If the formatted DirectCD disc is not closed, either by choice, or because it is RW and cannot be closed, you must install Adaptec's DirectCD Reader software on the computer you wish to read the CD from. This will allow Windows to make sense of the UDF format, the file system DirectCD uses.

2. If the CD-ROM is not MultiRead capable, you will not be able to read the CD, either with DirectCD Reader installed, or with the DirectCD disc "closed." This is because the data on a DirectCD disc is written in packets of information, rather than in tracks, like a standard CD. If the CD-ROM drive is not MultiRead capable, then it also means that the drive is not packet-tolerant, and it will not be able to access the information regardless of how it's prepared.

Using Adaptec's Easy CD Creator or CD Copier Deluxe

These two burning applications from Adaptec write to the CD in the standard track format, adding a Table of Contents to the end of the session. This method of writing is most widely recognized by other CD devices and will increase the chance for successful "disc interchange."

Even with this method, however, the preceding information about CD-RW media still applies. Using Easy CD Creator or CD Copier Deluxe with RW media may still create difficulties reading the information, unless the reader device is MultiRead capable. Using CD-R with this software, however, affords you the best chance of reading your created CDs on another computer and is the recommended method.

How do I clean my HP CD-Writer drive?

The HP CD-Writer Plus drive requires no maintenance or cleaning. If you simply keep your CDs clean, you will prevent most problems.

Warning

Do not attempt to use the CD-ROM cleaning CDs that use a small brush to sweep dirt off the laser mechanism. Do not use high-pressure air to clean the inside of the drive. These techniques will damage the HP CD-Writer Plus drive.

How do I create discs for other operating systems?

The process for setting up the software is simple. Click File on the menu, select CD Layout Properties, and then select ISO 9660 from the drop-down menu. This will set the software to burn the CD in the most universal format available. Even with the disc burned properly, there are some things to keep in mind:

1. The naming structure of any files you will be burning must meet the 8.3-character naming convention set forth in DOS. Additionally, if you select an option other than MS-DOS 8.3-character naming, the software will allow you to use more types of characters (*&%$#), but this will make the CD less likely to be readable on another operating system.

2. Remember that even though you can create a disc that another system can read, the code within the files may not make sense to a given operating system. For example, if you create a CD for a Macintosh computer containing a program written for Windows 98, the Mac's CD-ROM drive will be able to see it but the Mac will not be able to run the program.

How do I change CD device drive letters in Windows 95 and 98 and Windows NT?

After you physically install your CD recorder, Windows often places the original CD-ROM at a lower drive letter and gives the original drive letter to the HP SureStore CD-Writer. Some users prefer their devices to have specific drive letter associations, and occasionally, some programs will keep a record of what drive letter to use for certain processes. Both of these factors make it necessary to be able to change drive letters on certain devices. Windows allows the user control over the drive letter assignments.

Warning

Changing drive letter assignments can have adverse effects on a computer system if the letter being requested is already in use by another device. This is especially the case if the computer has network drives that are mapped and given letter assignments. Make sure to verify that the drive letter desired is not in use by another device.

Changing Drive Assignments in Windows 95 and 98

To change a drive assignment in Windows 95 and 98:

1. Right-click My Computer and choose Properties.

2. Click the Device Manager tab, and then click (+) next to CD-ROM. All CD devices should be listed here.

3. Double-click the CD-Writer in the list and then click the Settings tab.

4. Click the Starting drive letter and Ending drive letter fields and enter the desired letter.

If the starting drive letter and ending drive letter cannot be changed to the desired letter, usually either another device is using that letter or software present on the system is configuring these settings from a different location. If the system contains software that configures the drive letters elsewhere, it will be necessary to uninstall that software or to make the desired changes from within that software, instead of in Device Manager.

Changing Drive Assignments in Windows NT

To change a drive assignment in Windows NT:

1. Log in using an account with Administrative Rights on the system.

2. Click the Start button. Click Programs, then Administrative Tools, then Disk Administrator.

3. Left-click the rectangle representing the device that needs the letter change.

4. Click Assign Drive Letter. Choose the desired drive letter in the list box.

Why are files that are copied from a recorded CD to the hard drive assigned the Read-Only attribute on the hard drive?

This will always be the case with CD-R media, as they are read-only media. This is actually one of the more important features of CD technology in that data is virtually incorruptible once it's written to disc. It cannot be accidentally overwritten or erased when the disc has been closed. The most straightforward approach to resolving this problem is to change the attributes of the files after copying them to the hard drive. This procedure is accomplished by selecting the files individually or as a group, right-clicking the mouse button, and choosing "Properties." The dialog box that appears enables you to remove the "Read Only" attribute.

I was formatting a disc with DirectCD and the process was interrupted . . . now I can't use the disc! Can I fix this?

If power is lost while a CD-RW disc is being formatted, the disc will become unusable in any application, and it will fail if another format is attempted.

To solve this problem, use the Easy CD Creator Erase feature to fully erase the disc, then try the format operation again.

Can I play an audio CD on either my internal HP CD-Writer Plus drive or my CD-ROM if my sound card has only one input?

Yes. Use an audio "Y" cable connector. Some of these connectors require that a small switch be installed in the system case. Toggling the switch will enable you to select either drive for playback. Some newer sound cards allow two devices to be connected, so check with your sound card manufacturer before buying a "Y" cable connector.

Note

Some sound cards have more than one audio connector, but they're not suitable for connecting two devices—the extra connector is only to accommodate different styles of audio cables. Attaching more than one CD-ROM/CD-Writer to these types of sound cards is not recommended. Check with your sound card manufacturer before connecting more than one drive. For example, some versions of the Sound Blaster Live sound card have an SP/DIF digital input, which is not compatible with the output from the HP CD-Writer plus drive.

Why did my 10x HP CD-Writer Plus 9300/9310 drive include a blank 8x CD-R disc?

Early HP CD-Writer Plus 9300 series drives shipped with a blank 8x CD-R disc. Please be assured that the 8x-labeled media are fully compatible with your 10x drive. Be sure your computer system meets the minimum system requirements for the 9300 series drives.

Should I use CD-R or CD-RW for my project?

Table B.1 suggests which type of media you should use for various tasks.

Table B.1 Suggested Uses for CD-RW and CD-R Discs		
Task	*CD-RW*	*CD-R*
Create and update large documents, saving over previous versions.	X	
Transport work files to and from home.	X	
Back up your hard drive weekly.	X	
Continuously write, rewrite, and delete files.	X	
Distribute documents for CD-RW or MultiRead CD-ROM drives.	X	
Remove all files for completed projects from your hard drive.	X	
Distribute large presentations to virtually anyone, anywhere.		X
Store and share scanned photos and memorabilia.		X
Save your own music to CD.		X
Back up important computer files and archive them permanently.		X

Glossary

A

Adapter card

A circuit board that you plug into your computer to add functionality—for instance, you might install a SCSI adapter card in your computer to use an external SCSI CD-RW drive.

AIFF

A digital audio format that's very popular in the Macintosh world. You can use AIFF files to record CD-quality stereo sound in Red Book audio CD format.

B

Binary

Binary is the language used by computers. Binary data is composed of only two values, zero and 1.

Bootable CD

A CD-ROM containing the operating system and support files necessary to boot a computer without a hard drive. Bootable CD-ROMs are recorded in the *El Torito* format.

Byte

A single character of text stored in your computer's RAM or hard drive.

C

Caddy

A thin plastic box that held a CD within a CD-ROM drive; to load a disc, you first loaded it into the caddy, and then the caddy went into the drive. Caddy drives have been replaced by tray-loading drives.

Case

The metal chassis that surrounds your computer and holds all of the parts. Most computer cases have a separate cover that you can unscrew and remove; other cases are one-piece and open with a hinged door.

CD Extra

A CD Extra disc can contain both audio and data tracks. Because the audio track is recorded first on the disc, a CD Extra disc can also be played in a regular audio CD player.

CD-R

Short for *Compact Disc–Recordable*. A CD-R disc can store computer data and digital audio. Information is recorded by altering a layer of dye with a laser beam. CD-R discs can be recorded once; they cannot be reused like a CD-RW disc.

CD-ROM

Short for *Compact Disc–Read-Only Memory*. A CD-ROM is a compact disc recorded for use on a computer.

CD-ROM XA

A multisession CD-ROM XA disc can store separate recording sessions on the same disc. Older CD-ROM drives may not be able to read discs recorded in this format.

CD-RW

Short for *Compact Disc–Rewritable*. A CD-RW disc can store information like a CD-R disc, but the dye layer is replaced by a crystalline amorphous layer, so the disc can be erased and rewritten over and over.

Cost-per-megabyte

A measurement of the cost-efficiency of mass storage often quoted by the manufacturers of hard drives and removable drives. Cost-per-megabyte is calculated by determining the number of cents it costs to record one megabyte of data.

Crystalline layer

A layer of amorphous crystalline structure in a CD-RW disc that darkens or discolors when struck by a recorder's laser beam at high power. An opaque area within the crystalline layer prevents the laser in a CD-ROM drive from reflecting, so it acts the same as a pit on a commercially made CD-ROM. Unlike the dye in a CD-R disc, the crystalline layer can be "reset" and the disc can be used again.

D

Data buffer

An internal memory buffer built into every CD recorder that holds data from your hard drive until it's ready to be recorded. The temporary data storage provided by the data buffer helps maintain an efficient flow of data to the recorder.

Defragmenting

The process of reading files from your hard drive and rewriting them in contiguous form, one after another. If a file is written as a contiguous whole, it takes less time to read and send it to your CD recorder. Defragmenting utilities are available for both Windows and Mac OS.

Digital audio extraction

Most CD-ROM drives can extract the digital audio from the tracks on an existing audio CD. This must be done before recording the digital audio to a new audio CD.

DIP switches

Like jumpers, DIP switches are used to configure hardware devices. DIP switches may use a bank of either tiny sliding switches or rocker switches that can be set in different positions. You can set these switches with the tip of a pen.

Disc-at-Once

An advanced recording mode, where the laser write head writes the entire disc at once without turning the recording laser off between tracks. Older CD recorders may not be able to record discs in disc-at-once mode.

Disc image

A file saved to your hard drive that contains all of the information necessary to create a CD, ready to be recorded whenever you need it.

DVD

Short for *digital video disc*. Although similar in appearance to a standard compact disc, a DVD disc can hold anywhere from 4.7GB to 17GB. DVD discs can hold both computer data and movies in MPEG format.

Dye layer

A layer of dye in a CD-R disc that darkens or discolors when struck by a recorder's laser beam at high power. An opaque area within the dye layer prevents the laser in a CD-ROM drive from reflecting, so it acts the same as a pit on a commercially made CD-ROM.

E

EIDE

EIDE, which is short for *Enhanced Integrated Drive Electronics,* is the most common interface for connecting CD-ROM drives and CD recorders to today's PCs. A typical PC has both primary and secondary EIDE connectors. Each connector can handle two EIDE devices for a total of four drives.

El Torito format

The format standard used to record bootable CD-ROM discs.

External drive

A computer component that sits outside your computer and is connected by a cable to your computer; it has a separate external case and power cord.

F

FAQ

Short for *Frequently Asked Questions*. A text file containing the answers to the most common questions posed on a subject. Many Web sites, newsgroups, and mailing lists have a FAQ available for new arrivals to read.

Formatting

The process of preparing a hard drive to store data — if you're using Adaptec's DirectCD or recording a CD-RW disc, you'll have to format the blank disc first as well.

G

Gigabyte

A unit of data equal to 1,024MB (megabytes).

H

Hard drive

A computer component that provides permanent storage for your programs and data, enabling you to save and delete files whenever you like.

HFS

Short for *Hierarchical File System*. A CD-ROM file system used on the Macintosh.

HTML

Short for *Hypertext Markup Language*. The programming language used to create pages for use on the World Wide Web (which can also be used to create menu pages for your recorded CDs).

HTML Editor

A program used to create new HTML pages or edit existing pages.

HTML Tag

A separate line in an HTML file that determines the display or specifies the contents of the page.

I

Incremental multisession disc

A multisession disc that enables you to import data from the previous session for use in a new session (effectively "updating" the previous data that you've recorded).

Interface

A standard method of connecting a hardware device to your computer. Common interfaces for CD recorders include EIDE, SCSI, and USB.

Internal drive

A computer component that fits inside your computer's case, much like your floppy or hard drive.

ISO 9660

The standard CD-ROM file system recognized by virtually all operating systems in use today—the best choice for recording a CD-ROM with the best possible compatibility with a wide range of operating systems. ISO 9660 doesn't support long filenames.

J

Jewel box

A plastic storage case for a compact disc. Most audio CDs and blank CD-R/CD-RW discs are packaged in jewel boxes. Some CD recording programs can create a custom-printed insert for the front and back of a jewel box.

Joliet file system

A CD-ROM file system developed by Microsoft for Windows 95. Joliet supports long filenames of up to 64 characters, and names can include multiple periods and spaces.

Jumper

A *jumper* is small electrical crossover made of wire and plastic that connects two pins on a computer circuit board—this can include your computer's motherboard, an EIDE hard drive or CD recorder, or a SCSI device. To change the configuration of a computer component using jumpers, move the jumper to different positions to connect different sets of two pins as shown in the hardware documentation.

K

Kilobyte

A unit of data equal to 1,024 bytes.

L

Land

An area on the surface of a compact disc that reflects light. On a commercial disc, a land is simply a flat area; on a CD-R or CD-RW, a land is a clear area within the dye or crystalline layer.

Laser read head

All CD-ROM drives have a read head, which is a combination of the laser lens and the optical pickup and prism system that determines whether the beam was reflected or not. The read head is mounted on a movable track so that it can cover the entire surface of the disc.

Laser write head

Along with a laser read head, all CD recorders have a laser write head that can be toggled to high and low power levels — the different power levels can be toggled on and off to create the pits in a CD-R or CD-RW disc.

M

Master

An EIDE setting that indicates that the drive is the primary device on the EIDE cable. For example, an EIDE hard drive could be set to "single drive, master unit" (if it's the only drive on the cable) or "multiple drive, master unit" (if it's the primary drive and there is another device on the same cable).

Master disc

A glass disc created by a photoetching process. The master disc is used to create metal molds called stampers, which in turn are used to create compact discs.

Megabyte

A unit of data equal to 1,024KB (kilobytes).

Mixed-Mode disc

A Mixed-Mode disc has both digital audio tracks and a data track: the first track on the disc is recorded as computer data, while the following tracks are recorded as digital audio. A Mixed-Mode disc can't be played on a standard audio CD player.

Motherboard

The main circuit board in a computer that holds the processor, RAM chips, and most of the circuitry. Adapter cards plug into your motherboard.

MP3

A very popular digital audio format that's all the rage on the Web — you can record CD-quality stereo MP3 audio in Red Book audio CD format.

MPEG

Short for *Moving Pictures Expert Group*. MPEG format video is used on commercial DVD movie discs, and you can record your own Video CDs to watch MPEG format video clips.

Multisession

Discs recorded in multisession mode can carry separate recording sessions on the same disc. There are two different types of multisession disc: incremental (where only the last session is available) and multivolume (where all of the sessions can be accessed, but only one at a time).

Multitasking

Running more than one program or application on your computer at once.

Multivolume multisession disc

This type of multisession disc stores data in discrete volumes, each of which can be accessed. You can only read data from one volume at a time, and you can't modify the data stored on a session.

N

Network

A system of individual computers connected to each other, enabling data to be shared among machines. Computers connected to the network can also share resources such as printers, CD recorders, and modems.

P

Packet-writing

(Also called UDF, short for *Universal Disc Format*.) A method of recording data to a CD-RW drive without creating a layout; packet-writing software like Adaptec's DirectCD enables you to drag and drop files directly to the CD-RW drive icon in the same manner as you'd copy files to a floppy or hard drive.

Parallel port

Although the PC parallel port is traditionally used to connect a printer to your computer, there are CD recorders that connect to your parallel port as well. They are usually much slower and more prone to problems than drives that use other connection methods.

PCMCIA

Short for *Personal Computer Memory Card International Association,* also called PC cards. PCMCIA devices are used to connect hardware to your laptop or portable computer. A PC card can fit internally inside your laptop, or PCMCIA adapters can connect to external devices such as CD-ROM drives and CD recorders.

Pit

An area on the surface of a compact disc that scatters light and doesn't reflect it. On a commercial disc, a pit is a physical depression in the surface of the disc; on a CD-R or CD-RW, a pit is an opaque area within the dye or crystalline layer.

R

RAM

Short for *random access memory.* RAM modules store data needed by your computer to run your programs — once you've turned off your computer, however, you lose the data stored in RAM.

Random access

The file retrieval technique used by CD-ROM drives, CD recorders, and hard drives. A random-access drive can jump directly to a file no matter where it's recorded on the medium, and this process is much faster and more efficient than the sequential access used by tape drives.

Red Book

The international standard that specifies the layout of audio CDs and how they're recorded.

Restocking fee

A set amount of money charged by most online and local computer stores if you return an item.

S

SCAM

Short for *SCSI Configured Automatically.* A feature on some SCSI adapter cards: if all the devices on your drive chain are SCAM-compliant, you can set the card to automatically allocate SCSI ID numbers.

Screen printing

Most commercially made CD labels are screen-printed. The process involves adding layers of different-color ink through custom-made stencils to create a single multicolored image.

SCSI

Short for *Small Computer Systems Interface.* SCSI is the hard drive, CD-ROM, and CD recorder interface of choice for those who want speed, or who want to connect a large number of peripherals to their computers. Older Macintosh computers used SCSI hard drives, and it's been a popular interface for external peripherals for both PC and Macintosh.

SCSI ID

A unique number assigned to a SCSI device that identifies it to your SCSI adapter (and, in turn, to your computer's operating system). If you assign the same SCSI ID to two devices on the same computer, your computer will likely lock up.

Secure connection

Most online Web stores offer an encrypted (or secure) connection; when information is encrypted, it's much harder for a hacker to intercept your data as it's being transmitted to the Web site.

Slave

An EIDE setting that indicates that the drive is the primary device on the EIDE cable. For example, an EIDE hard drive could be set to "single drive, master unit" (if it's the only drive on the cable) or "multiple drive, master unit" (if it's the primary drive and there is another device on the same cable).

Slideshow

A computer program that displays digital images one after another on the computer's monitor.

Stampers

Metal molds used to create the pits and lands in a commercially manufactured compact disc.

Static electricity

Static electricity can damage any computer circuitry, so never touch a circuit board or open the case on your computer without first touching the metal frame of your computer. This discharges any static electricity on your body.

T

Terminator

All SCSI devices can be terminated with a switch or small resistor pack—if each end of a SCSI device chain isn't properly terminated, your computer won't be able to recognize the hardware.

Thumbwheel

A rotating selection control found on many SCSI drives that enables you to choose a unique SCSI ID for the device.

Track

On an audio CD, a track is a single section of audio (typically a single song) that you can jump to immediately. On a data CD, a track is simply a section of the CD-ROM that contains data—many CD-ROMs contain only a single data track that holds all of the information.

Track-at-Once

The most basic recording mode, where the laser write head writes each data and/or audio track individually; the recording laser is turned off between tracks.

U

UPC

Short for *Universal Product Code*. A unique number that identifies every commercially produced audio CD. Most computer audio CD player programs and audio CD cataloging programs can use the UPC number to identify the disc and recall the artist, title and track information.

USB

Short for *Universal Serial Bus*. USB ports are a popular method of connecting USB devices to most new PC and Macintosh computers. A USB device can be plugged in and used without rebooting your computer. USB supports a data transfer rate of up to 12 megabits per second.

V

Video CD

A recording format supported by most CD-RW drives that can store high-quality video discs for viewing on a video CD player, complete with menu system and freeze-frame.

Virtual memory

A method used by Windows and Mac OS to increase system RAM by temporarily using hard drive space. With virtual memory, your computer can run applications that require more RAM than you have available in your computer.

W

WAV

A standard format for digital sound developed by Microsoft. WAV files can be recorded in Red Book audio CD format using most CD recording software.

X

X factor

A speed benchmark used to indicate the speed of a CD recorder or CD-ROM drive. The X factor is the multiplier of the original transfer rate for a single-speed drive (150 kilobytes per second), so an 8x drive is eight times faster than an original single-speed CD-ROM drive.

Index

In CD

Your Online Source

- **Design a custom HP Pavilion PC system.** The "Customize Your Own System" feature allows

  you to personalize your HP Pavilion PC to your exact specifications.

- **Receive orders quickly.** Most orders are shipped the same day. Next-day and Saturday

  FedEx® delivery options are available.

ENTER OUR ONLINE SWEEPSTAKES

my2cents.idgbooks.com

Register This Book — And Win!

Visit **http://my2cents.idgbooks.com** to register this book and we'll automatically enter you in our fantastic monthly prize giveaway. It's also your opportunity to give us feedback: let us know what you thought of this book and how you would like to see other topics covered.

Discover IDG Books Online!

The IDG Books Online Web site is your online resource for tackling technology — at home and at the office. Frequently updated, the IDG Books Online Web site features exclusive software, insider information, online books, and live events!

10 Productive & Career-Enhancing Things You Can Do at www.idgbooks.com

- Nab source code for your own programming projects.

- Download software.

- Read Web exclusives: special articles and book excerpts by IDG Books Worldwide authors.

- Take advantage of resources to help you advance your career as a Novell or Microsoft professional.

- Buy IDG Books Worldwide titles or find a convenient bookstore that carries them.

- Register your book and win a prize.

- Chat live online with authors.

- Sign up for regular e-mail updates about our latest books.

- Suggest a book you'd like to read or write.

- Give us your 2¢ about our books and about our Web site.

You say you're not on the Web yet? It's easy to get started with IDG Books' *Discover the Internet,* available at local retailers everywhere.